Visual Storytelling with D3

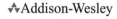

Visual Storytelling with D3

An Introduction to Data Visualization in JavaScript™

Ritchie S. King

✦Addison-Wesley

Upper Saddle River, NJ • Boston • Indianapolis • San Francisco
New York • Toronto • Montreal • London • Munich • Paris • Madrid
Capetown • Sydney • Tokyo • Singapore • Mexico City

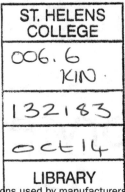
Many of the designations used by manufacturers and sellers to distinguish their products are claimed as trademarks. Where those designations appear in this book, and the publisher was aware of a trademark claim, the designations have been printed with initial capital letters or in all capitals.

The author and publisher have taken care in the preparation of this book, but make no expressed or implied warranty of any kind and assume no responsibility for errors or omissions. No liability is assumed for incidental or consequential damages in connection with or arising out of the use of the information or programs contained herein.

For information about buying this title in bulk quantities, or for special sales opportunities (which may include electronic versions; custom cover designs; and content particular to your business, training goals, marketing focus, or branding interests), please contact our corporate sales department at corpsales@pearsoned.com or (800) 382-3419.

For government sales inquiries, please contact governmentsales@pearsoned.com.

For questions about sales outside the U.S., please contact international@pearsoned.com.

Visit us on the Web: informit.com/aw

Library of Congress Cataloging-in-Publication Data

King, Ritchie S.

  Visual storytelling with D3 : an introduction to data visualization in JavaScript / Ritchie S. King.

     pages   cm

  Includes bibliographical references and index.

  ISBN 978-0-321-93317-1 (pbk. : alk. paper) — ISBN 0-321-93317-6 (pbk. : alk. paper)

 1. Information visualization. 2. JavaScript (Computer program language) 3. Computer graphics. I. Title.

  QA76.9.I52K56 2015

  006.6—dc23   2014029209

ISBN-13: 978-0-321-93317-1
ISBN-10: 0-321-93317-6
Text printed in the United States on recycled paper at RR Donnelley in Crawfordsville, Indiana.
First printing, August 2014

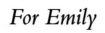
For Emily

Contents

Foreword

D3.js has quickly risen to become the underlying tool of choice for building data visualizations in JavaScript. It was written by Mike Bostock as a successor to the Protovis visualization library that he had previously created. Unlike other JavaScript visualization libraries and Protovis before it, D3 was designed to be a lower-level toolset for building visualizations or even for building higher level visualization libraries like Protovis. Because of this design philosophy, D3 gives programmers a much higher level of control over the structure, style, and behavior of their visualizations. With greater control comes a greater learning curve. This book was written to help ease you into working effectively with D3 and its author, Ritchie King, has a unique perspective on visualizations.

I first met Ritchie in 2011 when he was still a graduate student in NYU's highly selective Science, Health and Environmental Reporting (SHERP) program. He had just started his foray into data visualization but it was obvious he had a passion for it. A few years later, after he had graduated and was working as a reporter at *Quartz*, I bumped into him again. He told me about his work creating visualizations in D3 to go along with his reported stories and I realized that he would bring a fresh perspective to a book on D3. Instead of having a book written by a programmer about the mechanics of the library, it would be a book about conveying meaning through data visualization. It's exactly what I felt was missing from the available D3 literature. Ritchie has since moved on from *Quartz* to doing fantastic data-driven reporting at FiveThirtyEight.com, and he's brought that experience to bear in the content presented here.

This book is a terrific resource for both beginners and experienced programmers looking to learn how to create great looking data visualizations with D3. It begins with a discussion of how to select a data set and visualization and moves into the HTML building block D3 works with: SVG. The focus on introducing SVG before diving into D3 gives the reader foundational knowledge that is invaluable when learning more advanced topics like adding axes and interactive visualizations. Ritchie's writing style and focus on the visualization aspects of working with D3 make this book highly readable and much more than a basic tutorial on the specifics of the library. It's the perfect introduction to visualizations for both beginners and experts and I'm delighted to have it as part of the series.

—Paul Dix
Series Editor

Preface

Data, data, data. Piles and gobs of it are amassing everywhere faster than ever before. And with this grand swelling of information has come a sudden rise in the need for a discipline over two centuries old: Data visualization, the craft of communicating patterns and trends in raw data by transforming it into visual displays.

Traditionally, such displays have been rendered in ink, drawn onto the pages of books, newspapers, and academic journals, and frozen at the time of their printing. But more and more, data is being transformed into pixels and published online in interactive displays the viewer can change with the click of her mouse. Any modern practitioner of data visualization needs a tool to assist with that transformation—from information to a web page and from raw, immutable numbers to animated graphics.

Enter D3. Short for Data-Driven Documents, D3 not only helps you turn information into pixels, it enables you to create and manipulate web pages and graphics entirely based on data. It is a fantastic tool, and is exactly what the world, or at least the world of data visualization, needs.

First developed in 2011 by then Stanford graduate student Mike Bostock, along with his advisors Jeffery Heer and Vadim Ogievetsky, D3 is a freely available extension of JavaScript, a programming language that is absolutely ubiquitous on the Internet. The basic idea behind D3 is this: It provides a way to join data with elements on a web page and then manipulate those elements based on that data. Say you have five numbers you want to turn into a bar chart. All you need to do in D3 is join them up with five rectangle elements, then set the width of each rectangle to be proportional to the number it's connected to. It's really as simple as that.

Goals and Audience

Well, that's not quite true. D3 isn't totally easy. It is immensely powerful, but learning it can be a challenge. Fortunately, there are countless tutorials and examples freely available online, and many of the best ones were written by Mike Bostock himself. Still, although there is a vast and thriving D3 ecosystem out there, getting started can require a bit of work, especially if you don't have a lot of experience with JavaScript.

My main goal in writing this introductory textbook is to cover the D3 fundamentals in an accessible but nevertheless comprehensive way. (I am assuming you have some experience with HTML and CSS coming into this. If you don't, I highly recommend you get up to speed on the basics.) My hope with this book is that it will get you to a place where you can readily interpret and learn from the code examples of others—in other words, a place from which you can comfortably enter the D3 ecosystem.

The book also has a secondary goal: to cover some basic principles for making good data visualizations. Bad charts and infographics are rife on the web, even though data visualization, like any craft, has a set of best practices and time-honored techniques. In a sense, every visualization tells a story, so if you're planning on making one, it's crucial to think carefully about what story you want to tell and how best to tell it if you want your visualization to be good. Hopefully this book will give you a few ideas for how to go about doing that.

How This Book Is Structured

The organization of the book is fairly straightforward—it simply walks through the entire process of building an animated, interactive graphic in D3, including the initial conception of that graphic, finding the right data to use, and coming up with a strong design. As the process and the book advance, each subsequent chapter adds a layer of sophistication. Here are more details on what each chapter contains:

- **Chapter 1: Visual Storytelling and D3**—This first chapter provides a brief introduction to data visualization and why it's such a powerful means of communication. It also introduces D3 and discusses what makes it such an excellent tool for visualizing data on the web.

- **Chapter 2: Finding a Data-Driven Story and Telling It Visually**—This chapter covers how to find and tell a data story, including getting your hands on the relevant data and some style guidelines for making strong visualizations. The example chart, an interactive multi-year bar chart of the world's age distribution that is built throughout the rest of the book, is introduced.

- **Chapter 3: Scalable Vector Graphics**—Chapter 3 is an introduction to scalable vector graphics (SVG), a web standard for creating beautifully rendered graphical elements, which D3 can manipulate with ease. Part of the example chart is built entirely in SVG in this chapter.

- **Chapter 4: Shaping Web Pages with D3 Selections**—Getting started with D3 and using it to select and manipulate elements on a page is the subject of Chapter 4. The SVG chart from Chapter 3 is recreated with D3.

- **Chapter 5: Data-Joins: Enter**—Chapter 5 provides an introduction to the heart-and-soul of D3, data-joins. Again, data-joins are used to recreate the example chart.

- **Chapter 6: Sizing Charts and Adding Axes**—D3's methods for automatically scaling charts and generating axes are covered and applied to the example chart.

- **Chapter 7: Loading and Filtering External Data**—Creating charts from external, standalone datasets is something you'll do all the time with D3. This chapter explains how to do it and why D3 loads data asynchronously.
- **Chapter 8: Making Charts Interactive and Animated**—In this chapter, interactive buttons (one for each year in the data set) are added to the example chart, as are transitions, which cause the bars of the chart to grow and shrink in response to the buttons being clicked.
- **Chapter 9: Adding a Play Button**—A play button, which, upon being clicked, automatically cycles throughout all of the years in the dataset is built.
- **Chapter 10: Striking Out on Your Own**—The book ends with a wrap-up chapter that provides some guidance on how best to enter the D3 ecosystem.
- **Appendix A: JavaScript for Beginners**—This appendix serves as a very brief introduction to some JavaScript basics for the uninitiated.
- **Appendix B: Cleaning the Population Distribution Data**—Appendix B provides step-by-step instructions for how to download and clean the sample dataset used to build the example in the book.

Note that while the book is in color, certain Kindle devices do not display color, so the digital edition of this book will appear in grayscale on those devices.

Conventions

Code listings and inline code and function names will appear in a monospace font like this.

A Final Word

I was still very much a D3 beginner when I set out to write this book. I bring that up for two reasons. One is that, as I was writing, the things that initially confused me about D3 were still very fresh in my mind and I did my best to address them. I hope I was successful. The second is to say that you can do this. If I was able to do it, then I know you can do it too.

Acknowledgments

To start with, I have to thank my (now, at the time of publishing) wife, Emily Elert, who spent many a weekend fixing me lunches and taking care of the chores so that I could work on the book. The book is, of course, dedicated to her, but that's not quite enough. She deserves a prime spot in these acknowledgments as well. The thing is, I didn't fully appreciate going into the project how much of our leisure time together it would gobble up, but she did, and instead of treating me with all the bitterness she was entitled to, she was incredibly patient and supportive. And she even agreed to marry me along the way, which does not cease to amaze me one bit.

I also have to give a hearty thanks to Paul Dix, the series editor, right off the bat. This book, or at least my authorship of it, grew out of a casual conversation between us at a friendly get-together. You see, Paul is the fiancé of a good friend and grad school classmate of mine, and one night we were sharing some beers and talking programming and I mentioned that I had gotten really into using this super-sweet JavaScript library called D3. He paused and then asked, "And you're a writer?" "Yep," I replied. Another pause, even more pregnant than the first. "Do you want to write a book about D3?" Thank you, Paul, for taking that chance.

Thanks of course to my editor, Debra Williams Cauley, who demonstrated an uncanny ability to detect exactly when I really needed prodding to keep things moving forward. Or when I needed to join her for a sushi lunch to get some clarity on how the whole publishing thing works. She was also great at helping me triage some of the more substantive edits I received from reviewers toward the end of the writing process.

Speaking of reviewers, I owe a major debt of gratitude to them, naturally. To Kevin Quealy, Robert Mauriello, and Josh Peek for providing early feedback on my initial outlines of the text. To Robert, again, for making sure I didn't misrepresent any computer programming concepts in my quest to make the book as conversational as possible. To Alli Treman and Sasha Méndez for meticulously going through all of my code and catching some pretty embarrassing mistakes. And, especially, to Lynn Cherny, who gave me some very insightful feedback that undoubtedly made the book much better.

A very special thanks goes out to Chris Zahn, who put up with my ongoing failure to master the book-drafting workflow. I turned in some horribly formatted chapters, but he always helped clean them up and was super nice about it.

Taking a step back from book production a little bit, I have to bring up Kevin Quealy once more and also Amanda Cox. Those two not only got me interested in data visualization in the first place (by teaching a stunningly good data journalism class that I took at NYU) but have also helped me advance my career every step of the way. I owe them a lot. And as human beings, they couldn't be more awesome.

I'd also like to thank David Yanofsky, who was the other half of the two-person graphics team at Quartz when I worked there. Yano taught me a ton about D3 and JavaScript in general and he helped me build my first interactive graphic. He's also an incorrigible punster, which I admire. Thanks, bud.

And last, but certainly not least, I have to thank Mike Bostock for writing such a profoundly good library for making web-based visualizations. And also for constantly publishing elegant and beautiful examples of how to use that library to the fullest. Thank you, good sir!

About the Author

Ritchie S. King is a reporter and visual journalist at FiveThirtyEight.com, focusing on data visualization and interactive features. Prior to that, he occupied a similar role at *Quartz* (qz.com). In a previous life, he was a chemical engineer at a startup that was trying to turn wood chips and switchgrass into fuel. Though he left the world of engineering to become a journalist, he's still into math and likes to muck with data. His stories and graphics have appeared in the *New York Times*, *Bloomberg Businessweek*, *Popular Science*, and *IEEE Spectrum*.

1

Visual Storytelling and D3

This first chapter serves as a very basic primer on data visualization, a survey of how to harness its power to tell strong visual stories, and a brief introduction to D3. It describes the qualities that make charts so uniquely good at conveying quantitative information. It includes a discussion of good visualization design. Finally, it introduces D3: what it does, what it does well, what you shouldn't use it for, and the tools that you'll need to get started.

Visualization, Visualized

I could kick this introduction off with a paragraph or two describing how, in a world increasingly flush with data, data visualization is growing ever-more popular. I could cite some relevant stats, such as the fact that a free online course on data visualization offered at the beginning of 2013 attracted over 5,000 students. I could assert that journalists, especially on the web, are increasingly using charts to tell their stories and support their arguments, and that web developers and IT departments are looking for new ways to incorporate visualization into the products they design. I could state simply that more than ever before, people who create content want to make charts and data visualizations, and their audiences want to look at them.

But why make that point with words when a chart could do a much better job?

The line chart in Figure 1.1 shows that online searches for "infographic"—a pop term for charts and data visualizations (and also some graphical marketing materials)—have increased 100-fold since the beginning of 2009. It shows that popular interest in infographics didn't really take off until the beginning of 2010 but grew rapidly in the subsequent three years. It shows how in recent months, the frequency with which people search for "infographic" has fluctuated more than in the past, potentially peaking in months when an especially popular infographic is published.

It shows all of these things and more. The chart in Figure 1.1 tells a multifaceted story about people's interest in infographics. And, in doing so, it demonstrates the online rise of the medium in a faster and more elegant way than a list of stats and claims ever could.

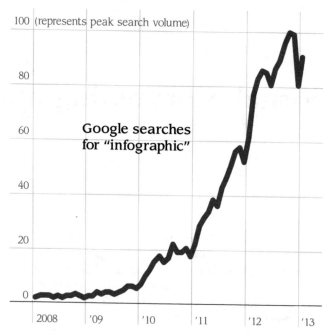

Figure 1.1   Infographics have grown pretty hip. Data from Google Trends.

Indeed, it's this peerless capacity to express information and tell data-rich stories that has earned charts and data visualization a spot in the limelight. They are more popular, easier to make, and more useful than ever. And that's why you're here.

Charts Give Data a Form—That Form Tells a Story

Why are charts so good at telling stories? Because *charts give data a visual form, which we can interpret in great detail, often at a glance.*

Take another look at Figure 1.1. Because I transformed the Google search data into a line chart—a standard graphical form—we have what looks like a partial drawing of a really jagged mountain instead of a list of numbers. This is really useful, because it makes thinking and talking about the patterns in the data as easy as thinking and talking about the shape of that mountain. It *climbs steeply* right there (2010), it *peaks* over there (late 2012), then it *drops off* a little to the right…. We've transformed Google search statistics into something we understand intuitively—height, or altitude.

Giving data a form…that's powerful stuff, even when it comes to topics that might seem super boring or intimidating on the surface. For example, US government debt. Believe it or not, I'm about to show you a chart of US debt that will fascinate you—guaranteed.

US debt as percentage of gross domestic product, 1855—2011

Year	%	Year	%	Year	%	Year	%	Year	%	
1855	0.9%	1887	11.2	1919	33.4	1951	63.7	1983	33.1	Reagan tax cuts
1856	0.7	1888	10.2	1920	27.3	1952	61.8	1984	34.0	
1857	0.9	1889	8.6	1921	31.6	1953	60.2	1985	36.4	
1858	1.2	1890	7.8	1922	31.1	1954	60.7	1986	39.5	
1859	1.5	1891	7.0	1923	25.2	1955	55.5	1987	40.6	
1860	1.9	1892	6.6	1924	23.5	1956	51.2	1988	41.0	
1861	7.2	1893	6.8	1925	21.6	1957	48.1	1989	40.6	
1862	16.8	1894	7.9	1926	19.0	1958	49.5	1990	42.1	
1863	23.8	1895	7.9	1927	18.0	1959	47.0	1991	45.3	
1864	25.6	1896	8.5	1928	17.0	1960	44.8	1992	48.1	
1865	31.0	1897	8.0	1929	14.9	1961	44.6	1993	49.3	
1866	31.4	1898	8.4	1930	16.5	1962	42.9	1994	49.2	
1867	31.4	1899	7.5	1931	22.3	1963	41.4	1995	49.1	
1868	30.5	1900	6.6	1932	34.5	1964	39.0	1996	48.4	
1869	30.0	1901	5.7	1933	39.1	1965	36.5	1997	45.9	
1870	27.9	1902	5.4	1934	44.0	1966	33.7	1998	43.0	
1871	25.7	1903	5.0	1935	42.9	1967	33.4	1999	39.4	
1872	24.4	1904	4.7	1936	43.0	1968	31.2	2000	34.7	
1873	23.2	1905	4.3	1937	40.1	1969	28.5	2001	32.5	
1874	24.0	1906	4.0	1938	42.8	1970	28.0	2002	33.6	
1875	23.7	1907	4.0	1939	43.0	1971	28.1	2003	35.6	
1876	24.1	1908	4.3	1940	42.7	1972	27.4	2004	36.8	The Great Recession
1877	23.9	1909	3.8	1941	43.3	1973	26.0	2005	36.9	
1878	25.5	1910	3.7	1942	62.0	1974	23.9	2006	36.6	
1879	23.0	1911	3.6	1943	77.1	1975	25.3	2007	36.3	
1880	18.4	1912	3.4	1944	95.7	1976	27.5	2008	40.5	
1881	16.8	1913	3.2	1945	112.7	1977	27.8	2009	54.1	
1882	14.3	1914	3.5	1946	102.6	1978	27.4	2010	62.8	
1883	13.5	1915	3.3	1947	90.4	1979	25.6	2011	67.7	
1884	13.3	1916	2.7	1948	79.9	1980	26.1			
1885	13.2	1917	13.3	1949	81.4	1981	25.8			
1886	12.4	1918	30.2	1950	73.7	1982	28.7			

(Side labels: The Civil War, 1861–1865; World War I, 1914–1918; The Great Depression & World War II, 1930–1945.)

Figure 1.2 US debt as a percentage of GDP (Source: Congressional Budget Office).

But first, a tiny bit of background on debt: A government tends to borrow more money (i.e., rack up more debt) when it's at war (because wars are expensive) and during recessions (to stimulate the economy). Also, if a government cuts taxes without cutting an equivalent amount of spending, then it has to borrow money to make up the difference.

Let's take a look at US government debt throughout history. We'll start with a boring old table, just so we can see the data before and after visualization. Figure 1.2 shows US government debt for every year from 1855 to 2011. It isn't just a list of

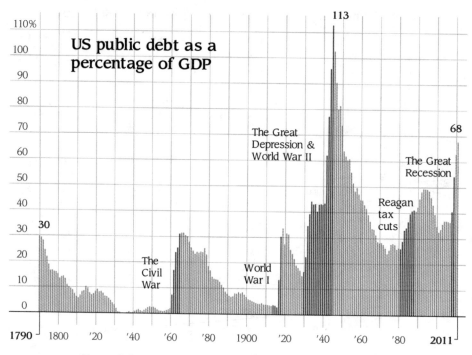

Figure 1.3 Debt to GDP, visualized (Source: Congressional Budget Office).

dollar values. The country grew a lot in those 156 years, and the amount of money it needed to, say, pull itself out of an economic slump, grew with it. To put the numbers on an even playing field, the debt is divided by the size of the economy, or the gross domestic product (GDP). The result is a list of values that can be compared meaningfully—how much the United States was borrowing as a percentage of its size.

Personally, I think the table itself is interesting (it helps that the years of major debt increases are highlighted in red). You can see that the United States has had debt since its very beginnings, and that during the last year of World War II, the country was borrowing an amount greater than the total value of its economy.

Now take a look at similar data, visualized in Figure 1.3.

Talk about mountains! When you chart the debt as a portion of GDP, the more dramatic changes really stick out (quite literally). You can immediately see the sharp increases during the Civil War and World War I, a jump followed by a plateau during the Great Depression, the huge peak during World War II, the slower climb during the Reagan era, and the sudden spike during the Great Recession. And most importantly, you can compare every value in this chart to every other value in an instant.

This visualization is so much more than a collection of numbers that describe US debt. It's an entire history of the United States in a shape the size of an index card that can be interpreted in seconds. Visualization has given the data a form and that form tells a story.

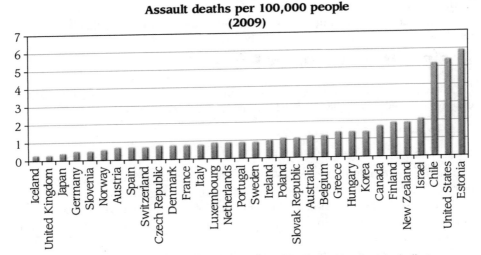

Figure 1.4 Assault deaths per capita in OECD countries (not including Mexico).

Quality: It Is All about Content

So what makes data visualization good? Sweet colors and hip typefaces, of course! It's gotta look *awesome*.

I jest. It's nice when a graphic looks awesome, but *what really makes a graphic good is its content*. In the section above, I mentioned that transforming data into a chart can make seemingly boring topics really interesting. This is true, but only if those seemingly boring topics are secretly fascinating deep down, like US debt. You can't take a completely mundane set of numbers, jazz them up with a whimsical font and some electric blue accents, and expect the result to be exciting. A boring story is a boring story.

On the other hand, if the data is extremely interesting, as long as you visualize it in a form that makes sense, you don't have to worry a ton about making your graphic pretty. Take Figure 1.4, which shows assault deaths per 100,000 people in 32 countries.

It's just an ugly bar chart that I threw together in Excel. But the data is interesting: When it comes to deaths caused by assault, the US looks a lot more like Chile and Estonia than other wealthy countries in the world. The chart would look a lot better if it were horizontal, so the country names could be read from left to right. It would also be nice if the bars didn't have that goofy color gradient. But really, these issues are minor compared to the power of the data on display. For its economic class, the US is unusually violent, and the bar chart in Figure 1.4 succeeds in expressing that point.

That's not to say you should just find really powerful datasets and visualize them in Excel. The number of graphical forms you can make in Excel is pretty limited, and everything the program does offer is static. Aside from that, it's good to make your charts look good, and it's essential to make sure the form you use expresses your data well.

But, as the cliché goes, content is king. It doesn't matter how aesthetically superb a data visualization is if the information it conveys is simply not compelling.

Design: It Is All about Form

Let's take a step back for a second and think about what it actually means to visualize data. Merriam-Webster gives two definitions for the word visualize:[1]

1. To see or form a mental image (of).
2. To make (an internal organ or part) visible by radiographic visualization.

The first definition is the one you're probably most familiar with. Maybe your baseball or softball coach used to tell you to "visualize yourself making contact with the ball." In this context, "visualize" means "imagine." When you visualize yourself hitting that ball, the visual you construct only exists inside your head. Of course, that's not true for data visualization.

The second definition gets us closer. A radiographic visualization is, for example, an X-ray. When a technician takes an X-ray of, say, your left forearm, she shoots X-rays at the limb, and whatever passes through gets picked up by a detector on the other side. Out comes a picture of your radius and hopefully not too fractured ulna.

That X-ray is a kind of data visualization. It's a two-dimensional schematic map in which every location on the image corresponds to a location on your forearm. Places that readily absorb X-rays appear nearly white, places that don't absorb them are nearly black, and everywhere in between is some shade of grey. Of course, the white areas reveal the shapes of your calcium-rich, X-ray-absorbing bones.

When you visualize data, it's a lot like making an X-ray: You take information and you encode it visually on a page, screen, or some other two-dimensional surface (for the most part). But there's a major difference: With data visualizations it's up to you to design the encoding. In an X-ray, it's always true that the position on the image represents the position in your body, and the color represents X-ray absorption. With data visualization, position and color can mean whatever you want them to. And while X-rays are a fairly realistic depiction of a physical object, data visualizations usually involve *an abstract arrangement of graphical elements*, such as circles, rectangles, and lines, whose attributes—size, position, color, etc.—*vary in some way* to represent different values in a dataset.

In the chart of US debt over time (Figure 1.3), the graphical element of choice is a bar or rectangle and the key attribute is its height. Each of the 221 years in the dataset is assigned its own bar, and the height of that bar is set to be proportional to the ratio of US debt to GDP. As a secondary attribute, color is used to highlight significant periods of increasing debt.

The element/attribute combination is the central component of a graphic's form. Choosing the right combination is the key to good visualization design.

---

1. http://www.merriam-webster.com/dictionary/visualize

Visual Storytelling

You might be wondering why this book is called "Visual Storytelling with D3" and not, say, "Data Visualization with D3." What is this storytelling business all about, anyway?

It's tempting to think that communicating an idea is a lot cleaner or more objective if you do it with data. After all, nobody can argue with the numbers!

There's certainly some truth to that, and, of course, whenever you're trying to prove a point, it helps to have some hard data on your side. But the fact of the matter is, when you turn a raw spreadsheet into something else you almost always have to make a judgment call (or at the very least a design decision). You choose what's worth showing, or, if you're showing everything in your dataset, you choose what to give visual emphasis. With a few exceptions, you are crafting the dataset into some sort of message or story, told visually.

Now building a dashboard that displays the value of a few stocks or the traffic of a few websites is hardly an act of storytelling in the traditional sense. But finding the right layout involves editorial decisions and craft. A visualization often conveys not only data but a perspective on that data. And that's worth keeping in mind.

Enter D3

Enough background for now. You know what data visualizations are, so let's shift gears and talk about the best tool around for making them on the web: D3.

Short for data-driven documents, D3 is a library of the programming language JavaScript, written by the immensely talented and insanely prolific Mike Bostock. True to its name, D3 enables you to bind data to web documents and then manipulate those documents based on that data. Cool. But what does that mean?

Let's start with the bit about D3 being a JavaScript library. D3 is not a piece of software that you download, like Adobe Illustrator; it's not a programming environment like R, where you do analysis and generate plots from a command line; and it's not an online tool like Google Charts or Tableau Public that lets you go to a website, plug in numbers, and create stock visualizations. Instead, it's a completely open source extension of JavaScript, just as every library is an extension of the language that it's written in. D3 expands the capabilities of JavaScript (in ways that are especially useful for data visualization).

If you're relatively new to programming, this answer might be a little unsatisfying. What is a library, physically, and what's in it? The answer is a bunch of functions and methods (which are a lot like functions). Functions and methods exist to store useful sequences of code so they can be easily reused over and over again. A library is essentially a suite of functions, each of which is designed to work in concert with the others. If it's a good library, the functions collectively provide a new way of using a programming language.

D3, being a library, is a list of functions and methods and their definitions (the sequences of commands they store). That list comes in the form of a JavaScript file.

You can take a peek at it right now, if you like. Just go to http://d3js.org/d3.v3.js. There's version 3...open source, as advertised.

So how do you access it? You access it by creating a webpage that runs that Java-Script file. When your browser runs d3.v3.js, it learns all of D3's functions and methods so you can use them in your own code. If somebody else looks at your webpage, her browser will be directed to run d3.v3.js, and then it too will understand D3's functions.

Those functions are powerful. D3 is definitely a library that enables coders to use JavaScript in a completely different way.

Its biggest innovation is right there in the name: data-driven documents. D3 makes it possible to bind data to web documents and then use the data to manipulate those documents. A web document is technically anything that can be located and rendered by a browser. This includes any HTML webpage, but also, importantly SVG, or scalable vector graphics, images.

You may have worked with SVGs before. If you're a designer, then the chances are close to 100%. SVG is a vector graphics format: The resolutions of SVGs self-adjust for any zoom level, so they never look pixelated. Underlying those graphics is a web document encoded in a markup language that is very similar to HTML. Instead of <p> tags for paragraphs and <h1> tags for headers, SVG has a <circle> tag for circles and a <line> tag for lines.

One of the things that make D3 so great for data visualizers is that you can use it to marry data with an SVG document, which means you can join individual data points to SVG elements such as circles, rectangles, and paths. You can then format and position those elements based on the joined data.

I'm going to say this again just to make sure it hits home. D3 enables you to directly set the attributes of graphical elements in SVG, a gorgeous web-based format, according to numbers in a data set! When you use D3, you are using data to directly control exactly what your browser is displaying. And that is D3 in a nutshell.

Things You Designers Will Love about D3

If you're a designer and you have a lot of experience with tools like Adobe Illustrator or Inkscape, then you'll love D3 for how elegantly it can create, destroy, and format SVG elements. You've no doubt downloaded SVG files from the web countless times and messed around with them in your design software. With D3, you'll be digging down to the SVG markup itself, perhaps for the first time, but the logic and naming conventions will be familiar. The interior color of a shape is called the "fill," and the line around the perimeter is called the "stroke." You can group objects together, apply gradients, create clipping paths, and change the opacity of things. Once you learn the basic syntax, the rest will be second nature.

Things You Coders Will Love about D3

If you're a coder, you'll love D3 for leveraging the power of existing web standards like HTML and SVG, instead of relying on plug-ins or a proprietary framework.

Web-based visualization tools that came before it, such as Protovis, Flare, and the JavaScript InfoViz Toolkit, all relied on their own, distinct ways of structuring graphics on a page (in technical terms, they used their own scene graphs). What D3 does instead is provide a way to directly manipulate the web's native scene graph—the document object model—using data.

D3 also adopts some useful conventions from other JavaScript libraries. For instance, it enables you to chain methods the same way you can with jQuery.

Things for Which You Should Not Use D3

I've probably made it sound like D3 is the only tool that you, as a builder of data visualizations, could ever possibly need. Unfortunately, that isn't the case. When you get to the point where you have a fully formed idea of how to display the data you want to display, D3 can take you the rest of the way there. But it can't help you find a story or figure out the best visual way to tell that story. (This isn't entirely true. People who are really good at using D3, such as Mike Bostock (its creator) and Shan Carter of *The New York Times*, use it to make bare bones prototypes of graphics, particularly in cases where the form is experimental.)

D3 also isn't built for scraping data off the web. The programming language Python has a couple of libraries that are really good at doing that.

D3 is not a good tool for sorting through data or doing basic data analysis. Spreadsheet applications such as Excel, OpenOffice Calc, and Google Drive's spreadsheet app are useful and accessible tools for doing this kind of work. For more advanced analysis, the statistical programming environment R is incredibly robust and powerful.

The other thing that D3 isn't built for is quickly making bar charts, maps, or other standard charts. If you want a plug-and-play chart generator for the web, something like Tableau is a better fit. In computing and software, there's always a trade-off between power and ease of use. Compared to R, Microsoft Excel, with its graphical interface, is a breeze to learn and use, but it can't do nearly as much. D3, like R, was designed to be powerful and robust: You can use it to create a multitude of graphical forms and to customize your visualizations to a much greater extent than you can with Tableau. But the trade-off is that they are both a lot harder to learn, and when it comes to D3 in particular, you can't use it to create a chart in two minutes or less.

Notes on Using D3

You are free to use D3 to make something for fun or something to sell without having to pay any royalties or even mention D3 by name. It's totally open. But D3 doesn't support all browsers, because not all browsers support web standards. The so-called modern browsers—Google Chrome, Mozilla Firefox, Opera, Safari, and Internet Explorer 9 and above—all do.

Anybody that looks at a project you've made in D3 can access all of the data behind it. Usually, this level of transparency isn't an issue: If you're building a visualization for everyone to see, then you probably aren't trying to keep the data a secret. But it's something to keep in mind if your source has asked you not to distribute their raw data.

Tools You Will Need

To build stuff in D3, you have to get your hands dirty writing some code. So, if you don't already have one, you'll need a good text editor. Why not use a word processor like Microsoft Word or the text editor that came with your computer? Because they aren't made for programming, so they don't do anything to make your life easier.

One very simple—but very useful—feature that a good programming text editor usually has is called syntax highlighting. Programming languages have different elements that are sort of like parts of speech: While English has nouns, pronouns, verbs, and adjectives, JavaScript has functions, numerals, strings, and operators. A text editor with syntax highlighting displays those different elements in different colors, which makes it infinitely easier to see what's going on in the code and to fix any problems with it.

Text editor preferences vary widely. The website tutorialzine.com has a really useful overview of a variety of text editors, some of which are totally free (see http://tutorialzine.com/2012/07/battle-of-the-tools-which-is-the-best-code-editor/).

The other thing you'll need to build stuff in D3 is a set of browser-based developer tools, including a web inspector and a JavaScript console. Developer tools let you change the HTML, CSS, and JavaScript of a page and see the results instantaneously. This saves you the trouble of, say, guessing the font size you want to use for a line of text, putting it into your markup, saving, realizing it's too small, trying another font size, saving again, etc. The JavaScript console, as we'll see, is critical for debugging.

The good news is that all modern browsers have developer tools available. Google Chrome, Safari, Opera, and Internet Explorer 9 and above all have developer tools built in to the browser. Firefox has an add-on called Firebug. In the chapters ahead, we'll rely heavily on the web inspector and the console.

Summary

Data visualization can be an extremely powerful way to tell a story because it gives information a form that readers can often interpret in an instant. However, that story is only as interesting as the information behind it. The crux of good visualization design is choosing a good combination of graphical elements and their attributes for displaying the data you want to display. It turns out that D3's specialty is pairing data sets up with graphical elements. Short for data-driven documents, D3 is an open-source library of JavaScript. D3 is nice for designers because it makes it possible for you to do a lot with SVG, a familiar graphical format, and it's nice for coders because it relies solely on web standards. To build stuff in D3, you need two key tools: a good text editor and a browser with developer tools.

2

Finding a Data-Driven Story and Telling It Visually

How do you find a data-driven story and how do you design graphics that will tell that story well? This chapter focuses on those two questions. It does so by introducing an example story idea, describing how to find relevant data, and then discussing possible ways to visualize that data. The example will extend well beyond this chapter. In fact, the rest of the book will explain how to build one of those visualizations using D3.

Getting Started

So you want to make a data visualization. Great! But where do you begin? How do you find a story, rich in data, to tell in graphics?

Typically, your data-driven story will have one of two beginnings: It'll start with either a dataset or a question.

New datasets are being released and updated all of the time. For example, New York City has a nonemergency municipal hotline (the number is 311) that residents call to, say, lodge a noise complaint, report an illegally parked vehicle, or notify authorities of a stray animal. The city maintains a running list of all of these calls: what kind of complaint each call was, which city agency the call was relayed to, the location of the complaint, etc. This list is updated every day and is completely publicly available. As a visual storyteller, you could at any point decide, "hey, I'd like to do something with that 311 data," or "maybe it's about time I updated my 311 graphic."

If you are starting with a question, that question is usually quantitative in nature, naturally. "How much does a musician typically make off of her music from album sales, concert tickets, and streaming services such as Spotify?" That's a question. And because it starts with the words "how much," it's one that is fairly ripe for data visualization treatment.

If you start with a question, you have to search for data that can answer it. Once you find that data, you are essentially where you would have been if you started with a dataset to begin with (though you probably have a better handle on the direction you want to take). What you have is a series of numbers or pieces of information that you want to display in some way. The next step is to inspect and analyze that data to find what, specifically, you think is worth showing. Often, the final question (or questions) you seek to answer look slightly different from the one you started with. The data that is available and what that data says have a tendency to constrain, broaden, or simply shift your initial scope. You analyze, you interpret, you change your direction, you analyze again, you build your story. It's an iterative process.

The data visualizations I've made that I've been the most satisfied with have all started with a question. Part of it might be that when you start with a question, your curiosity and your perspective drive the whole thing; if you start with a dataset, this isn't necessarily the case. In any event, when I was trying to think of an example to use in this book, I came up with a few questions. Here's the one that I settled on:

Is the World Getting Older?

I don't mean is planet Earth increasing in age—of course it is. I mean is the age distribution of all the humans living on this planet shifting away from childhood and adolescence and toward late adulthood? Is the population at large maturing? It's a basic question about a basic characteristic of people—their age—and in and of itself, it's actually pretty interesting. Who wouldn't want to know if the demographics of the world at large are changing?

As it turns out, it actually has to be true that the world will get older at some point. The world is fairly young now, because the rate at which new human beings are being born is high—about 2.6 children for every woman. Unless that rate continues apace (and it's not expected to), the world will start to age, be it in the next half-century or the 50 years after that. In a sense, the question isn't just "is the world getting older?" It's "is the world getting older *yet*?"

So, the question is, in part, one about population growth. If indeed the world is starting to get older, then population growth must be slowing down. Given the Earth's finite supply of resources, that's arguably a good thing.

But it gets even deeper. While a slower growing population would be good for the planet, an older world is, unfortunately, more challenging for us humans to support. When people get older, they tend to leave the workforce and become more dependent on social welfare to handle their living expenses and increasing medical costs. In many countries, it's the younger people still in the workforce who provide the money to fund those welfare programs. This is a problem in countries like Japan, where almost one out of every three people is aged 60 or older—either already retired or nearing retirement age. So, what happens when the ratio of retirees to workers grows really large around the world? How will we support our parents and grandparents?

Okay, whoa! What started off as a lighthearted question about whether or not the world is getting older got pretty real pretty fast. But the point is you might be interested in that question for a variety of reasons. You might be interested in the growth and composition of the population because you're concerned about the health of the environment; you might be a wonk who's interested in Social Security and the issue of crafting policy to support the elderly in a sustainable way; you might just be a person who's curious about raw demographics or data about the world at large; or you might be all of the above. And you can start with this question of global aging and build a data-driven, visual story that takes any of these angles. For the purposes of this book, I'm going to steer clear of the politically charged options and just focus on demographics.

But we're getting ahead of ourselves. Let's find some data.

Finding and Inspecting Data

There are tons of places to find raw data online. The United Nations, the World Bank, the International Monetary Fund, and the Organization for Economic Co-operation and Development (OECD) collect tons of information from countries around the world. Many of the world's major cities offer municipal data as well (like New York City and its 311 service requests). Those resources are all great, but they only represent the visible tip of the massive iceberg of data that's available online. In addition to the highly organized data on those sites, reams of data can be extracted programmatically (in other words, scraped) from websites and services like Twitter.

To answer the question of whether or not the world is getting older, I found some relevant data from the Population Division of the United Nations. The division has an estimated age breakdown for the entire world's population every five years starting in 1950 and going through 2010. The ages are divided into groups of five years: 0-4, 5-9, 10-14, and so on. Figure 2.1 shows what the data looks like.[1]

Reference date (as of 1 July)	Total population, both sexes combined, by five-year age group (thousands)						
	0–4	5–9	10–14	15–19	20–24	25–29	30–34
1950	337 251	269 704	260 697	238 747	222 005	194 256	167 209
1955	405 738	314 146	263 500	254 932	231 742	215 029	188 115
1960	433 231	381 461	308 046	258 324	248 292	225 859	209 154
1965	479 684	410 360	373 429	302 363	252 011	242 384	220 192
1970	520 790	461 057	405 234	368 391	296 285	246 786	237 369
1975	541 263	502 057	455 229	399 769	362 507	292 242	243 224
1980	545 877	524 690	497 005	450 683	394 321	357 215	288 242
1985	592 478	531 053	520 141	492 895	445 200	389 125	352 965
1990	644 696	578 491	527 461	516 614	486 853	439 086	384 823
1995	624 783	631 825	575 497	523 100	509 006	480 385	434 623
2000	604 456	613 690	628 646	571 501	516 100	502 205	474 365
2005	614 533	595 740	611 503	624 735	564 010	509 308	495 094
2010	642 161	607 380	592 696	606 056	617 394	559 498	503 170

Figure 2.1 The UN Population Division's data

1. The spreadsheet can be downloaded at http://esa.un.org/unpd/wpp/Excel-Data/EXCEL_FILES/1_Population/WPP2012_POP_F07_1_POPULATION_BY_AGE_BOTH_SEXES.XLS

Reference date (as of 1 July)	Total population, both sexes combined, by five-year age group (thousands)						
	0–4	5–9	10–14	15–19	20–24	25–29	30–34
2015	666 097	634 175	603 817	589 119	601 428	612 455	554 135
2020	668 233	658 727	630 771	600 313	584 685	596 785	607 140
2025	664 093	661 608	655 969	627 849	596 197	580 358	591 516
2030	663 764	658 124	659 148	653 250	623 697	591 710	575 328
2035	669 455	658 403	655 909	656 644	649 295	619 391	586 874
2040	677 340	664 644	656 412	653 602	652 946	645 199	614 732
2045	682 671	673 035	662 847	654 269	650 123	649 104	640 737
2050	684 194	678 836	671 418	660 852	650 994	646 532	644 911
2055	682 738	680 791	677 396	669 569	657 791	647 616	642 561
2060	680 700	679 723	679 483	675 686	666 704	654 591	643 861
2065	678 923	678 018	678 535	677 905	673 016	663 671	651 030
2070	677 165	676 526	676 936	677 082	675 425	670 154	660 295
2075	674 551	675 006	675 531	675 594	674 775	672 721	666 959
2080	669 948	672 593	674 081	674 288	673 451	672 228	669 713
2085	663 922	668 166	671 731	672 927	672 292	671 041	669 396
2090	656 828	662 292	667 357	670 663	671 072	670 013	668 379
2095	649 417	655 323	661 526	666 367	668 944	668 913	667 505
2100	641 628	648 019	654 592	660 608	664 779	666 901	666 552

Figure 2.2 The medium fertility projections

On top of that, the division has come up with projected age breakdowns for the future, again every five years, starting with 2015 and going all the way through 2100. Actually, they have a series of different projections, each of which involves a different assumption about birth rates in the future. There is a so-called high fertility scenario, in which birth rates are assumed to be relatively high, and a low fertility scenario in which they are assumed to be relatively low. There is also a medium fertility scenario, and a constant fertility scenario, which assumes that birth rates will stay exactly where they are today.

So which one should we use? Since it's the middle of the road projection, the medium fertility scenario is the best bet. The projected values for that scenario can be found in the same spreadsheet file as the estimates for years past—just on a different worksheet. Figure 2.2 shows what they look like.

You'll notice that all of the data is expressed as absolute population figures—in other words, we are looking at total numbers of people here. But what we really want are percentages. What portion of the total population was between ages 0 and 4 in 1950 and how does that compare to 2010? We can't just compare the total number of infants and toddlers for those two years, because the population at large was almost three times as big in 2010 as it was in 1950.

Translating these absolute numbers to percentages is straightforward: For every year, you take the number of 0-4 year olds and divide it by the total population in that year (which you can determine by adding the populations for all of the age groups together). Then you do the same thing for 5-9 year olds and 10-14 year olds, and so on. Appendix B has a step-by-step guide to cleaning up the UN Population Division data and converting it from absolute figures to percentages. After the conversion is done, the table looks something like Figure 2.3.

	A	B	C	D	E	F
1	year	0-4	5-9	10-14	15-19	20-24
2	1950	13.4%	10.7%	10.3%	9.5%	8.8%
3	1955	14.7%	11.4%	9.5%	9.2%	8.4%
4	1960	14.3%	12.6%	10.2%	8.5%	8.2%
5	1965	14.4%	12.3%	11.2%	9.1%	7.6%
6	1970	14.1%	12.5%	11.0%	10.0%	8.0%
7	1975	13.3%	12.3%	11.2%	9.8%	8.9%
8	1980	12.3%	11.8%	11.2%	10.1%	8.9%
9	1985	12.2%	10.9%	10.7%	10.1%	9.2%
10	1990	12.1%	10.9%	9.9%	9.7%	9.1%
11	1995	10.9%	11.0%	10.0%	9.1%	8.9%
12	2000	9.9%	10.0%	10.3%	9.3%	8.4%
13	2005	9.4%	9.1%	9.4%	9.6%	8.7%
14	2010	9.3%	8.8%	8.6%	8.8%	8.9%
15	2015	9.1%	8.7%	8.2%	8.0%	8.2%
16	2020	8.7%	8.5%	8.2%	7.8%	7.6%
17	2025	8.2%	8.2%	8.1%	7.8%	7.4%
18	2030	7.9%	7.8%	7.8%	7.8%	7.4%
19	2035	7.7%	7.5%	7.5%	7.5%	7.4%
20	2040	7.5%	7.4%	7.3%	7.2%	7.2%
21	2045	7.3%	7.2%	7.1%	7.0%	7.0%
22	2050	7.2%	7.1%	7.0%	6.9%	6.8%

Figure 2.3   The data expressed as percentages (and cut-off at 1950)

So now, we actually have all of the information we need to answer the question of whether or not the world is getting older. In fact, you can get a sense of it by just looking at Figure 2.3. From 2010 to 2050, the portion of 0-4 year olds is projected to drop from 9.3% to 7.2%, the portion of 5-9 years from 8.8% to 7.1%, that of 10-14 year olds from 8.6% to 7.0% and that of 15-19 year olds from 8.8% to 6.9%. If you take all of these age groups together, the total portion of people under 20 will go from 35.4% in 2010 to 28.2% in 2050. Let's look at the other end of the spectrum, shown in Figure 2.4.

Let's make the same comparison between 2010 and 2050 for these older age groups. If we combine them and look at the portion of people aged 60 and above, how is that projected to change over the next four decades? In 2010, that figure was only 11.1%, but by 2050, it's projected to be 21.2%! That's a huge increase. The world is certainly getting older. We have a data story.

Honing the Concept

Okay, so we have some data and we have a story. Before we start visualizing, we should think a little bit about what exactly we want to show.

We have some options. First, is it worth showing all of the five-year age groups, or should we combine them into larger groups, such as 0-19 years old and 60 years and older? Second, which years do we include? Do we start with 2010, or do we start earlier? And do we end all the way out at 2100, or do we limit the projection to a year that is closer at hand?

	A	N	O	P	Q	R
1	year	60-64	65-69	70-74	75-79	80+
2	1950	2.9%	2.2%	1.5%	0.9%	0.6%
3	1955	2.8%	2.2%	1.5%	0.9%	0.6%
4	1960	2.8%	2.1%	1.5%	0.9%	0.6%
5	1965	2.9%	2.1%	1.4%	0.9%	0.6%
6	1970	2.9%	2.2%	1.5%	0.9%	0.7%
7	1975	2.9%	2.3%	1.6%	1.0%	0.8%
8	1980	2.7%	2.3%	1.7%	1.1%	0.9%
9	1985	2.9%	2.1%	1.7%	1.2%	1.0%
10	1990	3.0%	2.3%	1.6%	1.2%	1.1%
11	1995	3.0%	2.5%	1.8%	1.1%	1.2%
12	2000	3.1%	2.5%	1.9%	1.3%	1.2%
13	2005	3.0%	2.6%	2.0%	1.4%	1.4%
14	2010	3.4%	2.6%	2.1%	1.5%	1.6%
15	2015	4.0%	2.9%	2.1%	1.6%	1.7%
16	2020	4.1%	3.4%	2.4%	1.6%	1.9%
17	2025	4.5%	3.6%	2.9%	1.9%	2.0%
18	2030	4.8%	4.0%	3.0%	2.2%	2.3%
19	2035	4.8%	4.2%	3.4%	2.4%	2.8%
20	2040	4.8%	4.3%	3.6%	2.7%	3.2%
21	2045	5.2%	4.3%	3.8%	2.9%	3.6%
22	2050	5.6%	4.7%	3.7%	3.1%	4.1%

Figure 2.4 The older age groups

When you're answering these kinds of questions, your editorial judgment has to come into play. What do you think are the most interesting things about your data? Who is your audience, and what do they want to know?

With that in mind, is it worth showing all of the five-year age groups? I would say it could be, because the 80 and older age group seems to be growing at a much faster rate than all of the others. That's interesting, and if you incorporate that age group into a larger "60 and older" age group, that information will be lost. But if there is a chart form that would work really well for this data set only if the age groups are combined, then we might want to combine them.

On to the next question: Which year do we start with? I'm thinking we should start with 1950. That way we can show not only how the world is projected to age in the years to come, but how it has aged in decades past. Including those earlier years will show a longer-term trend and provide more context. It's also true, of course, that past years are, well, past. Determining population figures for years gone by surely involved some assumptions on the part of the UN, but not quite as many assumptions as it took to compute the projected populations of the future. We know more about the past than we do about the future, so the past figures are more solid, and adding more of them to the graphic will better ground it in reality.

So, which year do we end with? My thinking is that we don't go all the way out to 2100, because the further out you go, the more tenuous the projections become. I think we should stop at 2050, for the somewhat arbitrary reason that, if we do, our data will end at a nice, even number, and cover 100 years exactly. A not so arbitrary reason to stop at 2050 is that it's only about 35 years in the future, yet the UN projects there will be significant change in the age composition of the world between now and then.

Now that we've nailed down our scope, let's start designing a graphic!

Choosing a Form

In Chapter 1, we said that the crux of good data visualization design is choosing the right combination of graphical elements and attributes to represent data. Making that choice is the main step in giving a graphic form. And it's a graphic's form that does the bulk of the visual storytelling.

Of course, you don't always have to create a new form from scratch. There are plenty of tried and true forms out there from which you can choose—bar charts, line charts, scatterplots, radar plots, Sankey diagrams, slopegraphs, choropleth maps—the list goes on. In most cases, it makes sense to fall back on one of these trusty ole forms to get the job done.

But which one do you choose? Picking one form over another usually involves some trade-offs. Each form emphasizes certain things and deemphasizes others, allowing the viewer to make some comparisons across the dataset, but also sometimes inhibiting her capability to make others. Let's walk through some options for how we could display our age composition data.

Showing the Data as a Column Chart

Let's start with one of the most basic chart forms—a column chart. In a column chart, the graphical element of choice is a column (really, a vertically aligned rectangle). The length (height) of the column represents the number of elements that match a particular attribute (or attributes) of interest. Figure 2.5 shows a column chart for our age distribution data. In this example, people are our elements and the attributes of

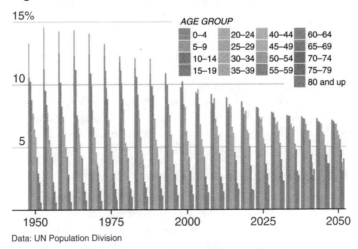

Data: UN Population Division

Figure 2.5 A column chart for our age data

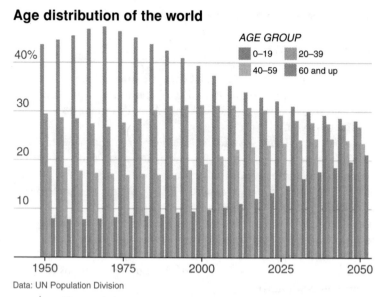

Figure 2.6 A column chart with four age groups

interest are age and time. Note that age is not being treated as a simple continuum here (1–80+) but as ordered categories of five years each (0-4, 5-9, etc.).

What do you think? Does this chart do a good job of showing that the world is getting older?

No, not really. Why? There are too many columns! The age distribution information gets buried. In the *Wall Street Journal Guide to Information Graphics* (2010, New York: W.W. Norton & Co.) Dona M. Wong (previously head of the paper's graphics department) suggests that when you have a column chart like this with multiple categories, you should limit the number of categories to four or fewer. That's good advice, and if we were to follow it, we would need to aggregate the 17 five-year age groups into four larger ones: 0-19 year-olds, 20-39 year olds, 40-59 year olds, and those 60 years and older. Figure 2.6 shows just such a chart.

A little clearer, yes? How does this chart fare overall? The overarching trend—that the world is getting older—is definitely possible to see. Though, of course, it doesn't show how fast the 80 and older age group is projected to rise because we limited ourselves to four age groupings. Let's take a look at some other options.

Showing the Data as a Stacked Column Chart

What if instead of putting the bars next to each other, we put them on top of each other? Figure 2.7 shows just such a chart—a so-called stacked column chart.

Like its unstacked brethren, the stacked column chart is a little hard to parse with all 17 age groups. Let's try aggregating the age groups again and see how it looks.

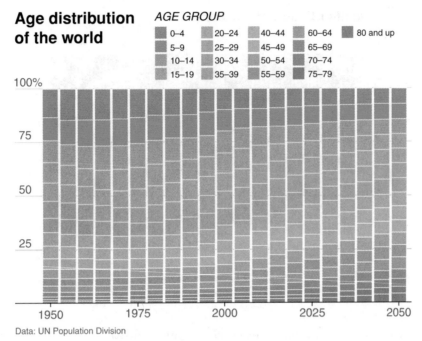

Age distribution of the world

AGE GROUP

0–4	20–24	40–44	60–64	80 and up
5–9	25–29	45–49	65–69	
10–14	30–34	50–54	70–74	
15–19	35–39	55–59	75–79	

Data: UN Population Division

Figure 2.7 A stacked column chart

Not bad. So, how does Figure 2.8 compare to its unstacked counterpart in Figure 2.6? It's much easier to interpret. You can see immediately that the portion of 0 to 19 year olds is shrinking and the 60 and above crowd is growing. As a chart form, the stacked column chart also does a much better job at conveying a sense of composition. It's immediately obvious that the different colors represent parts of a whole, whereas in Figure 2.3 it is not.

But the stacked column chart does have one drawback, compared to the normal column chart. Look at the year 2050. If you had to rank the different age groups from largest to smallest, what would you say? It's really hard to compare the values within a year, especially when they are close. The reason is that it's difficult for us to determine the difference in length between two objects when their ends aren't lined up. (W. Cleveland and R. McGill, Graphical Perception: Theory, Experimentation, and Application to the Development of Graphical Methods, *Journal of the American Statistical Association,* Vol. 79, No. 387, 1984.) In the column chart in Figure 2.3, all of the columns are flush with the baseline at the bottom, so we can compare the length of any two by just looking to see which one stands taller. But our ability to compare lengths is greatly compromised when we stack columns on top of each other.

Given the choice between only the column chart and the stacked column chart, which would you choose? Because there are trade-offs between the two, your editorial judgment has to come into play. If your goal is simply to answer the question "is the

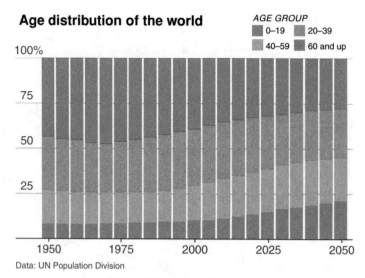

Figure 2.8 A simpler stack

world getting older?" then the stacked column chart is a better choice. It shows very clearly that the answer is "yes." If, on the other hand, being able to see the composition of any given year is important for the story you want to tell, then the column chart might be a good option.

Showing the Data as a Line Chart

But, of course, a column chart and stacked column chart aren't the only two options available. Let's see how the data looks if we use another workhorse in the data visualization world—a line chart.

The line chart in Figure 2.9 is really interesting, because you can see dips in the population cascade across the curves over time. For instance, there's a dip in 5-9 year olds in 1950, which then turns into a dip in 10-14 year olds in 1955, a dip in 15-19 year olds in 1960, and so on. Why is this dip there? The answer is World War II. Birth rates were lower while the war was in progress, from 1939 to 1944. Babies born during that time would have been roughly between 6 and 11 years old in 1950, and because there were relatively fewer of them, there's a visible dip in the 5-9 year-old population.

So that's super interesting, and something that wasn't apparent when we were just looking at the raw data. Visualization doesn't only help the audience see patterns in data, it can also help you, the data visualization designer, see such patterns. This is one of the reasons why data visualization design is often an iterative process—you sometimes discover things as you go along that make you want to shift your focus a little bit. It would be totally reasonable at this point to decide that you wanted whatever the final graphic was to show those population dips.

Age distridution of the world

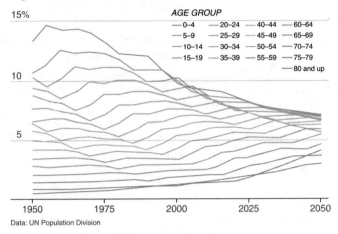

Data: UN Population Division

Figure 2.9   A line chart

Age distribution of the world

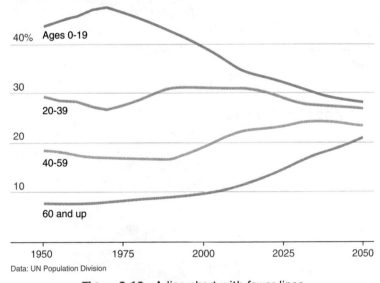

Data: UN Population Division

Figure 2.10   A line chart with fewer lines

Population dips aside, how good of a job does Figure 2.9 do at conveying the idea that the world is getting older? It's not great, actually. The chart gets a little confusing as time advances and the lines start to cross. There might just be too many lines. Again, let's see how it looks if we use broader age groups. Take a look at Figure 2.10.

Notice that the population dip from World War II is still there, but it's much less noticeable. Let's compare Figure 2.10 to the column chart in Figure 2.6. What do you see? They show the exact same trends in pretty similar ways, but in the column chart, it's like you have to read those trends between the columns, whereas in the line chart, they are shown plainly.

Now, let's compare Figure 2.10 with the simple stacked column chart in Figure 2.8. What are the pros and cons of each? Figure 2.8 does a really good job of conveying a sense of composition. But it doesn't allow you to look at an individual year and compare the relative sizes of the age groups. It also isn't very good at showing the trends of the age groups in the middle. Because the 0-19 age group is flush with the top of the chart and the 60 and up age group is flush with the bottom, it's easy to see how those age groups are changing over time. But with the age groups in the middle, not so much.

The line chart in Figure 2.10, on the other hand, is really good at showing both the trends of all the age groups over time and allowing you to compare the relative values of each age group for any year.

Showing the Data as a Pie Chart

Now, let's say we wanted to really focus on the age breakdown of the world in an individual year. How might we go about doing that? We could try a pie chart, as in Figure 2.11.

Pie charts are pretty controversial in the data visualization world—and for good reason. On one hand, the pie chart is arguably the least intimidating of all chart forms, which makes it a tempting option for any designer worried about frightening or boring her audience. But on the other hand, pie charts really are pretty bad at displaying data.

Age distribution of the world, 2010

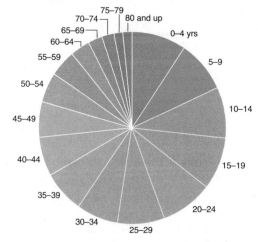

Data: UN Population Division

Figure 2.11 A pie chart

Age distribution of the world, 2010

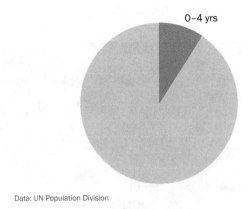

Data: UN Population Division

Figure 2.12   Just a single slice

With pie charts, the graphical elements you are relying on to convey information are, of course, pie-shaped slices of a circle. And what is the attribute that varies between them? It's the angle formed by the two straight sides of each slice. That angle is larger for bigger slices and smaller for smaller ones.

As it turns out, we humans are really bad at perceiving differences in angles. We tend to overestimate obtuse angles (those greater than 90°) and underestimate acute ones (less than 90°). We also tend to perceive the exact same pie slice as larger if it's oriented horizontally (with the point facing left or right, assuming the angle is less than 180°) than if it's oriented vertically (with the point facing up or down). When you are trying to compare slices of a circle that are all oriented differently—as in Figure 2.11—that's a real problem.

Some experts think you should only use pie charts to compare a single part to its whole, and not to compare parts with each other.[2] In other words, you should limit the number of slices shown on a pie chart to one. For example, Figure 2.12 is a pared down version of Figure 2.11 that highlights only the portion of the population that is between 0 and 4.

But is Figure 2.12 actually useful, or would it be if we made one of those pie charts for each age group and put them all side-by-side? No, not really. Alas, though it may be tempting to use them, pie charts are seriously limited in their utility.

Showing the Data as a Bar Chart

A better way to enable comparisons between age groups within a selected year is to make a simple bar chart for that year, as in Figure 2.13.

---

2. See, for example, http://www.excelcharts.com/blog/optimal-number-categories-pie-chart/

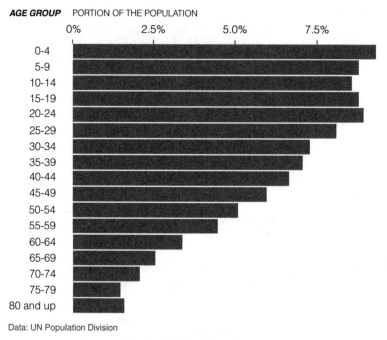

Age distribution of the world, 2010

Figure 2.13 A bar chart

Like column charts, bar charts consist of rectangles that vary in length. The difference between the two is that, in a bar chart the bar can run horizontally (as in Figure 2.13) or vertically. Also, each bar typically represents a single category of a single element or dimension. In Figure 2.13 time is not included as a second dimension as it was in the column chart in Figure 2.5. Figure 2.13 simply presents the percentage of people who fall into each age category at a particular point in time (2010). This yields a simpler graph since you are not trying to compare age groups across time.

> **Note**
>
> A note on using bar charts and column charts: Because they both show data via variations in the lengths of the rectangles, it's important that the entire length of every rectangle is actually shown. In practice, what this means is that the scale should always start at zero and the longest bar or column should extend very close to the maximum width or height available in the space allowed.

So how good is Figure 2.13? When it comes to showing with precision and clarity the age composition of a single year, it's the best chart form we've seen so far. Yet it doesn't allow us to compare across years, at least not as is. But don't fret: There's a way we can make a bar chart that will.

Showing the Data as a Small Multiple Bar Chart

What if we created a massive chart that consisted of a series of bar charts like the one shown in Figure 2.13, one for each year in our dataset? Well, if we made all of the bar charts the same size as the one in Figure 2.13, the chart would have to be pretty massive. But what if we combined age groups, shrunk the charts way down, and laid them out in a grid? Then we might have something. Take a look at Figure 2.14.

This kind of graphical layout—a series of small, similar charts clustered together—is varyingly called a trellis chart, grid chart, panel chart, lattice chart, or a small multiple. This last term is the one preferred by Edward Tufte, the influential information design theorist and writer. In his book, *Envisioning Information* (1990, Cheshire, Conn.: Graphics Press), Tufte writes:

> At the heart of quantitative reasoning is a single question: *Compared to what?* Small multiple designs, multivariate and data bountiful, answer directly by visually enforcing comparisons of changes, of the differences among objects, of the scope of alternatives. For a wide range of problems in data presentation, small multiples are the best design solution.

So what is this chart good at conveying, and what are its shortcomings? Again, just like a single bar chart, it's good at allowing the different age groups to be compared within an individual year. And, because the year increases as you go down a column (instead of across a row) you can compare between years, too (at least between the years in each column).

What it's not especially great at is showing the overall trend over time—that the population is getting older. That information is certainly there, but it doesn't pop out at you the way it does in some of the other chart forms we've seen.

So which of the chart forms we've looked at is best? Again, it all depends on what you want to convey. If you're only interested in showing very simply that the world is projected to get older, then either the stacked column chart in Figure 2.8 or the simple line chart in Figure 2.10 are fine options. If you want to enable comparison within years (at the expense of emphasizing the overall trend), then the small multiple bar chart is a good way to go. So there is no simple answer. Choosing a chart form depends on the type of data you have and what you are trying to say about that data.

Chart Suggestions—A Thought Starter

In the last few sections we looked at different ways of visualizing the same dataset, evaluated their pros and cons, and came up with a couple of recommendations, depending on the goals of the data visualization. But is that really a good way of going about designing graphics? Making full-fledged charts for a bunch of different forms and picking the one that works best? No, of course not.

It can help to make quick charts using programs like R or spreadsheet software like Excel, Open Office, or Google Drive to give you a sense of what the data looks like when visualized.

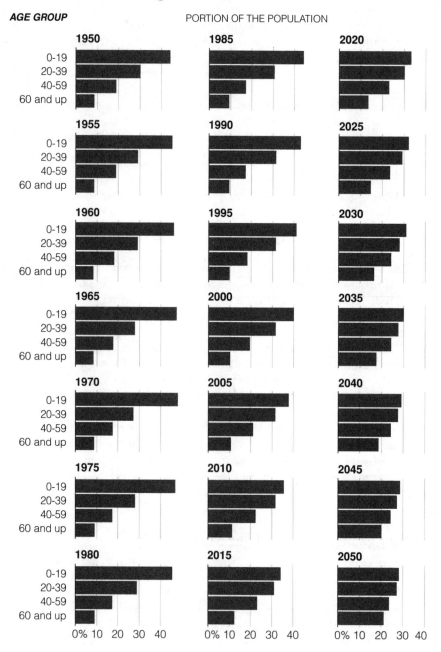

Age distribution of the world

Figure 2.14   A small multiple bar chart

> **Note**
>
> Personally, I make a lot of charts in R and then pull them into a program such as Ink-scape or Adobe Illustrator to put the final touches on. In fact, that's exactly how I made the charts in the previous section, and for those of you who have used ggplot2, you'll recognize the color scheme.

But as you gain experience, you'll gain an intuitive sense of what will work and what won't, before you start plotting. In the meantime, there's a handy diagram that you can use to help you get started choosing a form. It is shown in Figure 2.15 and was created by Dr. Andrew Abela (http://extremepresentation.typepad.com/blog/2006/09/choosing_a_good.html), a marketing professor and dean of the business school at Catholic University of America in Washington, D.C.

As the title says, this diagram is really just a thought starter. You shouldn't feel bound to it. But if you don't have a lot of experience designing data visualizations, it can help you gain a sense of when it is appropriate to use which of the most basic chart forms.

> **Note**
>
> An important note: The chart suggestions diagram says nothing about animation or interactivity. It assumes that the final product of your work as a chart designer will be an unmoving, unclickable chart, probably existing as an image file or embedded in a presentation. When animation and interactivity are on the table, the scope of what you can and cannot do changes entirely.

The Example We Will Build in This Book

So what should we do with this population data? We talked about a few good options in the previous section. But I don't think we should go with any of them! Well, not exactly, anyway.

The data visualization we are going to spend pretty much the remainder of the book building is going to look at lot like the one shown in Figure 2.16.

It looks almost identical to the single bar chart in Figure 2.13. But there are a couple of differences. First, the order of the age groups is flipped. Why? Because when it comes to age distribution charts, it's a bit of a convention to have the oldest age group on top and the youngest on the bottom. But more importantly, the chart will be interactive. Notice the text that says, "PLAY ALL YEARS," and the two rows containing all the years in our dataset. On the chart you'll be building, those years will be clickable, and when one of them is clicked, the bars will grow and or shrink until they are the right length for the selected year. When "PLAY ALL YEARS" is clicked, the chart will be set to 1950, and then advance automatically through each of the subsequent years to show how the age distribution has changed over time.

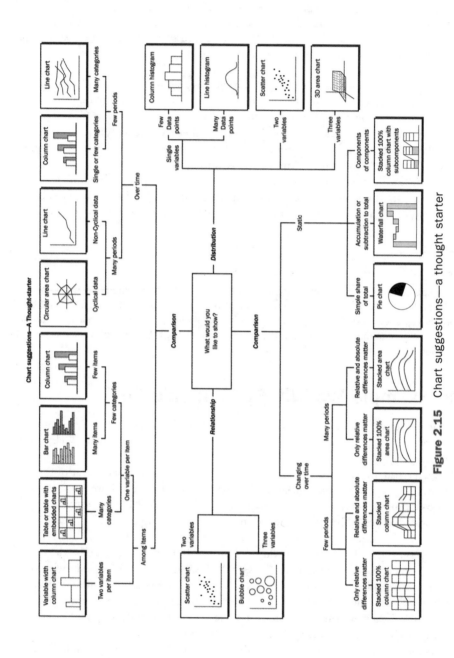

Figure 2.15 Chart suggestions—a thought starter

Age distribution of the world

▶ *PLAY ALL YEARS*

1950 1955 1960 1965 1970 1975 1980 1985 1990 1995 2000
2005 **2010** 2015 2020 2025 2030 2035 2040 2045 2050

AGE GROUP   *PORTION OF THE POPULATION*

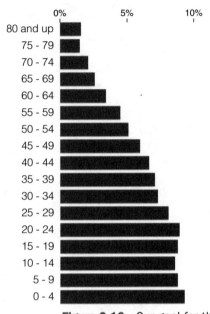

Figure 2.16   Our goal for this book

It's arguably not the best form for showing this data—the trend that the world is getting older won't be immediately apparent—but it's one that, admittedly, enables us to cover some important D3 ground. You'll learn how to use D3 to create a graphic on a webpage using a medium-sized dataset and how to make that graphic both interactive and animated. Sound exciting? Great! Let's get to it.

Summary

In this chapter I introduced the dataset we will use to build the central example data visualization of this book. But the chapter covered more than that. We talked about how to get started on a data story—by having some data in hand or by asking a question and finding data to answer it. We talked about inspecting the data that you have and how, when you do, you often come up with ideas for what to show in your graphic that you didn't have initially. Finally, we talked about using your editorial judgment to really refine your concept before you get to work on the design.

3

Scalable Vector Graphics

This chapter will serve as a primer on scalable vector graphics (SVG). It will go over how to create SVG elements and how to style them and transform them. After the basics have been covered, it will show how to build a bar chart of the global age distribution in 2010 from scratch in SVG. This chapter assumes rudimentary knowledge of HTML and CSS.

Peeking under the Hood

Toward the end of this chapter, we're going to start building the interactive bar chart of the world's age distribution described at the end of Chapter 2. (Only it won't be interactive—at least not by the end of this chapter. What we're really going to focus on is building a static version of the world's age distribution in 2010, and 2010 only.)

We're going to build that chart from scratch using SVG. You'll likely be creating and manipulating a lot of SVG elements if you use D3, and it's good to know a bit about what's going on under the hood.

So let's get started! This book assumes that you have some basic experience with HTML and CSS, so a lot of code will be passed off to you without much explanation. As long as you understand <p> tags, know what a <div> is, and have a basic grasp of CSS, you should be just fine.

What Is SVG, Exactly?

Graphics come in two basic flavors: vector and raster. A raster image is made up of a fixed number of square pixels (which, remember, is short for "picture elements") and each pixel is one color. JPEGs, PNGs, GIFs...all of the formats that digital photos typically come in are raster formats.

The telltale sign of a raster is that when you zoom in on it, it gets fuzzy—or more precisely, pixelated. The reason is rendering. When you are viewing an image at a 100% zoom level, each individual image pixel is being rendered into exactly one pixel on your computer's monitor. But if you blow the image up to 200% (which means that you are doubling both the width and the height, so quadrupling the area of the image) each image pixel takes up four pixels on your screen. Keep zooming and at some point, you'll actually be able to see that your image is made up of a bunch of little squares. That's pixelation.

Vectors images, instead of just telling your computer to make the pixel that is 50th from the top and 100th from the left magenta, describe an entire drawing: "Put a black curve on the left, a red rectangle on the right, and a blue circle with a yellow outline that is semi-transparent up top." It's up to your computer (or really, whatever piece of software you are using) to take these instructions and then tell your screen's pixels what to do. The beauty of this is that the instructions themselves can be really simple, and your screen's pixels are rendered differently at different zoom levels so the drawing is always crystal clear. No pixelation. (Then again, vectors are really only good for fairly basic shapes, not for encoding, say, an Ansel Adams landscape.)

SVG is just one type of vector format. But it's a really useful one, because it's a web standard, so web browsers can understand the instructions it provides (as long as the browser isn't Internet Explorer 8 or earlier). Since D3 is designed to work with web standards, it plays really well with SVG.

Playing with Circles in SVG

All SVGs are encoded in a human-readable programming language that's a lot like HTML. There are opening tags and closing tags, parents, children, the whole nine. In fact, nowadays, if you're building a webpage, you can insert a chunk of SVG markup right into your HTML and the graphic will appear in your browser (this is exactly what D3 does when you use it to make SVG-based graphics). This wasn't always the case; SVG support was a major addition to HTML5, at the time of this writing the latest standard. Now, there's no need to reference a separate file sitting at a different URL, as you would with an <img> tag. You can also use your browser's web inspector to see what's going on inside your SVG markup, which is extremely helpful for debugging.

With that in mind, let's start making some SVGs for the web!

Open up your text editor of choice (if you don't have a text editor, see Chapter 1 for more info). We're going to create an HTML file that we'll open up in the browser. Since we'll be playing around with SVG, let's call it **svg-sandbox.html**.

The first thing we want to do is declare that we are writing an HTML document. The World Wide Web Consortium (W3C) recommends using this preamble at the beginning of every page (and since they set the standards, we listen!):

```
<!DOCTYPE html>
```

If you don't, there's a chance the browser might render your code in some old-fashioned way, making everything look wonky. The DOCTYPE declaration tells the browser, "hey, I totally follow HTML web standards, so don't misread me!"

It's also a good idea to tell the browser what character encoding you're using. If you're trying to show some really unusual Unicode characters, you don't want the user's browser to interpret that code in ASCII, an encoding that is much more limited.

If her browser is set to the ASCII character encoding some of that Unicode could be lost in translation, producing a jumble of characters called mojibake. You can override that setting by specifying the character encoding directly in your HTML. Unicode is sort of the lingua franca of encodings—it's by far the most inclusive and the most used, so you should use it whenever possible.

```
<meta charset="utf-8">
```

Okay, here's the basic set up of **svg-sandbox.html**, with the DOCTYPE, character encoding, and a label just for fun:

```
<!DOCTYPE html>
<html>
        <head>
                <meta charset="utf-8">
        </head>
        <body>
                <p>SVG sandbox</p>
        </body>
</html>
```

The first thing we have to do to build an SVG image is create an <svg> element inside of <body>. Among other things, this sets aside some space on the page for the graphics. Let's go ahead and give it a width and a height.

```
<body>
        <p>SVG sandbox</p>
        <svg width="500px" height="500px"></svg>
</body>
```

See how similar SVG is to HTML? We can even give the <svg> element a width and height inline, right inside the tag. All of the shapes and text we'll create will go inside of that <svg> tag. Let's start with a circle, which we can create using a <circle> tag:

```
<svg width="500px" height="500px">
        <circle/>
</svg>
```

Now open **svg-sandbox.html** in your browser, and check out that circle! Wait, you don't see anything? Oh yeah, that's because we haven't told the browser anything about the circle—how big we want it to be, where it should be positioned, what color it should be…. We haven't set any of its attributes. But we can do that inline (i.e., inside of the <circle> tag), in the same way we style HTML elements inline.

```
<svg width="500px" height="500px">
        <circle cx="100" cy="50" r="20"/>
</svg>
```

The result is shown in Figure 3.1.

SVG sandbox

Figure 3.1 A basic SVG circle

SVG sandbox

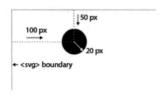

Figure 3.2 A diagram of the circle's position and size

Alright, now we've got a circle, black by default. As I'm sure you've guessed, r refers to the circle's radius. cx is the position of its center-point on the x-axis (left to right), and cy is the position of the center-point on the y-axis (from top to bottom). In SVG, units are in pixels by default, but you can change them to inches or centimeters or any other accepted measurement value if you like. (Try setting the radius to 100%!) Figure 3.2 shows the lay of the land (or sandbox) so far.

Inspecting SVG in the Web Inspector

Now that we have an SVG circle in our browser, we can inspect it with the browser's web inspector. I'll be using Chrome in this book, but all modern browsers either have a built-in web inspector or a free plugin you can download. In Chrome if you right-click on the circle and select "Inspect Element," the Developer Tools window will open. That markup in Figure 3.3 sure looks familiar.

SVG sandbox

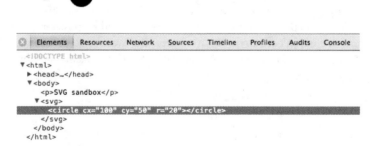

Figure 3.3 Looking at SVG elements with the Web Inspector

We can change the style attributes of our circle within the Web Inspector. Double-click on the 100 next to cx, change it to 0, and hit enter. Now the circle's center-point is 0 pixels from the left, and half of it is cut off (see Figure 3.4).

Styling SVG Elements with CSS

Position and size are great, but we should also add a little color to this circle, no? If you've done any graphic design and have some experience with programs like Adobe Illustrator, you'll recognize a lot of SVG's nomenclature. The interior color of a shape is called the "fill," and the line around the edge of a shape is called the "stroke." Figure 3.5 shows an example.

```
<svg width="500px" height="500px">
    <circle cx="100" cy="50" r="20" fill="darkmagenta" stroke="black"
stroke-width="5"/>
</svg>
```

Say we wanted to draw multiple circles, of various sizes, in different positions, but that all look the same. We could style all of those circles inline as shown in Figure 3.6.

```
<svg width="500px" height="500px">
    <circle cx="120" cy="50" r="20" fill="darkmagenta" stroke="black"
stroke-width="5"/>
```

SVG sandbox

Figure 3.4   Pushing the circle off the screen with the Web Inspector

SVG sandbox

Figure 3.5   A circle with a fill and a stroke

SVG sandbox

Figure 3.6   Three different circles with the same stroke and fill

```
        <circle cx="15" cy="50" r="10" fill="darkmagenta" stroke="black"
stroke-width="5"/>
        <circle cx="60" cy="100" r="50" fill="darkmagenta" stroke="black"
stroke-width="5"/>
</svg>
```

Or we could use CSS (another bonus of using SVG). Just as with HTML, using CSS makes it easier to apply styles to multiple elements (and thus, change the styling of multiple elements on the fly). So, while the code above works perfectly fine, you can make your life easier by assigning classes to each of the circles and styling them in one fell swoop.

```
<!DOCTYPE html>
<html>
<head>
<meta charset="utf-8">
<style>
.styled-circle
{
        fill: darkmagenta;
        stroke: black;
        stroke-width:5;
}
</style>
</head>
<body>
        <p>SVG sandbox</p>
        <svg width="500px" height="500px">
                <circle cx="120" cy="50" r="20" class="styled-circle"/>
                <circle cx="15" cy="50" r="10" class="styled-circle"/>
                <circle cx="60" cy="100" r="50" class="styled-circle"/>
        </svg>
</body>
</html>
```

There are a couple of things to note: One is that you can only use CSS for style properties, such as fill and stroke. You can't use CSS for defining the position or size of an SVG element. So, if you are drawing 100 circles and each has a radius of 5, you still have to define r for each one individually. But don't worry: D3 makes it possible to do this with one short line of code.

The second thing is that SVG styles and HTML styles are different and have different names, even though sometimes the properties they refer to are similar. To create an outline around a <div> in HTML, you would use the border property, since

<div>s don't have strokes. To avoid confusion, Scott Murray[1] suggests putting svg in front of classes associated with SVG elements, like so:

```
svg .styled-circle {
    /* Styling goes here */
}
```

This limits the CSS selector to elements that are children of any <svg> elements on your page (and are also classed styled-circle). But mostly, it serves as a reminder to use SVG properties.

Other Shapes

I hope I haven't given you the impression that SVG is all circles all the time (see Figures 3.7 through 3.12). Here's a reference list of basic SVG elements, how to position and size them, and some notes on using them. I've included the old familiar circle so you'll have everything in one handy reference.

Rectangles

Tag

<rect>

Position and Size

x	Horizontal location of the rectangle's top-left corner
y	Vertical location of the rectangle's top-left corner
width	The rectangle's width
height	The rectangle's height

```
<svg width="500px" height="500px">
    <rect x="0" y="0" width="100" height="20"/>
</svg>
```

Rounded Rectangles

Tag

<rect>

Figure 3.7 A rectangle

---

1. Murray, Scott. *Interactive Data Visualization for the Web*. Sebastopol, CA: O'Reilly Media Inc., 2013.

Figure 3.8 A rounded rectangle

Position and Size

x	Horizontal location of the rectangle's top-left corner
y	Vertical location of the rectangle's top-left corner
width	The rectangle's width
height	The rectangle's height
rx	Radius of curvature for the horizontal component of the round corners
ry	Radius of curvature for the vertical component of the round corners

```
<svg width="500px" height="500px">
    <rect x="0" y="0" width="100" height="50" rx="10" ry="10"/>
</svg>
```

Note
Rounded rectangles generally look best when rx and ry are equal.

Circles

Tag
`<circle>`

Position and Size

cx	Horizontal location of the circle's center-point
cy	Vertical location of the circle's center-point
r	The circle's radius

```
<svg width="500px" height="500px">
    <circle cx="50" cy="25" r="20"/>
</svg>
```

Figure 3.9 A circle

Ellipses

Tag

`<ellipse>`

Position and Size

cx	Horizontal location of the ellipse's center-point
cy	Vertical location of the ellipse's center-point
rx	The ellipse's radius along its horizontal axis
ry	The ellipse's radius along its vertical axis

```
<svg width="500px" height="500px">
      <ellipse cx="50" cy="25" rx="40" ry="20"/>
</svg>
```

Figure 3.10   An ellipse

Polygons

Tag

`<polygon>`

Position and Size

points	A series of x and y coordinates describing the location of the polygon's angles

```
<svg width="500px" height="500px">
      <polygon points="100,0 50,50 150,50"/>
</svg>
```

Figure 3.11   A polygon

Note

Polygons are always closed shapes. So, if you specify three points, the third will automatically be connected to the first.

Lines

Tag

`<line>`

Position and Size

x1	Horizontal position of the start-point
y1	Vertical position of the start-point
x2	Horizontal position of the end-point
y2	Vertical position of the end-point

```
<svg width="500px" height="500px">
      <line x1="0" y1="0" x2="200" y2="50" stroke="black"/>
</svg>
```

Figure 3.12 A line

> **Note**
> You have to give the stroke a color for the line to be visible.

Paths

Tag

`<path>`

Position and Size

d	Tells your browser how to draw the path

Paths are almost like a separate language. Every other shape in SVG can be created with a path element: They can make straight lines, they can make curves, and they can be closed and filled in. I won't go over all of the details, but here's an example to give you a taste (it is shown in Figure 3.13):

```
<svg width="500px" height="500px">
      <path d="M 0 50 q 50 -50 100 0 1 -100 0" stroke="black"
fill="none"/>
</svg>
```

Figure 3.13 A path

Every path has one (often quite long) value for the attribute d. There are letters and numbers in that value that say how the path should be drawn. In the example above, M is short for "moveto," meaning that the imaginary cursor drawing the path should move to, in this case, 0 pixels from the left and 50 from the top. q then tells the cursor to draw a quadratic Bézier curve that arcs to a point 50 pixels over and 50 pixels up and then arcs back down to a point that is 100 pixels to the right of where it started, but vertically aligned. l then says to draw a line 100 pixels to left, completing the shape (which sort of resembles a setting sun).

See what I mean? Like a language unto itself. And I've just scratched the surface. If you want to learn more about paths, you should check out the specifications, which were written by the World Wide Web Consortium (http://www.w3.org/TR/SVG11/paths.html). Fortunately, D3 makes drawing paths a lot simpler than hardcoding them in SVG.

> **Note**
>
> Paths, like circles and rectangles, have a black fill by default in SVG. If you don't want a fill, you have to set fill to "none."

SVG Text

In addition to shapes, you can also use SVG to draw text. But why would you want to when you can use a good ol' <p> tag? If you're building a graphic in D3 that has labels you want to change and move around, SVG text can be easier to use. You can also rotate SVG text, or make the text travel along an arc, or any other path (though you should do those things sparingly, because it makes the text harder to read). Here's the skinny on SVG text:

```
<body>
        <svg width="500px" height="500px">
                <text x="10" y="25" font-size="20">SVG sandbox, now in SVG
only</text>
        </svg>
</body>
```

And the text generated is shown in Figure 3.14.

Note that the SVG <text> tag is not self-closing. The text you want to draw goes in between the opening and closing tags, just like with a <p> tag.

All of the basic text attributes have the same names in SVG as they do in HTML: font-size, font-family, font-weight, font-style. That is, except color. With SVG text, as with shapes, the color is called the fill. And yes, you can add strokes around your text:

```
<svg width="500px" height="500px">
        <text x="10" y="50" font-size="40" fill="lightgrey" stroke="red"
font-family="Comic Sans MS">Party like it's 1999!</text>
</svg>
```

SVG sandbox, now in SVG only

Figure 3.14   SVG text

Party like it's 1999!

Figure 3.15   SVG text getting wild

The result is shown in Figure 3.15.

The x and y attributes specify the position of the text's anchor point. By default, the anchor point marks the start of the text and is vertically aligned with the text's baseline. Here's a snippet that makes the anchor point and baseline visible:

```
<svg width="500px" height="500px">
    <text x="10" y="50" font-size="40" fill="grey">Anchors away! Or
not...</text>
    <circle cx="10" cy="50" r="4" fill="magenta"/>
    <line x1="10" y1="50" x2="420" y2="50" stroke="magenta"/>
</svg>
```

Figure 3.16 shows you what it looks like.

Because the anchor point is aligned with the baseline, you need to remember to set the y coordinate so that your text has enough space up top. If you set y to 0, then you'll only see tails.

```
<svg width="500px" height="500px">
    <text x="10" y="0" font-size="40">Where did all my text go?</text>
</svg>
```

You can change the position of the anchor by setting the text-anchor attribute. Text-anchor is set to start by default, but if you want to center-align your text, you can set it to middle and if you want to right-align it, you can set it to end.

```
<svg width="500px" height="500px">
    <text x="10" y="20" text-anchor="start">This text is</text>
    <text x="10" y="35" text-anchor="start">aligned</text>
    <text x="10" y="50" text-anchor="start">to the left</text>
    <text x="300" y="20" text-anchor="middle">This text is</text>
    <text x="300" y="35" text-anchor="middle">aligned</text>
    <text x="300" y="50" text-anchor="middle">to the center</text>
    <text x="590" y="20" text-anchor="end">This text is</text>
    <text x="590" y="35" text-anchor="end">aligned</text>
    <text x="590" y="50" text-anchor="end">to the right</text>
</svg>
```

Anchors away! Or not...

Figure 3.16   It's not leaving that spot

Figure 3.17 shows start, middle, and end text anchors.

One disadvantage of SVG text, as you may have realized, is that you have to know where you want your line breaks to be. In the example in Figure 3.17, I had to create three separate text elements for the block of text at the left, three for the block in the center, and three for the right. Unlike HTML, SVG has no way of simply drawing a box for a chunk of text to go into that will break it up in lines automatically.

One last thing about SVG text: You can add links using an <a> tag. The SVG <a> tag differs from its HTML counterpart in two ways: 1) You have to write `xlink:href="your-link-here"` instead of `href="your-link-here"` and 2) by default, if you hover your cursor over a link in SVG, it will turn into a pointer, but other than that, the link won't be formatted any differently from the surrounding text. Here's a snippet that creates a link and formats it to look like a standard link in HTML:

```
<head>
<style>
svg a {
      fill:blue;
}
svg a:visited{
      fill:purple;
}
svg a:hover{
      text-decoration:underline;
}
</style>
</head>
<body>
      <svg width="500px" height="500px">
            <text x="10" y="20">Here's where to go to <a
xlink:href="http://www.w3schools.com/svg/svg_text.asp">learn more
about SVG text</a>, including how to rotate it</text>
      </svg>
</body>
```

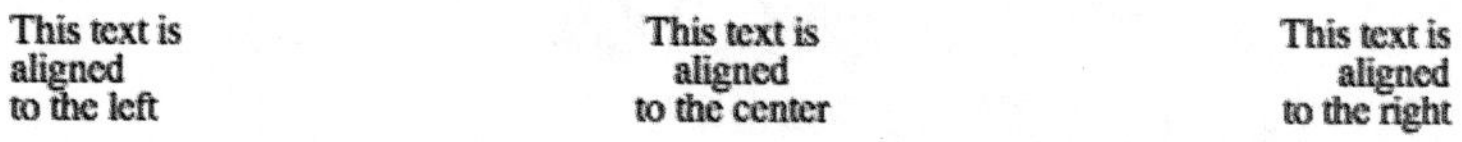

This text is
aligned
to the left

This text is
aligned
to the center

This text is
aligned
to the right

Figure 3.17   Examples of the different text anchors

SVG Style Properties

SVG has a slew of style properties you can use for designing graphics. We've gone over some of them, such as fill and stroke, but here are a few more details.

Color and Transparency

In SVG, you can set the color of a fill or a stroke in a few different ways.

Color Names	Blue	DarkMagenta	BlanchedAlmond
HEX	#0000FF	#8B008B	#FFEBCD
RGB	rgb(0,0,255)	rgb(139,0,139)	rgb(255,235,205)

```
<svg width="500px" height="500px">
    <circle cx="50" cy="50" r="20" fill="BlanchedAlmond"/>
    <circle cx="100" cy="50" r="20" stroke="#0000FF" stroke-width="5"
fill="none"/>
    <circle cx="150" cy="50" r="20" fill="rgb(139,0,139)"/>
</svg>
```

Figure 3.18 shows the three different circles.

You can also make SVG elements transparent:

opacity	A number between 0 and 1, where 0 is invisible and 1 is completely opaque, changes the opacity of both the fill and the stroke
fill-opacity	Only changes the opacity of the fill
stroke-opacity	Only changes the opacity of the stroke
RGBA	An RGB color that includes an alpha value, which is also between 0 and 1 and functionally equivalent to opacity

```
<svg width="500px" height="500px">
    <circle cx="50" cy="50" r="40" fill="rgb(0,0,255)" opacity="0.5"/>
    <circle cx="100" cy="50" r="40" fill="rgba(0,0,255,0.5)"/>
</svg>
```

Figure 3.19 shows an example of using transparency.

Figure 3.18 Circles colored in different ways with different notations

Figure 3.19 Overlapping transparent circles

When making graphics in SVG, I prefer to use `opacity` instead of RGBA. For one, it makes it easier to look at your code and see which elements are transparent and which ones aren't. Also, if you're using D3 and changing the opacity of different elements without changing their color, you don't have to unnecessarily reset the color with every change.

Stroke Properties

When it comes to strokes, you have the option of setting the color, width, and opacity, and also making the stroke dashed or changing the caps on the end from flat to round.

stroke	Sets the color of a stroke
stroke-width	Sets the thickness
stroke-opacity	Sets the opacity
stroke-linecap	Sets the shape of the endpoints of a stroke. The options are butt (the default), round, and square
stroke-dasharray	Creates a pattern of dashes and gaps for the stroke to be drawn in

```
<head>
<style>
.linecap-demo{
      stroke:darkmagenta;
      stroke-width:5;
}
</style>
</head>
<body>
      <svg width="500px" height="500px">
            <text x="0" y="20" font-weight="bold">Linecaps</text>
            <text x="0" y="50">Butt</text>
            <line x1="60" y1="45" x2="200" y2="45" class="linecap-demo"
stroke-linecap="butt"/>
            <text x="0" y="70">Round</text>
            <line x1="60" y1="65" x2="200" y2="65" class="linecap-demo"
stroke-linecap="round"/>
            <text x="0" y="90">Square</text>
            <line x1="60" y1="85" x2="200" y2="85" class="linecap-demo"
stroke-linecap="square"/>
      </svg>
</body>
```

Figure 3.20 shows examples of various linecap styles.

A stroke dasharray is a sequence of numbers separated by spaces that sets the widths of the stroke's alternating dashes (sections of line) and gaps (sections of no line).

Linecaps

Figure 3.20 Linecap styles

Dasharrays

Figure 3.21 Dasharray styles

For example, a dasharray of "5 5" will travel along the page for 5 pixels, disappear for 5 pixels, and then pick the path back up for another 5 pixels, and so on. The dasharray can be as long and as weird as you like, and when the stroke reaches the length covered by the array (which is 10 pixels in the example above) it starts over.

```
<head>
<style>
.dasharray-demo{
      stroke:darkmagenta;
      stroke-width:3;
}
</style>
</head>
<body>
      <svg width="500px" height="500px">
            <text x="0" y="20" font-weight="bold">Dasharrays</text>
            <text x="100" y="50" text-anchor="end">1 1</text>
            <line x1="110" y1="45" x2="350" y2="45" class="dasharray-
demo" stroke-dasharray="1 1"/>
            <text x="100" y="70" text-anchor="end">10 4 4 4</text>
            <line x1="110" y1="65" x2="350" y2="65" class="dasharray-demo"
stroke-dasharray="10 4 4 4"/>
            <text x="100" y="90" text-anchor="end">5 10 1 20 30 5</text>
            <line x1="110" y1="85" x2="350" y2="85" class="dasharray-demo"
stroke-dasharray="5 10 1 20 30 5"/>
      </svg>
</body>
```

Figure 3.21 shows examples of various dasharray styles.

Figure 3.22 Drawing order

Drawing Order and Groups

Unlike Adobe Illustrator or Inkscape, SVG doesn't have layers. But it does draw stuff in order. It starts with the first element in your code and then goes down the line. If there is overlap between two elements, the one that appears lower down in your code will be in front.

```
<style>
svg text{
      text-anchor:middle;
      fill:lightgrey;
}
svg rect{
      fill:crimson;
      opacity:0.5;
}
</style>
<body>
      <svg width="500px" height="500px">
             <text x="100" y="35">Text on bottom</text>
             <rect x="0" y="0"/ width="200" height="60"/>
             <rect x="250" y="0" width="200" height="60"/>
             <text x="350" y="35">Text on top</text>
      </svg>
</body>
```

Two different examples of drawing order are shown in Figure 3.22.

One thing you can do in SVG that you'll be familiar with if you're a designer is to group elements together. You do this with a <g> tag. We'll learn the real value of groups when we dig into D3, but one benefit to grouping objects that you'll appreciate now is that you can apply styles to a group and they'll automatically be applied to all of the elements within that group.

```
<head>
<style>
.blue-group{
      fill: blue;
      stroke-width: 3;
}
```

```
.red-group{
        fill: red;
        stroke-width: 4;
        font-weight:bold;
}
.green-group{
        fill: green;
        stroke-width: 2;
        font-family: Arial;
        fill-opacity:0.5;
}
</style>
</head>
<body>
        <svg width="500px" height="500px">
                <g class="blue-group">
                        <text x="0" y="20">Blue group</text>
                        <rect x="0" y="40" width="50" height="50" rx="10" ry="10"/>
                        <polygon points="80,30 70,70 130,50"/>
                        <line x1="60" y1="75" x2="120" y2="90" stroke="blue"/>
                </g>
                <g class="red-group">
                        <text x="200" y="20">Red group</text>
                        <rect x="200" y="40" width="50" height="50" rx="10" ry="10"/>
                        <polygon points="280,30 270,70 330,50"/>
                        <line x1="260" y1="75" x2="320" y2="90" stroke="red"/>
                </g>
                <g class="green-group">
                        <text x="400" y="20">Green group</text>
                        <rect x="400" y="40" width="50" height="50" rx="10" ry="10"/>
                        <polygon points="480,30 470,70 530,50"/>
                        <line x1="460" y1="75" x2="520" y2="90" stroke="green"/>
                </g>
        </svg>
</body>
```

Figure 3.23 shows examples of grouping.

I gave you a lot to chew on in that snippet above, and it's worth taking the time to study it. Why do all the <line> elements have strokes defined inline instead of in the CSS? That's right—because otherwise, each of the text objects would also have a stroke around it.

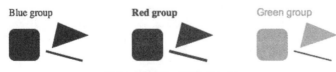

Figure 3.23 SVG groups

Transformations

SVG elements can be moved around, rotated, and manipulated in other ways using the transform property. Here's a selection of transform functions (arguments in brackets are optional):

translate (tx[,ty])	Redefines the coordinate system of the SVG element such that 0,0 refers to the location at tx,ty. If ty is undefined, it defaults to 0.
rotate(angle [,cx,cy])	Rotates the element clockwise by a number of degrees equal to angle. cx and cy define the point around which the element will be rotated. They default to 0,0.
scale (sx[,sy])	Rescales the element by a factor of sx horizontally and sy vertically. If sy is not defined, it is set equal to sx, so the scaling is proportional.

Those definitions are pretty technical, and it might not be too clear what they mean. Let's start with translate. The translate transformation redefines the coordinate system of an SVG element. Okay. Why would you want to do that? The last example from the previous section gives us a good reason.

When I created that example, I started with the blue group. Then I copied that chunk of SVG code to make the red group. I had to change the copied group's class from blue-group to red-group, then change the text element so it would say "Red group," and the stroke of the <line> so that it also would be red. After doing all of that, I had to increase the x coordinates for each of individual elements by 200 so the red group would be shifted to the right and not sit on top of the blue group. I did the exact same thing for the green group, substituting "green" for "red" and 400 for 200.

If I had used translate, I could have kept the x coordinates the same and instead shifted the coordinate systems for both the red group and the green group to the right (the CSS in this example is the same as above):

```
<svg width="500px" height="500px">
    <g class="blue-group">
        <text x="0" y="20">Blue group</text>
        <rect x="0" y="40" width="50" height="50" rx="10" ry="10"/>
        <polygon points="80,30 70,70 130,50"/>
        <line x1="60" y1="75" x2="120" y2="90" stroke="blue"/>
    </g>
    <g class="red-group" transform="translate(200)">
        <text x="0" y="20">Red group</text>
        <rect x="0" y="40" width="50" height="50" rx="10" ry="10"/>
        <polygon points="80,30 70,70 130,50"/>
        <line x1="60" y1="75" x2="120" y2="90" stroke="red"/>
    </g>
    <g class="green-group" transform="translate(400)">
        <text x="0" y="20">Green group</text>
```

```
                <rect x="0" y="40" width="50" height="50" rx="10" ry="10"/>
                <polygon points="80,30 70,70 130,50"/>
                <line x1="60" y1="75" x2="120" y2="90" stroke="green"/>
        </g>
</svg>
```

The `<text>` element in the red group has an x coordinate of 0. But because the group has been translated over 200 pixels, 0 actually refers to 200 on your screen. If, of course, I decided that 200 pixels was too much spacing, I would only have to change that one value inside the translate function to move the whole group somewhere else.

Here's another example using those same three groups that involves rotating and scaling (again, I've omitted the CSS because it hasn't changed from the original example):

```
<svg width="500px" height="500px">
        <g class="blue-group" transform="scale(1.2)">
                <text x="0" y="20">Blue group</text>
                <rect x="0" y="40" width="50" height="50" rx="10" ry="10"/>
                <polygon points="80,30 70,70 130,50"/>
                <line x1="60" y1="75" x2="120" y2="90" stroke="blue"/>
        </g>
        <g class="red-group" transform="translate(200)">
                <text x="0" y="20">Red group</text>
                <rect x="0" y="40" width="50" height="50" rx="10" ry="10"/>
                <polygon points="80,30 70,70 130,50"/>
                <line x1="60" y1="75" x2="120" y2="90" stroke="red"/>
        </g>
        <g class="green-group" transform="translate(200,120) rotate(90)">
                <text x="0" y="20">Green group</text>
                <rect x="0" y="40" width="50" height="50" rx="10" ry="10"/>
                <polygon points="80,30 70,70 130,50"/>
                <line x1="60" y1="75" x2="120" y2="90" stroke="green"/>
        </g>
</svg>
```

Figure 3.24 shows examples of transformed groups.

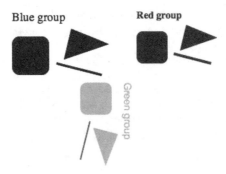

Figure 3.24   Transformed groups

Building a Bar Chart in SVG

Now we have all the tools we need (more even) to build a basic bar chart in SVG. So, let's take a look at the population distribution around the world in 2010.

Age Group	Percent of Population
0–4 years old	9.3%
5–9	8.8%
10–14	8.6%
15–19	8.80%
20–24	8.90%
25–29	8.10%
30–34	7.30%
35–39	7.10%
40–44	6.60%
45–49	6.00%
50–54	5.10%
55–59	4.50%
60–64	3.40%
65–69	2.60%
70–74	2.10%
75–79	1.50%
80 and up	1.60%

Recall from the previous chapter that we decided to make this a horizontal (instead of vertical) bar chart, and that the 80 and up age group will go on top and 0-4 will go on the bottom. Here's the snippet that we need to get started. Let's call our file **pop2010.html**:

```
<!DOCTYPE html>
<html>
<head>
<meta charset="utf-8">
<style>
</style>
</head>
<body>
        <svg width="500px" height="500px">
                <!-- 80 and up -->
                <rect x="0" y="0" height="20" width=""/>
                <!-- 75-79 -->
                <rect x="0" y="25" height="20" width=""/>
                <!-- 70-74 -->
                <rect x="0" y="50" height="20" width=""/>
                <!-- 65-69 -->
```

```
            <rect x="0" y="75" height="20" width=""/>
            <!-- 60-64 -->
            <rect x="0" y="100" height="20" width=""/>
            <!-- 55-59 -->
            <rect x="0" y="125" height="20" width=""/>
            <!-- 50-54 -->
            <rect x="0" y="150" height="20" width=""/>
            <!-- 45-49 -->
            <rect x="0" y="175" height="20" width=""/>
            <!-- 40-44 -->
            <rect x="0" y="200" height="20" width=""/>
            <!-- 35-39 -->
            <rect x="0" y="225" height="20" width=""/>
            <!-- 30-34 -->
            <rect x="0" y="250" height="20" width=""/>
            <!-- 25-29 -->
            <rect x="0" y="275" height="20" width=""/>
            <!-- 20-24 -->
            <rect x="0" y="300" height="20" width=""/>
            <!-- 15-19 -->
            <rect x="0" y="325" height="20" width=""/>
            <!-- 10-14 -->
            <rect x="0" y="350" height="20" width=""/>
            <!-- 5-9 -->
            <rect x="0" y="375" height="20" width=""/>
            <!-- 0-4 -->
            <rect x="0" y="400" height="20" width=""/>
        </svg>
    </body>
</html>
```

We have 17 bars, one for each of the age groups. Each one is 20 pixels tall, and there is 5 pixels of space in between them. We haven't set the widths yet, because the width is the attribute we're using to represent our data. So, first we have to figure out how to take those percentage values and translate them into pixels.

As a first attempt, we could simply plug the numbers in as is:

```
<svg width="500px" height="500px">
        <!-- 80 and up -->
        <rect x="0" y="0" height="20" width="1.6"/>
        <!-- 75-79 -->
        <rect x="0" y="25" height="20" width="1.5"/>
        <!-- 70-74 -->
        <rect x="0" y="50" height="20" width="2.1"/>
        <!-- 65-69 -->
        <rect x="0" y="75" height="20" width="2.6"/>
        <!-- 60-64 -->
        <rect x="0" y="100" height="20" width="3.4"/>
        <!-- 55-59 -->
```

```
<rect x="0" y="125" height="20" width="4.5"/>
<!-- 50-54 -->
<rect x="0" y="150" height="20" width="5.1"/>
<!-- 45-49 -->
<rect x="0" y="175" height="20" width="6.0"/>
<!-- 40-44 -->
<rect x="0" y="200" height="20" width="6.6"/>
<!-- 35-39 -->
<rect x="0" y="225" height="20" width="7.1"/>
<!-- 30-34 -->
<rect x="0" y="250" height="20" width="7.3"/>
<!-- 25-29 -->
<rect x="0" y="275" height="20" width="8.1"/>
<!-- 20-24 -->
<rect x="0" y="300" height="20" width="8.9"/>
<!-- 15-19 -->
<rect x="0" y="325" height="20" width="8.8"/>
<!-- 10-14 -->
<rect x="0" y="350" height="20" width="8.6"/>
<!-- 5-9 -->
<rect x="0" y="375" height="20" width="8.8"/>
<!-- 0-4 -->
<rect x="0" y="400" height="20" width="9.3"/>
</svg>
```

When we do that we get the graph shown in Figure 3.25.

Figure 3.25 Not quite big enough

Hmm...those bars look pretty stubby. It's kind of hard to see the difference between them. Clearly they need to be bigger. Let's try multiplying each of the numbers by 10. This will increase the width of each bar but keep its size exactly the same relative to the others.

```
<svg width="500px" height="500px">
        <!-- 80 and up -->
        <rect x="0" y="0" height="20" width="16"/>
        <!-- 75-79 -->
        <rect x="0" y="25" height="20" width="15"/>
        <!-- 70-74 -->
        <rect x="0" y="50" height="20" width="21"/>
        <!-- 65-69 -->
        <rect x="0" y="75" height="20" width="26"/>
        <!-- 60-64 -->
        <rect x="0" y="100" height="20" width="34"/>
        <!-- 55-59 -->
        <rect x="0" y="125" height="20" width="45"/>
        <!-- 50-54 -->
        <rect x="0" y="150" height="20" width="51"/>
        <!-- 45-49 -->
        <rect x="0" y="175" height="20" width="60"/>
        <!-- 40-44 -->
        <rect x="0" y="200" height="20" width="66"/>
        <!-- 35-39 -->
        <rect x="0" y="225" height="20" width="71"/>
        <!-- 30-34 -->
        <rect x="0" y="250" height="20" width="73"/>
        <!-- 25-29 -->
        <rect x="0" y="275" height="20" width="81"/>
        <!-- 20-24 -->
        <rect x="0" y="300" height="20" width="89"/>
        <!-- 15-19 -->
        <rect x="0" y="325" height="20" width="88"/>
        <!-- 10-14 -->
        <rect x="0" y="350" height="20" width="86"/>
        <!-- 5-9 -->
        <rect x="0" y="375" height="20" width="88"/>
        <!-- 0-4 -->
        <rect x="0" y="400" height="20" width="93"/>
</svg>
```

Figure 3.26 shows the new result.

That's a little better. We could try multiplying by 20 and keep going until we get an overall width that looks good. But what if instead of sizing our bars by trial and error, we want our chart to take up a predefined area?

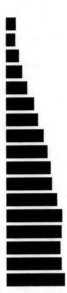

Figure 3.26 Better

Say we want the whole thing to be 400 pixels wide. The largest value, and thus
the biggest bar, in our data set is 9.3, the percentage of the world's population that is
between 0 and 4 years old. So we want a value of 9.3 to translate into 400 pixels. How
do we do that? Multiplication again: 400 divided by 9.3 is 43.0. If we multiply all of
the values by 43, then we'll re-size the whole thing proportionally and the largest bar
will be 400 pixels wide.

We could do the math for each of the values in our data set, and set the widths
accordingly. But an easier way to do it is to put all of the <rect> elements into a group
and then use the scale transform function, like so:

```
<svg width="500px" height="500px">
    <g transform="scale(43,1)">
            <!-- 80 and up -->
            <rect x="0" y="0" height="20" width="1.6"/>
            <!-- 75-79 -->
            <rect x="0" y="25" height="20" width="1.5"/>
            <!-- 70-74 -->
            <rect x="0" y="50" height="20" width="2.1"/>
            <!-- 65-69 -->
            <rect x="0" y="75" height="20" width="2.6"/>
            <!-- 60-64 -->
            <rect x="0" y="100" height="20" width="3.4"/>
            <!-- 55-59 -->
            <rect x="0" y="125" height="20" width="4.5"/>
            <!-- 50-54 -->
            <rect x="0" y="150" height="20" width="5.1"/>
```

```
<!-- 45-49 -->
<rect x="0" y="175" height="20" width="6.0"/>
<!-- 40-44 -->
<rect x="0" y="200" height="20" width="6.6"/>
<!-- 35-39 -->
<rect x="0" y="225" height="20" width="7.1"/>
<!-- 30-34 -->
<rect x="0" y="250" height="20" width="7.3"/>
<!-- 25-29 -->
<rect x="0" y="275" height="20" width="8.1"/>
<!-- 20-24 -->
<rect x="0" y="300" height="20" width="8.9"/>
<!-- 15-19 -->
<rect x="0" y="325" height="20" width="8.8"/>
<!-- 10-14 -->
<rect x="0" y="350" height="20" width="8.6"/>
<!-- 5-9 -->
<rect x="0" y="375" height="20" width="8.8"/>
<!-- 0-4 -->
<rect x="0" y="400" height="20" width="9.3"/>
    </g>
</svg>
```

Figure 3.27 shows the result.

In the previous code, the scale function increases the size of the bars by a factor of 43 along the x-axis, but keeps them the same size along the y-axis (multiplying all the values by 1).

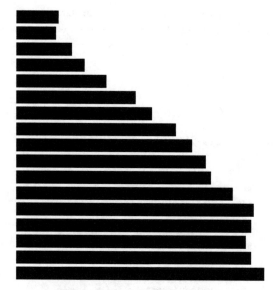

Figure 3.27 Mind your scales

That's a nice looking set of bars there. We should really add some labels and an axis, though, so other people can actually extract some meaning from them. But oops...the bars start in the top-left corner, and there isn't any room around the edges. Don't fret, we can use `translate` to shift the bars over and down, and then put some labels on the side:

```
<svg width="500px" height="500px">
    <g transform="translate(100,30) scale(43.1,1)">
        <!-- 80 and up -->
        <rect x="0" y="0" height="20" width="1.6"/>
        <!-- 75-79 -->
        <rect x="0" y="25" height="20" width="1.5"/>
        <!-- 70-74 -->
        <rect x="0" y="50" height="20" width="2.1"/>
        <!-- 65-69 -->
        <rect x="0" y="75" height="20" width="2.6"/>
        <!-- 60-64 -->
        <rect x="0" y="100" height="20" width="3.4"/>
        <!-- 55-59 -->
        <rect x="0" y="125" height="20" width="4.5"/>
        <!-- 50-54 -->
        <rect x="0" y="150" height="20" width="5.1"/>
        <!-- 45-49 -->
        <rect x="0" y="175" height="20" width="6.0"/>
        <!-- 40-44 -->
        <rect x="0" y="200" height="20" width="6.6"/>
        <!-- 35-39 -->
        <rect x="0" y="225" height="20" width="7.1"/>
        <!-- 30-34 -->
        <rect x="0" y="250" height="20" width="7.3"/>
        <!-- 25-29 -->
        <rect x="0" y="275" height="20" width="8.1"/>
        <!-- 20-24 -->
        <rect x="0" y="300" height="20" width="8.9"/>
        <!-- 15-19 -->
        <rect x="0" y="325" height="20" width="8.8"/>
        <!-- 10-14 -->
        <rect x="0" y="350" height="20" width="8.6"/>
        <!-- 5-9 -->
        <rect x="0" y="375" height="20" width="8.8"/>
        <!-- 0-4 -->
        <rect x="0" y="400" height="20" width="9.3"/>
    </g>
    <g>
        <text x="0" y="45">80 and up</text>
        <text x="0" y="70">75-79</text>
        <text x="0" y="95">70-74</text>
```

```
              <text x="0" y="120">65-69</text>
              <text x="0" y="145">60-64</text>
              <text x="0" y="170">55-59</text>
              <text x="0" y="195">50-54</text>
              <text x="0" y="220">45-49</text>
              <text x="0" y="245">40-44</text>
              <text x="0" y="270">35-39</text>
              <text x="0" y="295">30-34</text>
              <text x="0" y="320">25-29</text>
              <text x="0" y="345">20-24</text>
              <text x="0" y="370">15-19</text>
              <text x="0" y="395">10-14</text>
              <text x="0" y="420">5-9</text>
              <text x="0" y="445">0-4</text>
       </g>
</svg>
```

Figure 3.28 shows the bars with labels.

Now we need to make an axis. Let's create a tick mark every 2.5% using the `<line>` element. So, we'll need one at 0, 2.5%, 5.0%, and 7.5%. We'll need to figure out where the right positions are in our pixel space. It would be handy if we could use

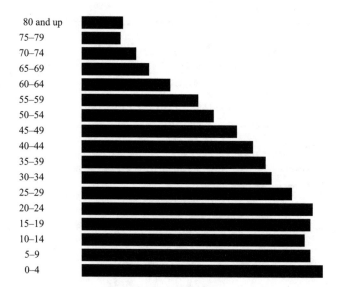

Figure 3.28 With labels

the old scale trick we used for the bars, but we can't. (I'll leave it to you to figure out why.) So, we have to multiply each of the values by 43 instead.

```
<g transform="translate(100,30)" stroke="black">
        <line x1="0" y1="0" x2="0" y2="-10"/>
        <line x1="107.75" y1="0" x2="107.75" y2="-10"/>
        <line x1="215.5" y1="0" x2="215.5" y2="-10"/>
        <line x1="323.25" y1="0" x2="323.25" y2="-10"/>
</g>
```

Let's also go ahead and add some labels on those tick marks. Here's the complete code:

```
<svg width="500px" height="500px">
        <g transform="translate(100,30) scale(43.1,1)">
                <!-- 80 and up -->
                <rect x="0" y="0" height="20" width="1.6"/>
                <!-- 75-79 -->
                <rect x="0" y="25" height="20" width="1.5"/>
                <!-- 70-74 -->
                <rect x="0" y="50" height="20" width="2.1"/>
                <!-- 65-69 -->
                <rect x="0" y="75" height="20" width="2.6"/>
                <!-- 60-64 -->
                <rect x="0" y="100" height="20" width="3.4"/>
                <!-- 55-59 -->
                <rect x="0" y="125" height="20" width="4.5"/>
                <!-- 50-54 -->
                <rect x="0" y="150" height="20" width="5.1"/>
                <!-- 45-49 -->
                <rect x="0" y="175" height="20" width="6.0"/>
                <!-- 40-44 -->
                <rect x="0" y="200" height="20" width="6.6"/>
                <!-- 35-39 -->
                <rect x="0" y="225" height="20" width="7.1"/>
                <!-- 30-34 -->
                <rect x="0" y="250" height="20" width="7.3"/>
                <!-- 25-29 -->
                <rect x="0" y="275" height="20" width="8.1"/>
                <!-- 20-24 -->
                <rect x="0" y="300" height="20" width="8.9"/>
                <!-- 15-19 -->
```

```
                    <rect x="0" y="325" height="20" width="8.8"/>
                    <!-- 10-14 -->
                    <rect x="0" y="350" height="20" width="8.6"/>
                    <!-- 5-9 -->
                    <rect x="0" y="375" height="20" width="8.8"/>
                    <!-- 0-4 -->
                    <rect x="0" y="400" height="20" width="9.3"/>
            </g>
            <g>
                    <text x="0" y="45">80 and up</text>
                    <text x="0" y="70">75-79</text>
                    <text x="0" y="95">70-74</text>
                    <text x="0" y="120">65-69</text>
                    <text x="0" y="145">60-64</text>
                    <text x="0" y="170">55-59</text>
                    <text x="0" y="195">50-54</text>
                    <text x="0" y="220">45-49</text>
                    <text x="0" y="245">40-44</text>
                    <text x="0" y="270">35-39</text>
                    <text x="0" y="295">30-34</text>
                    <text x="0" y="320">25-29</text>
                    <text x="0" y="345">20-24</text>
                    <text x="0" y="370">15-19</text>
                    <text x="0" y="395">10-14</text>
                    <text x="0" y="420">5-9</text>
                    <text x="0" y="445">0-4</text>
            </g>
            <g transform="translate(100,30)" stroke="black">
                    <line x1="0" y1="0" x2="0" y2="-10"/>
                    <line x1="107.75" y1="0" x2="107.75" y2="-10"/>
                    <line x1="215.5" y1="0" x2="215.5" y2="-10"/>
                    <line x1="323.25" y1="0" x2="323.25" y2="-10"/>
            </g>
            <g transform="translate(100,30)" text-anchor="middle">
                    <text x="0" y="-15">0</text>
                    <text x="107.75" y="-15">2.5%</text>
                    <text x="215.5" y="-15">5.0%</text>
                    <text x="323.25" y="-15">7.5%</text>
            </g>
    </svg>
```

Figure 3.29 shows our example with an axis.

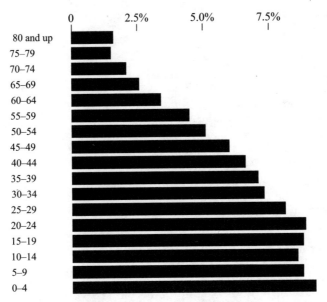

Figure 3.29   Now, with an axis

That looks pretty good! Here's a much more polished version with a heading and some labels at the top (in HTML) and all of the styling done in CSS instead of inline:

```
<!DOCTYPE html>
<html>
<head>
        <meta charset="utf-8">
        <style>
                body {
                        font-family: Helvetica;
                }
                svg {
                        width:500px;
                        height:500px;
                }
                .top-label {
                        font-size: 13px;
                        font-style: italic;
                        text-transform: uppercase;
                        float: left;
                }
                .age-label {
                        text-align: right;
                        font-weight: bold;
                        width: 90px;
                        padding-right: 10px;
                }
```

```
                    .clearfix {
                            clear:both;
                    }
                    .bar {
                            fill: DarkSlateBlue;
                    }
                    .bar-label {
                            text-anchor: end;
                    }
                    .axis-label {
                            text-anchor: middle;
                            font-size: 13px;
                    }
        </style>
</head>
<body>
        <h2>Age distribution of the world, 2010</h2>
        <div class="top-label age-label">
                <p>age group</p>
        </div>
        <div class="top-label">
                <p>portion of the population</p>
        </div>
        <div class="clearfix"></div>
        <svg>
                <g transform="translate(100,30) scale(43.1,1)"
class="bar">
                        <!-- 80 and up -->
                        <rect x="0" y="0" height="20" width="1.6"/>
                        <!-- 75-79 -->
                        <rect x="0" y="25" height="20" width="1.5"/>
                        <!-- 70-74 -->
                        <rect x="0" y="50" height="20" width="2.1"/>
                        <!-- 65-69 -->
                        <rect x="0" y="75" height="20" width="2.6"/>
                        <!-- 60-64 -->
                        <rect x="0" y="100" height="20" width="3.4"/>
                        <!-- 55-59 -->
                        <rect x="0" y="125" height="20" width="4.5"/>
                        <!-- 50-54 -->
                        <rect x="0" y="150" height="20" width="5.1"/>
                        <!-- 45-49 -->
                        <rect x="0" y="175" height="20" width="6.0"/>
                        <!-- 40-44 -->
                        <rect x="0" y="200" height="20" width="6.6"/>
                        <!-- 35-39 -->
                        <rect x="0" y="225" height="20" width="7.1"/>
                        <!-- 30-34 -->
                        <rect x="0" y="250" height="20" width="7.3"/>
                        <!-- 25-29 -->
```

```
            <rect x="0" y="275" height="20" width="8.1"/>
            <!-- 20-24 -->
            <rect x="0" y="300" height="20" width="8.9"/>
            <!-- 15-19 -->
            <rect x="0" y="325" height="20" width="8.8"/>
            <!-- 10-14 -->
            <rect x="0" y="350" height="20" width="8.6"/>
            <!-- 5-9 -->
            <rect x="0" y="375" height="20" width="8.8"/>
            <!-- 0-4 -->
            <rect x="0" y="400" height="20" width="9.3"/>
        </g>
        <g class="bar-label">
            <text x="90" y="45">80 and up</text>
            <text x="90" y="70">75-79</text>
            <text x="90" y="95">70-74</text>
            <text x="90" y="120">65-69</text>
            <text x="90" y="145">60-64</text>
            <text x="90" y="170">55-59</text>
            <text x="90" y="195">50-54</text>
            <text x="90" y="220">45-49</text>
            <text x="90" y="245">40-44</text>
            <text x="90" y="270">35-39</text>
            <text x="90" y="295">30-34</text>
            <text x="90" y="320">25-29</text>
            <text x="90" y="345">20-24</text>
            <text x="90" y="370">15-19</text>
            <text x="90" y="395">10-14</text>
            <text x="90" y="420">5-9</text>
            <text x="90" y="445">0-4</text>
        </g>
        <g transform="translate(100,30)" stroke="black">
            <line x1="0" y1="0" x2="0" y2="-10"/>
            <line x1="107.75" y1="0" x2="107.75" y2="-10"/>
            <line x1="215.5" y1="0" x2="215.5" y2="-10"/>
            <line x1="323.25" y1="0" x2="323.25" y2="-10"/>
        </g>
        <g transform="translate(100,30)" class="axis-label">
            <text x="0" y="-15">0</text>
            <text x="107.75" y="-15">2.5%</text>
            <text x="215.5" y="-15">5.0%</text>
            <text x="323.25" y="-15">7.5%</text>
        </g>
    </svg>
</body>
</html>
```

Figure 3.30 shows the finished product.

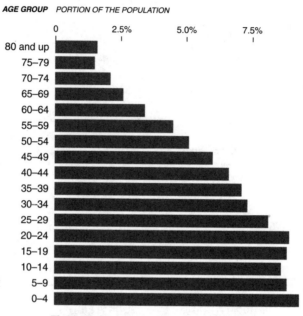

Figure 3.30 The fruits of your labor

Congratulations! Chances are, you've just hard-coded your first graphic entirely in SVG. With any luck, it'll be your last.

A lot of what we just did was super tedious (just look at how long and repetitive the code is), which is disheartening considering we were only working with 17 data points. What if we had 217? The good news is that D3 makes the most tedious parts of hard-coding in SVG incredibly simple (once you know how to do it).

For example, you don't have to do any math to figure out what factor to use for scaling charts to a larger size. You can set a desired width for your chart and then tell D3 to find the largest value in your data set (you don't even have to know what it is) and it will create a scale you can apply to all of your values. And, as far as axes go, D3 can make those for you; you don't have to draw the lines yourself.

Without further ado, let's dig into some JavaScript!

Summary

One of the major advantages of SVG as a graphical format is that it can be scaled without losing resolution. SVG is a markup language, very much like HTML. Basic SVG tags tell the browser to draw shapes, lines, and text. Classes can be assigned to SVG elements, and they can be styled with CSS. There are myriad styles and transforms that allow users of SVG to endlessly customize their graphics.

4

Shaping Web Pages with D3 Selections

In this chapter we are going to dive in to D3 (finally!). Specifically, we're going to cover something called selections. On the most basic level, selections are D3's way of letting you access a web page so you can make changes to it. Selections give you the keys to the web page document so you can drive it! Remember, although D3 is an amazing tool for creating data visualizations, it doesn't have a basic function for generating charts. Instead, it provides a bunch of ways to manipulate the contents of a web page, based on data. But it's up to you to create the shapes and lines you need to make an intelligible data visualization.

Getting Set Up with D3

D3 is a JavaScript library, a large-ish text file filled with JavaScript code that defines a bunch of functions and methods. (If you don't know what a function or a method is, you should definitely read Appendix A on basic JavaScript before continuing.)

To be able to use D3, you need to do what is called referencing the library in your HTML file. That's just a technical way of saying your markup needs to have a link to the D3 library file where all the functions and methods are defined. Otherwise, when you try to use one of those functions, your browser will have no idea what you're talking about. The reference looks like this...

```
<script src="http://d3js.org/d3.v3.min.js"></script>
```

...and it goes in the body of your HTML. (Note: This reference is for version 3 of D3.) Your browser will follow that link when it opens up your web page and run the JavaScript file, making those functions and methods available for you to use both in your script and in the JavaScript console.

Listing 4.1 shows a snippet of code you can use to get started building a web page using D3.

Listing 4.1   *A starter snippet*

```html
<!DOCTYPE html>
<html>
<head>
<meta charset="utf-8">
<style>
      /* Your CSS goes here */
</style>
</head>
<body>
<script src="http://d3js.org/d3.v3.min.js"></script>

      <!-- Your HTML goes here -->
<script>
      // Your JavaScript goes here
</script>
</body>
</html>
```

All of the "Your X goes here" statements above are comments, so your machine won't try to interpret them as code. (The reason the symbols surrounding each comment are different is that each one is written in a different language.)

Note that while you reference the D3 library before your HTML, the JavaScript you write goes below your HTML. Why? Because you use D3 to manipulate elements on the web page, and you need to create those elements first!

Making Selections

So what is a selection, exactly? Well, it's a selection of elements from your web page's DOM, or Document Object Model. The DOM is the hierarchical, HTML-based structure that underpins every web page. When your browser is rendering a web page, it is interpreting the underlying DOM.

When you take a peek at the DOM (which you can do with the Web Inspector), it looks a lot like an HTML file, and it sometimes mirrors the HTML file being loaded exactly. But there's a big difference between a static HTML file and the DOM. The DOM always represents the current state of a web page. It's initial state could be defined by a static HTML file, but then change based on, say, some JavaScript.

Back to selections. What kinds of elements can a selection be? It could be a single <div>, it could be all of the page's paragraph elements, it could be everything with the class myClass, it could be an SVG circle, or it could even be the entire body of the page.

The best way to understand what selections are and how they work is to use them. So, put the following code into a file called **selections.html** and open it up in your browser (see Figure 4.1). Then we can create some selections in the console!

Is this a circle?

Yeah, looks like it

Figure 4.1 Looks like a circle to me, too

```html
<!DOCTYPE html>
<html>
<head>
<meta charset="utf-8">
<style>
      /* Your CSS goes here */
</style>
</head>
<body>
<script src="http://d3js.org/d3.v3.min.js"></script>
      <div id="header">
            <p>Is this a circle?</p>
      </div>
      <svg width="500px" height="40px">
            <circle r="20" cx="50" cy="20"/>
      </svg>
      <div class="footer">
            <p>Yeah, looks like it</p>
      </div>
<script>
      // Your JavaScript goes here
</script>
</body>
</html>
```

D3 has two methods for creating selections: d3.select() and d3.selectAll().
Let's start with d3.select(), which only selects one element at a time. Open up the
console, which you can do in Chrome by going to View > Developer > JavaScript
Console. Type d3.select("p") into the console. Figure 4.2 shows what you should
see.

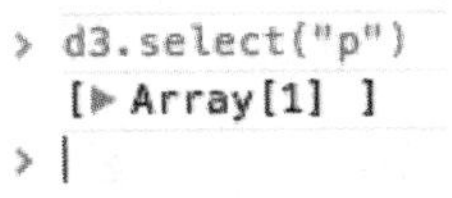

```
> d3.select("p")
  [▶ Array[1]  ]
> |
```

Figure 4.2 A D3 selection

```
> d3.select("p")[0][0]
  <p>Is this a circle?</p>
>
```

Figure 4.3   The element inside

```
> d3.select("p").text()
  "Is this a circle?"
> |
```

Figure 4.4   Paragraph text on display

This is a circle, eh?

Yeah, looks like it

```
×   Elements   Resources   Network   Sources   Timeline
> d3.select("p").text("This is a circle, eh?")
  [▶ Array[1] ]
> |
```

Figure 4.5   Translated to Canadian English

Doesn't look like much—but that's it! That's our selection, an array with another array inside of it. Selections always look like this, but don't worry about why for now. Let's just take a peek inside. We can peel back the layers by indexing into the array: Enter d3.select("p")[0][0] into the console. The result is shown in Figure 4.3.

Yep—that looks familiar. It's the markup for the first paragraph at the top of **selections.html**. You may have figured out what d3.select() did in this case: Since the method was passed the argument "p", it went hunting for paragraph elements. And the way d3.select() works is that it always creates a selection out of the first match it finds.

So now that we have a selection, what can we do with it? So many things! Creating and then changing selections is what D3 is all about. D3 has scores and scores of methods that are built to operate on selections and modify the element or elements inside. One such method is text(). Type d3.select("p").text() into the console, and you should get what is shown in Figure 4.4.

As you can see, text() returns whatever text is stored inside of your selection. (Or, to be more precise, it returns the text inside of the opening and closing tags of the element stored inside of your selection.) Pretty cool. Now for some magic: You can change that text by passing an argument to the text() method. Try

d3.select("p").text("This is a circle, eh?").

Figure 4.5 shows what you'll get.

Congratulations! You have officially used D3 to drive a web document. Two Ds down, one to go!

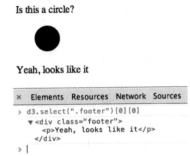

Is this a circle?

Yeah, looks like it

```
×  Elements  Resources  Network  Sources
> d3.select(".footer")[0][0]
  ▼<div class="footer">
     <p>Yeah, looks like it</p>
   </div>
> |
```

Figure 4.6   Selecting by class

Using CSS Selectors to Create Selections

Let's try selecting some of the other elements on the page. Go ahead and refresh **selections.html** so that it is no longer in "Canadian English." Say we wanted to select the second <div> element. Since d3.select("div") will always pick the first <div> it comes across, we have to use something else to hone in on the second. In this case, the second <div> is the only element on the page with the class "footer". We can take advantage of this by typing d3.select(".footer"). The result is shown in Figure 4.6.

You should recognize the convention D3 uses to select by class: .className. Prefacing a class name with a period—that's straight from CSS. In fact, D3 always employs CSS selectors to make selections. That term—**selector**—may be new to you, but what it refers to should be familiar. The selector for paragraph elements, for example, is p. The selector for elements with the id "myID" is #myID. Collectively, selectors are CSS's nomenclature for referring to elements. I'm sure you've used them countless times.

SVG elements also have CSS selectors, which is why you can use CSS to style them. Those selectors, just like the selectors for HTML elements, are the names of SVG tags. The selector for a rectangle, which has the tag <rect>, is rect. The selector for a group, which has the tag <g>, is g. If you're selecting an SVG element by class, then of course, the convention is the same: .className.

Try typing d3.select("circle") into the console. Of course, d3.select ("circle").text() doesn't do much, but we'll learn some methods in the next section you can use to manipulate SVG elements.

Creating Selections from Other Selections

It's also possible to create a selection from another selection. Say we wanted to select the second paragraph element in **selections.html**. If we use d3.select("p") it will always return the first paragraph. And the second paragraph has no class or id, so we can't use one of those to hone in on it. What we can do instead is select the second <div> using its class name and then select the first paragraph within that <div>:

```
d3.select(".footer").select("p")
```

In the code above, D3 is only hunting for paragraph elements within the `<div>` that has the class `footer`.

Assigning Selections to Variables

One final note about selections: Since they are arrays, you can assign them to variables. Try typing the following into the console:

```
var myGraf = d3.select("p")
myGraf.text()
```

Changing a Selection's Attributes

Being able to change the text inside of an HTML element is pretty cool. But what if you wanted to change the font size or reformat the element in some other way? Or, what if you wanted to adjust an SVG shape, which has no text?

D3 has a really useful method that enables you to change the attributes of a selection—it's called `attr()`. (I find that saying function and method names out loud or in my head actually makes me feel more comfortable using them. But abbreviating the word "attribute" after the "r" produces a fragment that's difficult to say (unless you're French). So, many people pronounce `attr` such that it rhymes with "hatter.")

The SVG circle in **selections.html** hasn't gotten a lot of play, so let's use `attr()` on it. First, since we'll be referencing the circle quite a bit, let's create a variable for the selection just to make things easy. Type the following into the console:

```
var myCircle = d3.select("circle");
```

Now type this:

```
myCircle.attr("fill", "red");
```

You will get what is shown in Figure 4.7.

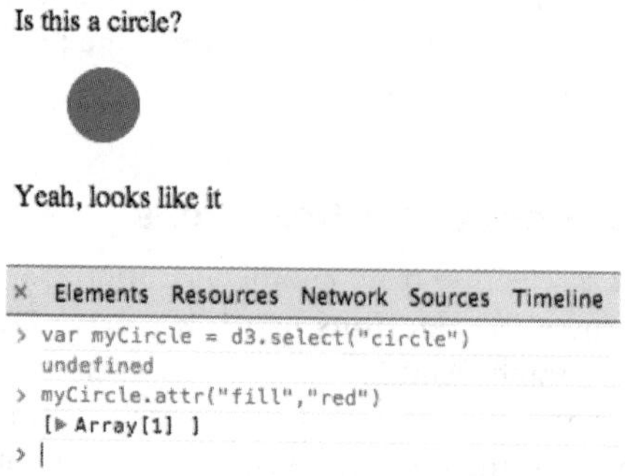

Is this a circle?

Yeah, looks like it

```
✕  Elements  Resources  Network  Sources  Timeline
> var myCircle = d3.select("circle")
  undefined
> myCircle.attr("fill","red")
  [▶ Array[1] ]
> |
```

Figure 4.7 It is a circle, and now it's red

It should be pretty obvious what happened here: attr() changed the fill attribute of the circle to red. Terrific! Now, say you wanted to change the radius, too. To do that, type:

```
myCircle.attr("r",5)
```

Figure 4.8 shows the change in the radius.

You can also use attr() to add a stroke, even though no stroke is defined in the markup.

```
myCircle.attr("stroke", "black")
```

Figure 4.9 shows the circle with a stroke around it.

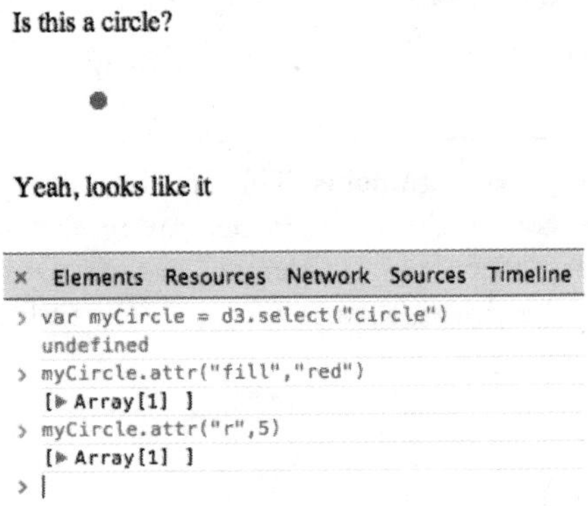

Is this a circle?

●

Yeah, looks like it

```
✕  Elements  Resources  Network  Sources  Timeline
> var myCircle = d3.select("circle")
  undefined
> myCircle.attr("fill","red")
  [▶ Array[1] ]
> myCircle.attr("r",5)
  [▶ Array[1] ]
> |
```

Figure 4.8 And now it looks like a dot

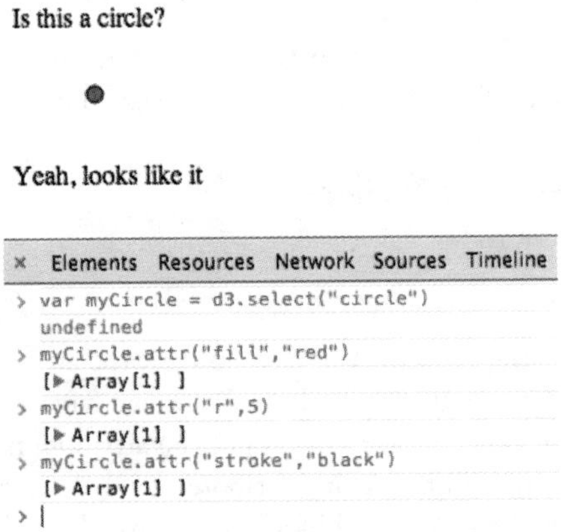

Is this a circle?

●

Yeah, looks like it

```
✕  Elements  Resources  Network  Sources  Timeline
> var myCircle = d3.select("circle")
  undefined
> myCircle.attr("fill","red")
  [▶ Array[1] ]
> myCircle.attr("r",5)
  [▶ Array[1] ]
> myCircle.attr("stroke","black")
  [▶ Array[1] ]
> |
```

Figure 4.9 Stroke of genius

How `attr()` Works

It's worth looking into how `attr()` works. You use attributes all the time in HTML, but, like selectors, the term itself might not mean much to you. Attributes in HTML (and in SVG) go in the start tag, and on the most basic level add some additional qualities to the element in question or apply some formatting to it. They generally look like this:

```
<tag attribute="value"></tag>
```

Here are some examples of the attributes used in **selections.html**:

Markup	Attribute	Value
`<div id="header">`	id	`"header"`
`<svg width="500px" height="40px">`	width, height	`"500px"`, `"40px"`
`<circle r="20" cx="50" cy="20"/>`	r, cx, and cy	`"20"`, `"50"`, and `"20"`
`<div class="footer">`	class	`"footer"`

`attr()` works by taking two arguments. The first argument is the name of the attribute and the second is the value. It then inserts that attribute/value pair into the start tag of the selected element in the DOM. So, for `myCircle.attr("fill", "red")`, it turns our circle element from

```
<circle r="20" cx="50" cy="20"/>
```

to

```
<circle r="20" cx="50" cy="20" fill="red"/>
```

But you don't have to take my word for it. Refresh **selections.html** and change the fill of the circle to red using `attr()`. Then inspect the circle using your web inspector. You should have what is shown in Figure 4.10.

(Recall that `<circle/>` is equivalent to `<circle></circle>`.) Now, say you want to change the radius of the circle again. The thing is, the circle element already has an r attribute. So what does `attr()` do in this case? Don't worry: It's smart enough to simply change the value of an attribute that is already defined. So if you type in `myCircle.attr("r", 5)`, you will get

```
<circle r="5" cx="50" cy="20" fill="red"/>
```

and not

```
<circle r="20" cx="50" cy="20" fill="red" r="5"/>
```

A quick note on conventions: Inside the element tag, the attribute names are never in quotes but the values always are. In the markup above, we have r="5" instead of r=5 or "r"="5". However, in our D3 code, we always put the attribute name in quotes. Why? Because otherwise JavaScript will think the attribute name is a variable. If we typed `myCircle.attr(r, 5)`, the browser would look for a variable within your JavaScript code called r. After not finding one, it would return an error. So, instead, you have to pass in

Figure 4.10 How `attr()` changes the DOM

the attribute name surrounded by quotes. Then D3 strips the quotes off and inserts the attribute, along with its corresponding value, into the selected element's start tag.

As for the attribute value, if you also surround it in quotes, then D3 will stick it into the start tag with the quotes still on. But you can also pass in a number and D3 will automatically add quotes. So, `myCircle.attr("r", 5)` is equivalent to `myCircle.attr("r", "5")`. The nice thing about using numbers is that it makes it easier to do math: You could do `myCircle.attr("r", 2 + 3)`. If this doesn't seem super useful right now, just wait—by the end of the chapter it will.

Using `attr()` to Apply Classes and Style Rules

You can use `attr()` to apply classes and ids, because classes and ids are both attributes. Say you wanted to add the class `myGraf` to the first paragraph element in **selections. html**. You would simply type:

```
d3.select("p").attr("class", "myGraf")
```

Now, say you actually had some style rules defined for the class `myGraf` in your CSS. After assigning that class to the first paragraph, it would then be styled according to your CSS.

You can also use `attr()` to style HTML elements. When you apply a style to an HTML element inline, your markup generally looks like this:

```
<element style="property: value"></element>
```

So, to change the font of the first paragraph in **selections.html** to Arial, you would change the markup to:

```
<p style="font-family: Arial">Is this a circle?</p>
```

You can use `attr()` to insert that bit of inline styling into the start tag. Try

```
d3.select("p").attr("style", "font-family: Arial");
```

Not bad, but D3 has a better method for styling HTML elements—`style()`. With `style()`, you can change the font of the first paragraph by typing:

```
d3.select("p").style("font-family", "Arial");
```

The method is just like `attr()`, but it assumes you are talking about the style attribute and takes the property name and property value as its two arguments. The result is code that is both simpler to type and easier to read.

D3 Strives to be Declarative

The `attr()` and `style()` methods are designed to be really straightforward to use. If you want the fill of your selection to be red, you type `attr("fill", "red");`. If you want the font family of your selection to be Arial, you type `style("font-family","Arial");`. Pretty simple.

D3 is all about what is called declarative programming: You tell your machine what you want to happen instead of telling it how to make it happen. With `attr()` you name the attribute and the value and D3 takes care of the rest.

Declarative code is not only simpler to write, it's also a lot easier to read. If you're looking back at your code and you see

```
myCircle.attr("fill", "red");
```

it's obvious what's going on.

Chaining Methods

One nice declarative feature of D3 is that it allows you to chain methods together (if you've ever used jQuery, method chaining should be familiar to you). As an example, let's go back to our SVG circle. Refresh **selections.html** in your browser. Create a selection for the circle and again call it `myCircle`:

```
var myCircle = d3.select("circle");
```

Okay, now let's say you wanted to change a bunch of the circle's attributes. Here's how you might do it based on what we've learned so far:

```
myCircle.attr("fill", "red");
myCircle.attr("r", 10);
myCircle.attr("stroke", "black");
myCircle.attr("stroke-width", 2);
```

This should yield what is shown in Figure 4.11.

This worked, but there's an easier way: You can simply type out one long statement by chaining the methods. So instead, try:

Is this a circle?

Yeah, looks like it

```
 ×   Elements  Resources  Network  Sources  Timeline
 >  var myCircle = d3.select("circle")
    myCircle.attr("fill","red")
    myCircle.attr("r",10)
    myCircle.attr("stroke","black")
    myCircle.attr("stroke-width",2)
    [▶ Array[1] ]
 > |
```

Figure 4.11   It is a circle, but it looks a lot different

```
d3.select("circle").attr("fill", "red").attr("r", 10).attr("stroke", "black").
attr("stroke-width", 2);
```

You can make that statement look a lot nicer by inserting some line breaks and indentations into the code, neither of which affects the JavaScript at all:

```
d3.select("circle")
    .attr("fill", "red")
    .attr("r", 10)
    .attr("stroke", "black")

    .attr("stroke-width", 2);
```

It should be pretty clear what this method chaining is doing—it's applying all of those attr() calls to the selection at the beginning of the chain. The semicolon signifies the end of the chain, so it's important to make sure that only the last line has one. Otherwise, you'll get an error.

D3 lets you chain other methods, too—chaining isn't limited only to attr(). For example:

```
d3.select("p")
    .attr("class", "myGraf")
    .style("font-family", "Arial")
    .style("color", "blue")
    .text("Did all this chaining work?");
```

Figure 4.12 shows the result of that chaining.

Creating New Selections in the Middle of a Chain

It's also possible to introduce new selections in the middle of these long chains, something you'll do a lot when you use D3. As soon as you introduce a new selection, all of the subsequent methods will act on that selection instead of the initial selection. Consider this example:

Did all this chaining work?

Yeah, looks like it

```
×  Elements  Resources  Network  Sources  Timeline
>  d3.select("p")
      .attr("class","myGraf")
      .style("font-family","Arial")
      .style("color","blue")
      .text("Did all this chaining work?");
   [▶ Array[1] ]
> |
```

Figure 4.12 Chaining a series of different methods together

Is this a circle?

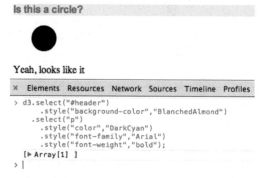

Yeah, looks like it

```
×  Elements  Resources  Network  Sources  Timeline  Profiles
>  d3.select("#header")
      .style("background-color","BlanchedAlmond")
    .select("p")
      .style("color","DarkCyan")
      .style("font-family","Arial")
      .style("font-weight","bold");
   [▶ Array[1] ]
> |
```

Figure 4.13 A chain with a new selection

```
d3.select("#header")
    .style("background-color", "BlanchedAlmond")
  .select("p")
    .style("color", "DarkCyan")
    .style("font-family", "Arial")
    .style("font-weight", "bold");
```

Figure 4.13 shows the result.

The chain above proceeds like this: An initial selection is created for the `<div>` with the id header, the background color of that `<div>` is changed to blanched almond, a new selection is created for the first paragraph in that `<div>`, and then three different styles are applied to that paragraph.

Notice that I've only indented the line with `.select("p")` halfway. That's a personal preference (inspired by Mike Bostock), and it's purely for legibility. You can see that a new selection is introduced in the middle of the chain because it's poking out to the left. And you know that the methods that follow will be applied to that selection and not the initial selection.

Chains and Variable Assignment

One last thing about chaining methods: You can actually create a selection, apply a chain of methods to it, and assign that selection to a variable all in one fell swoop. For example, in

```
var myCircle = d3.select("circle")
        .attr("fill", "red")
        .attr("r", 10)
        .attr("stroke", "black")
        .attr("stroke-width", 2);
```

the circle selection is created, all of the attribute changes are applied, and then it is assigned to the variable myCircle for later use.

If a new selection is introduced in the middle of your chain, then whatever the working selection is at the end of the chain will be assigned to the variable. For example, in

```
var myGraf = d3.select("#header")
        .style("background-color", "BlanchedAlmond")
    .select("p")
        .style("color", "DarkCyan")
        .style("font-family", "Arial")
        .style("font-weight", "bold");
```

the selection assigned to myGraf is the paragraph element (but the background color of the <div> is still changed to BlanchedAlmond).

Appending New Elements

So far, we've used D3 to do a lot of cool things to the DOM. But everything we've done has involved making changes to elements that are already there. We haven't added any new elements or taken any away.

D3 makes doing those things easy with the methods remove() and append(). Let's start with remove(). Refresh **selections.html** and type d3.select("body").remove(); into the console. Whoa. Everything disappeared! If you go to the Web Inspector, you should have what is shown in Figure 4.14.

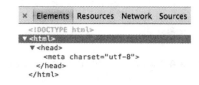

Figure 4.14 It's like a ghost DOM in here

Easy enough. If you wanted to get rid of the first <div>, you would type d3.select("div").remove(), and so on.

Now let's add some elements. The method append() adds a child element to whatever the selection is. Refresh **selections.html** and type the following into the console:

```
d3.select("#header").append("p")
        .text("(I am an appended paragraph)")
        .style("font-style", "italic")
        .style("color", "grey");
```

Figure 4.15 shows the result.

There are three important things to know about append(). First, the argument you pass to append() is the tag for the element you want to add, in quotes. In our example, that argument is "p", so we've created a paragraph element. If we wanted to append a <div>, we would use append("div"), and for an SVG rectangle we would use append("rect").

The second thing to note is that append() always adds the new element to the end (hence the word append). In our example, we appended a new paragraph to the first <div>, and it shows up as the last paragraph in that <div> (see Figure 4.16).

The third is that append() returns a selection. In other words, it introduces a new selection to the chain. That is why the text() method call and the two style() method calls in our example operate on the freshly appended paragraph element and not the <div> that was initially selected.

Is this a circle?

(I am an appended paragraph)

Yeah, looks like it

```
✕  Elements  Resources  Network  Sources  Timeline  Profiles
>  d3.select("#header").append("p")
        .text("(I am an appended paragraph)")
        .style("font-style","italic")
        .style("color","grey");
   [▶ Array[1] ]
> |
```

Figure 4.15 A new, appended paragraph

Is this a circle?

(I am an appended paragraph)

●

Yeah, looks like it

```
×  | Elements  Resources  Network  Sources  Timeline  Profiles  Audits  Console
<!DOCTYPE html>
▼<html>
  ▶ <head>…</head>
  ▼<body>
      <script src="http://d3js.org/d3.v3.min.js"></script>
    ▼<div id="header">
        <p>Is this a circle?</p>
        <p style="font-style: italic; color: rgb(128, 128, 128);">(I am an appended paragraph)</p>
      </div>
    ▶ <svg height="40px">…</svg>
    ▶ <div class="footer">…</div>
    </body>
</html>
```

Figure 4.16   Appended elements go to the back of the line

Putting It All Together

Okay, now we've got quite an arsenal at our disposal. In fact, we have all the tools we need to create a web page entirely with D3. So let's do it. Put **selections.html** aside for a second and create a new page called **selections2.html**. Begin with the starter snippet in Listing 4.1.

Now, instead of doing things in the console, we're going to do our D3 coding inside the second script tag in **selections2.html**. Why? Because when you change the DOM from the console, all those changes are erased as soon as you refresh the page, and that's clearly not what we want.

Let's recreate **selections.html**, except using D3 instead of HTML. I'll go through how to do it step-by-step, but I encourage you to try it on your own first.

The very first element inside the body of **selections.html** is a <div> with the id header. That shouldn't be too hard to create with append(). But what do we append the <div> to? Whatever the parent element should be. If you look back at the structure of **selections.html**, the parent element of that first <div> is the body of the page itself. Type the following statement inside the second script tag in **selections2.html**:

```
d3.select("body").append("div")
      .attr("id", "header");
```

Once you've created that <div>, you can select it and append a paragraph element to it. Add the following code to your script, hit save, and open up the page in your browser to make sure it's working:

```
d3.select("div").append("p")
      .text("Is this a circle?");
```

Great. Now on to the <svg> element. Go back to selecting the body and then append an <svg> element with a height of 40 pixels.

```
d3.select("body").append("svg")
      .attr("height", 40);
```

And then add a <circle> to it:

```
d3.select("svg").append("circle")
      .attr("r", 20)
      .attr("cx", 50)
      .attr("cy", 20);
```

And then finish up by adding that last <div> along with its paragraph.

```
d3.select("body").append("div")
      .attr("class", "footer");

d3.select(".footer").append("p")
      .text("Yeah, looks like it");
```

There it is—a complete recreation of **selections.html** in D3.
Here is a more succinct way to write all of that code.

```
var body = d3.select("body")

body.append("div")
   .attr("id","header")
  .append("p")
   .text("Is this a circle?");

body.append("svg")
   .attr("height",40)
  .append("circle")
   .attr("r",20)
   .attr("cx",50)
   .attr("cy",20);

body.append("div")
   .attr("class","footer")
  .append("p")
   .text("Yeah, looks like it");
```

If you understand everything that's going on in that code above, you've successfully absorbed this chapter so far.

Selecting Multiple Elements with d3.selectAll()

We've covered d3.select() in detail in this chapter, but we haven't covered its sister method, d3.selectAll(). You'll use d3.selectAll() a lot—much more than

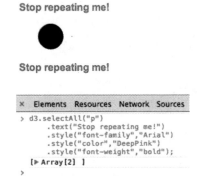

Figure 4.17 Now it's really getting circular

`d3.select()`. But you'll mostly use it when computing data-joins, which we'll cover in the next chapter. For now, I'll just introduce the method briefly.

`d3.selectAll()` is a way to create a selection of multiple elements. Where, say, `d3.select("p")` will return a selection with the first paragraph element on the page, `d3.selectAll("p")` will return a selection with all the paragraph elements. You can still use all of the same methods, such as `attr()` and `text()`, on selections created with `d3.selectAll()`. But when you do, the changes will be applied to all of the elements in your selection.

Let's go back to **selections.html** (or **selections2.html** if you like). Open it up in your browser and type the following into the console:

```
d3.selectAll("p")
      .text("Stop repeating me!")
      .style("font-family", "Arial")
      .style("color", "DeepPink")
      .style("font-weight", "bold");
```

Figure 4.17 presents the result.

Building a Bar Chart with Selections

Okay, now let's build the same population bar chart we did back in Chapter 3, but this time, let's do it in D3. The most straightforward way to do that, given what we know at this point, is to go through the markup from **pop2010-svg.html** tag-by-tag and recreate it in D3 using selections, `append()`, `attr()`, and the other methods we've covered in this chapter.

Here's a snippet for you to get started with. Let's call this file **pop2010-D3.html**.

```
<!DOCTYPE html>
<html>
<head>
```

```
<meta charset="utf-8">
<style>
        body {
                font-family: Helvetica;
        }
        svg {
                width: 500px;
                height: 500px;
        }
        .top-label {
                font-size: 13px;
                font-style: italic;
                text-transform: uppercase;
                float: left;
        }
        .age-label {
                text-align: right;
                font-weight: bold;
                width: 90px;
                padding-right: 10px;
        }
        .clearfix {
                clear: both;
        }
        .bar {
                fill: DarkSlateBlue;
        }
        .bar-label {
                text-anchor: end;
        }
        .axis-label {
                text-anchor: middle;
                font-size: 13px;
        }
</style>
</head>
<body>
<script src="http://d3js.org/d3.v3.min.js"></script>
<script>
        // Your JavaScript goes here
</script>
</body>
</html>
```

You'll notice that the CSS above is taken straight from **pop2010-svg.html**. As we build the chart in D3, we can use attr() to apply classes to the elements we create. For the sake of both convenience and consistency, I'm planning on using the exact same class names when we build the chart in D3 as I did when we built it in SVG.

Since we want all those elements to be styled in exactly the same way, we can use the same CSS.

I won't show screenshots of the bar chart as we go. Each of the pieces we build in D3 should look identical to the corresponding elements in **pop2010–svg.html**, so you can use that as a reference.

Let's start with the HTML at the top:

```
<h2>Age distribution of the world, 2010</h2>
<div class="top-label age-label">
        <p>age group</p>
</div>
<div class="top-label">
        <p>portion of the population</p>
</div>
<div class="clearfix"></div>
```

All of the top-level elements in the snippet above are children of the body element. So, if we want to create these elements with D3, we need to append them to the body of the document. Here's how we might do that:

```
d3.select("body").append("h2")
        .text("Age distribution of the world, 2010");

d3.select("body").append("div")
        .attr("class", "top-label age-label");

d3.select("body").append("div")
        .attr("class", "top-label");

d3.select("body").append("div")
        .attr("class", "clearfix");
```

It's a little tedious (and inefficient) to select the document body every time we append something to it, so we can create a variable:

```
var body = d3.select("body");

body.append("h2")
        .text("Age distribution of the world, 2010");

body.append("div")
        .attr("class", "top-label age-label");
body.append("div")
        .attr("class", "top-label");
body.append("div")
        .attr("class", "clearfix");
```

Now, let's add the paragraphs. We want to append them to their respective <div>s. We could create a variable for each of those <div>s, but in this particular case, it's probably easier to just stick them right into the chain.

```
body.append("div")
        .attr("class", "top-label age-label")
    .append("p")
        .text("age group");

body.append("div")
        .attr("class", "top-label")
    .append("p")
        .text("portion of the population");
```

Excellent! Now on to the SVG. Here's the snippet for the bars:

```
<svg>
        <g transform="translate(100,30) scale(43.1,1)" class="bar">
                <!-- 80 and up -->
                <rect x="0" y="0" height="20" width="1.6"/>
                <!-- 75-79 -->
                <rect x="0" y="25" height="20" width="1.5"/>
                <!-- 70-74 -->
                <rect x="0" y="50" height="20" width="2.1"/>
                <!-- 65-69 -->
                <rect x="0" y="75" height="20" width="2.6"/>
                <!-- 60-64 -->
                <rect x="0" y="100" height="20" width="3.4"/>
                <!-- 55-59 -->
                <rect x="0" y="125" height="20" width="4.5"/>
                <!-- 50-54 -->
                <rect x="0" y="150" height="20" width="5.1"/>
                <!-- 45-49 -->
                <rect x="0" y="175" height="20" width="6.0"/>
                <!-- 40-44 -->
                <rect x="0" y="200" height="20" width="6.6"/>
                <!-- 35-39 -->
                <rect x="0" y="225" height="20" width="7.1"/>
                <!-- 30-34 -->
                <rect x="0" y="250" height="20" width="7.3"/>
                <!-- 25-29 -->
                <rect x="0" y="275" height="20" width="8.1"/>
                <!-- 20-24 -->
                <rect x="0" y="300" height="20" width="8.9"/>
                <!-- 15-19 -->
                <rect x="0" y="325" height="20" width="8.8"/>
                <!-- 10-14 -->
                <rect x="0" y="350" height="20" width="8.6"/>
                <!-- 5-9 -->
                <rect x="0" y="375" height="20" width="8.8"/>
                <!-- 0-4 -->
                <rect x="0" y="400" height="20" width="9.3"/>
        </g>
```

So, first things first. We need to append an <svg> element to the document body. And since we know we'll be appending a lot of things to that <svg> element, we can go ahead and create a variable for it:

```
var svg = body.append("svg");
```

Then, we want to append a group to that <svg> element, and again it makes sense to assign it to a variable, because we'll be appending 17 separate rectangles to it.

```
var barGroup = svg.append("g")
        .attr("transform", "translate(100,30) scale(43,1)")
        .attr("class", "bar");
```

Now for the rectangles.

```
barGroup.append("rect")
        .attr("x", 0)
        .attr("y", 0)
        .attr("height", 20)
        .attr("width", 1.6);

barGroup.append("rect")
        .attr("x", 0)
        .attr("y", 25)
        .attr("height", 20)
        .attr("width", 1.5);

barGroup.append("rect")
        .attr("x", 0)
        .attr("y", 50)
        .attr("height", 20)
        .attr("width", 2.1);

barGroup.append("rect")
        .attr("x", 0)
        .attr("y", 75)
        .attr("height", 20)
        .attr("width", 2.6);

barGroup.append("rect")
        .attr("x", 0)
        .attr("y", 100)
        .attr("height", 20)
        .attr("width", 3.4);

barGroup.append("rect")
        .attr("x", 0)
        .attr("y", 125)
        .attr("height", 20)
        .attr("width", 4.5);
```

```
barGroup.append("rect")
        .attr("x", 0)
        .attr("y", 150)
        .attr("height", 20)
        .attr("width", 5.1);

barGroup.append("rect")
        .attr("x", 0)
        .attr("y", 175)
        .attr("height", 20)
        .attr("width", 6.0);

barGroup.append("rect")
        .attr("x", 0)
        .attr("y", 200)
        .attr("height", 20)
        .attr("width", 6.6);

barGroup.append("rect")
        .attr("x", 0)
        .attr("y", 225)
        .attr("height", 20)
        .attr("width", 7.1);

barGroup.append("rect")
        .attr("x", 0)
        .attr("y", 250)
        .attr("height", 20)
        .attr("width", 7.3);

barGroup.append("rect")
        .attr("x", 0)
        .attr("y", 275)
        .attr("height", 20)
        .attr("width", 8.1);

barGroup.append("rect")
        .attr("x", 0)
        .attr("y", 300)
        .attr("height", 20)
        .attr("width", 8.9);

barGroup.append("rect")
        .attr("x", 0)
        .attr("y", 325)
        .attr("height", 20)
        .attr("width", 8.8);

barGroup.append("rect")
        .attr("x", 0)
        .attr("y", 350)
```

```
        .attr("height", 20)
        .attr("width", 8.6);

barGroup.append("rect")
        .attr("x", 0)
        .attr("y", 375)
        .attr("height", 20)
        .attr("width", 8.8);

barGroup.append("rect")
        .attr("x", 0)
        .attr("y", 400)
        .attr("height", 20)
        .attr("width", 9.3);
```

Okay, that's a lot of rectangles. By now, you've probably got the hang of going through SVG markup and translating it into D3 using append() and attr(). Go ahead and do it for the rest of the chart. I'll put the code here, but I encourage you to try it on your own.

```
<!DOCTYPE html>
<html>
<head>
<meta charset="utf-8">
<style>
        body {
                font-family: Helvetica;
        }
        svg {
                width: 500px;
                height: 500px;
        }
        .top-label {
                font-size: 13px;
                font-style: italic;
                text-transform: uppercase;
                float: left;
        }
        .age-label {
                text-align: right;
                font-weight: bold;
                width: 90px;
                padding-right: 10px;
        }
        .clearfix {
                clear: both;
        }
        .bar {
                fill: DarkSlateBlue;
```

```
        }
        .bar-label {
                text-anchor: end;
        }
        .axis-label {
                text-anchor: middle;
                font-size: 13px;
        }
</style>
</head>
<body>
<script src="http://d3js.org/d3.v3.min.js"></script>
<script>
        var body = d3.select("body");

        body.append("h2")
                .text("Age distribution of the world, 2010");

        body.append("div")
                .attr("class", "top-label age-label")
          .append("p")
                .text("age group");

        body.append("div")
                .attr("class", "top-label")
          .append("p")
                .text("portion of the population");

        body.append("div")
                .attr("class", "clearfix")

        var svg = body.append("svg");

        var barGroup = svg.append("g")
                .attr("transform", "translate(100,30) scale(43,1)")
                .attr("class", "bar");

        barGroup.append("rect")
                .attr("x", 0)
                .attr("y", 0)
                .attr("height", 20)
                .attr("width", 1.6);

        barGroup.append("rect")
                .attr("x", 0)
                .attr("y", 25)
                .attr("height", 20)
                .attr("width", 1.5);

        barGroup.append("rect")
                .attr("x", 0)
                .attr("y", 50)
```

```
        .attr("height", 20)
        .attr("width", 2.1);

barGroup.append("rect")
        .attr("x", 0)
        .attr("y", 75)
        .attr("height", 20)
        .attr("width", 2.6);

barGroup.append("rect")
        .attr("x", 0)
        .attr("y", 100)
        .attr("height", 20)
        .attr("width", 3.4);

barGroup.append("rect")
        .attr("x", 0)
        .attr("y", 125)
        .attr("height", 20)
        .attr("width", 4.5);

barGroup.append("rect")
        .attr("x", 0)
        .attr("y", 150)
        .attr("height", 20)
        .attr("width", 5.1);

barGroup.append("rect")
        .attr("x", 0)
        .attr("y", 175)
        .attr("height", 20)
        .attr("width", 6.0);

barGroup.append("rect")
        .attr("x", 0)
        .attr("y", 200)
        .attr("height", 20)
        .attr("width", 6.6);

barGroup.append("rect")
        .attr("x", 0)
        .attr("y", 225)
        .attr("height", 20)
        .attr("width", 7.1);

barGroup.append("rect")
        .attr("x", 0)
        .attr("y", 250)
        .attr("height", 20)
        .attr("width", 7.3);
```

```
barGroup.append("rect")
        .attr("x", 0)
        .attr("y", 275)
        .attr("height", 20)
        .attr("width", 8.1);

barGroup.append("rect")
        .attr("x", 0)
        .attr("y", 300)
        .attr("height", 20)
        .attr("width", 8.9);

barGroup.append("rect")
        .attr("x", 0)
        .attr("y", 325)
        .attr("height", 20)
        .attr("width", 8.8);

barGroup.append("rect")
        .attr("x", 0)
        .attr("y", 350)
        .attr("height", 20)
        .attr("width", 8.6);

barGroup.append("rect")
        .attr("x", 0)
        .attr("y", 375)
        .attr("height", 20)
        .attr("width", 8.8);

barGroup.append("rect")
        .attr("x", 0)
        .attr("y", 400)
        .attr("height", 20)
        .attr("width", 9.3);

var barLabelGroup = svg.append("g")
        .attr("class", "bar-label")

barLabelGroup.append("text")
        .attr("x", 90)
        .attr("y", 45)
        .text("80 and up");

barLabelGroup.append("text")
        .attr("x", 90)
        .attr("y", 70)
        .text("75-79");
```

```
barLabelGroup.append("text")
        .attr("x", 90)
        .attr("y", 95)
        .text("70-74");

barLabelGroup.append("text")
        .attr("x", 90)
        .attr("y", 120)
        .text("65-69");

barLabelGroup.append("text")
        .attr("x", 90)
        .attr("y", 145)
        .text("60-64");

barLabelGroup.append("text")
        .attr("x", 90)
        .attr("y", 170)
        .text("55-59");

barLabelGroup.append("text")
        .attr("x", 90)
        .attr("y", 195)
        .text("50-54");

barLabelGroup.append("text")
        .attr("x", 90)
        .attr("y", 220)
        .text("45-49");

barLabelGroup.append("text")
        .attr("x", 90)
        .attr("y", 245)
        .text("40-44");

barLabelGroup.append("text")
        .attr("x", 90)
        .attr("y", 270)
        .text("35-39");

barLabelGroup.append("text")
        .attr("x", 90)
        .attr("y", 295)
        .text("30-34");

barLabelGroup.append("text")
        .attr("x", 90)
        .attr("y", 320)
        .text("25-29");
```

```
barLabelGroup.append("text")
        .attr("x", 90)
        .attr("y", 345)
        .text("20-24");

barLabelGroup.append("text")
        .attr("x", 90)
        .attr("y", 370)
        .text("15-19");

barLabelGroup.append("text")
        .attr("x", 90)
        .attr("y", 395)
        .text("10-14");

barLabelGroup.append("text")
        .attr("x", 90)
        .attr("y", 420)
        .text("5-9");

barLabelGroup.append("text")
        .attr("x", 90)
        .attr("y", 445)
        .text("0-4");

var axisTickGroup = svg.append("g")
        .attr("transform", "translate(100,30)")
        .attr("stroke", "black");

axisTickGroup.append("line")
        .attr("x1", 0)
        .attr("y1", 0)
        .attr("x2", 0)
        .attr("y2", -10);

axisTickGroup.append("line")
        .attr("x1", 107.75)
        .attr("y1", 0)
        .attr("x2", 107.75)
        .attr("y2", -10);

axisTickGroup.append("line")
        .attr("x1", 215.5)
        .attr("y1", 0)
        .attr("x2", 215.5)
        .attr("y2", -10);

axisTickGroup.append("line")
        .attr("x1", 323.25)
        .attr("y1", 0)
        .attr("x2", 323.25)
        .attr("y2", -10);
```

```
        var axisLabelGroup = svg.append("g")
                .attr("transform", "translate(100,30)")
                .attr("class", "axis-label");

        axisLabelGroup.append("text")
                .attr("x", 0)
                .attr("y", -15)
                .text("0");

        axisLabelGroup.append("text")
                .attr("x", 107.75)
                .attr("y", -15)
                .text("2.5%");

        axisLabelGroup.append("text")
                .attr("x", 215.5)
                .attr("y", -15)
                .text("5.0%");

        axisLabelGroup.append("text")
                .attr("x", 323.25)
                .attr("y", -15)
                .text("7.5%");
</script>
</body>
</html>
```

Woohoo! You've made a bar chart from scratch, completely in D3. Congratulations!

But wait…this hardly seems like an improvement. Our **pop2010-svg.html** file was only 119 lines long, including comments, but **pop2010-D3.html** is 312 lines long. We've nearly tripled our work! What good is this D3, anyway?

Of course, we aren't using D3's full capabilities just yet—on the contrary, we're hardly using any of them. But even more importantly, we aren't using JavaScript the way we should be either. There are a lot of things we can do to make the code above both shorter and more useful.

Use Variables

The first thing we should do is use variables instead of hard-coding the same numbers in over and over again. Well-chosen variables are like levers in a factory or dials on a sound board—they are the inputs you shift or turn to tweak your output. Let's look again at the section of our code where we create the rectangles (I'm only going to include four of them instead of all 17, but the changes we make to these four should be made to all of the bars):

```
barGroup.append("rect")
        .attr("x", 0)
        .attr("y", 0)
        .attr("height", 20)
        .attr("width", 1.6);
```

```
barGroup.append("rect")
        .attr("x", 0)
        .attr("y", 25)
        .attr("height", 20)
        .attr("width", 1.5);

barGroup.append("rect")
        .attr("x", 0)
        .attr("y", 50)
        .attr("height", 20)
        .attr("width", 2.1);

barGroup.append("rect")
        .attr("x", 0)
        .attr("y", 75)
        .attr("height", 20)
        .attr("width", 2.6);
```

Do you see any opportunities for creating useful variables? Height, right? Its value is 20 in every case (it would be weird if our bars had different heights). Let's create a variable called barHeight and use that instead of the number for each bar:

```
var barHeight = 20;
barGroup.append("rect")
        .attr("x", 0)
        .attr("y", 0)
        .attr("height", barHeight)
        .attr("width", 1.6);

barGroup.append("rect")
        .attr("x", 0)
        .attr("y", 50)
        .attr("height", barHeight)
        .attr("width", 1.5);

barGroup.append("rect")
        .attr("x", 0)
        .attr("y", 100)
        .attr("height", barHeight)
        .attr("width", 2.1);

barGroup.append("rect")
        .attr("x", 0)
        .attr("y", 150)
        .attr("height", barHeight)
        .attr("width", 2.6);
```

Now, if we decided we wanted our bars to be fatter or skinnier than 20 pixels, we could just change that number at the top (turn that height dial, shift that height lever), and it would change the height of all four of them.

Using variables is not that different from using CSS, really. With CSS, you give a bunch of different elements a class, and when you change the formatting rules for that class, the formatting of all of those elements changes. Modifying things once is a lot easier than doing it a bunch of times, whether it means going through your markup and tweaking everything inline, or going through your D3 script and tweaking everything "in-chain."

Do Math

You might be thinking that we should just use CSS more in our code: After all, you could use a CSS rule to define the height of those bars. You don't need to whip up a variable in JavaScript.

But there are some basic things you can do in JavaScript that you can't do in CSS—math is one of them. Take a look at the y attribute for the rectangles above. The first one is 0, then 25, then 50, then 75. The idea is that, going down the page, we want a bar to start every 25 pixels. As the code exists now, we've already done the math to figure out each bar's vertical position. Turns out, that was a bit of a waste of time. JavaScript can do that math for us, and we should always take advantage of that capability. We're humans after all, and when it comes to math, we make a lot more mistakes than computers.

If we define a variable called barSpacing and set it equal to 25, we can set the y attribute for each of the bars as follows:

First bar	.attr("y", 0)
Second bar	.attr("y", barSpacing)
Third bar	.attr("y", 2 * barSpacing)
Fourth bar	.attr("y", 3 * barSpacing)

Great, now we have another variable we can tweak.

Use Better Variables

So, now we have two variables at our disposal: barHeight and barSpacing. As it turns out, this isn't really a useful set of dials to have. Why? I'll tell you. Say we wanted to set barHeight to 30. If we didn't change barSpacing as well, then the bars would overlap. That's no good. It would be much more useful to be able to control the bar height and the size of the gap in between the bars—and then just make the spacing equal to the sum of those two values.

Easy enough:

```
var barHeight = 20,
    barGap = 5,
    barSpacing = barHeight + barGap;
```

```
barGroup.append("rect")
        .attr("x", 0)
        .attr("y", 0)
        .attr("height", barHeight)
        .attr("width", 1.6);

barGroup.append("rect")
        .attr("x", 0)
        .attr("y", barSpacing)
        .attr("height", barHeight)
        .attr("width", 1.5);

barGroup.append("rect")
        .attr("x", 0)
        .attr("y", 2 * barSpacing)
        .attr("height", barHeight)
        .attr("width", 2.1);

barGroup.append("rect")
        .attr("x", 0)
        .attr("y", 3 * barSpacing)
        .attr("height", barHeight)
        .attr("width", 2.6);
```

Use a Variable for Your Data

In general, when you're doing stuff with data in JavaScript, it's a good idea for that data to be stored in its own variable, usually an array. You might decide you want to modify your code to use that data in a place you didn't before, or you might just want to swap that data out for new data. In either case, it doesn't help to have your data scattered across multiple D3 chains.

Here's an array we can use for our data:

```
var popData = [1.6, 1.5, 2.1, 2.6, 3.4, 4.5, 5.1, 6.0, 6.6, 7.1, 7.3, 8.1,
        8.9, 8.8, 8.6, 8.8, 9.3];
```

The first value is the percentage of the population that was 80 years old or older in 2010—the data we are representing with our top bar. Likewise, the last value in the array is the one we are representing with our bottom bar—that same percentage of people from age 0 to age 4.

Now, to access these values when setting the widths of the bars, we just need to index into the array.

First bar	`.attr("width", popData[0])`
Second bar	`.attr("width", popData[1])`
Third bar	`.attr("width", popData[2])`
Fourth bar	`.attr("width", popData[3])`

Make Your Constraints Explicit

We've been messing around with just the bars, but let's go up a level and take a look at the group to which they belong:

```
var barGroup = svg.append("g")
        .attr("transform", "translate(100,30) scale(43,1)")
        .attr("class", "bar");
```

There's a weird number tucked away in that bit of code—43. Do you remember where it came from? We needed to figure out how to scale the bars so they would take up 400 pixels of width. So we took the biggest value in our data set—9.3—that would make for the biggest bar, and we divided 400 by that number to get the factor we needed for scaling.

But what if we decided we wanted the bars to take up only 300 pixels or 500? We would have to divide that new width by 9.3 to get a new scaling factor, and it would be a pain to do this every time.

What makes more sense is to just make that constraint—the maximum width we want our bars to take up—explicit. In other words, make it a variable. Then we can derive other values, such as the scaling factor, from it:

```
var popData = [1.6, 1.5, 2.1, 2.6, 3.4, 4.5, 5.1, 6.0, 6.6, 7.1, 7.3, 8.1,
        8.9, 8.8, 8.6, 8.8, 9.3];

var width = 400,
        scaleFactor = width / popData[16];
```

Now, to actually put that scaleFactor variable to use, we have to do some concatenation. In our code, we give the group barGroup a transform attribute with the following value:

```
"translate(100,30) scale(43,1)"
```

We want to create a string that is similar, but uses the scaleFactor variable instead of 43. So, we have to concatenate. Remember that JavaScript does automatic type conversion—if you add a number (or a variable that represents a number) to a string, it will convert the number into a string and then concatenate:

```
"translate(100,30) scale(" + scaleFactor + ",1)"
```

You'll encounter a lot of this kind of concatenation when you use D3, since many key methods take strings as arguments. It can look a little weird—you're probably not used to seeing quotation marks immediately after an open parenthesis or immediately before a comma—but don't be intimidated by the weirdness. If you go through step by step and just try to parse the statement (by converting the variables to numbers in your mind and concatenating them with the text), you shouldn't have any problems. This is a perfect example of how useful syntax highlighting can be: If strings and variables are different colors in your text editor, then it's a lot easier to parse weird concatenations.

Use Loops

The last thing we can do to make **pop2010-D3.html** better, knowing what we know now, is to use loops to get rid of some of the redundancy. Let's take a look at the updated code for our bars. Does any of it seem a little repetitive to you?

```
var popData = [1.6, 1.5, 2.1, 2.6, 3.4, 4.5, 5.1, 6.0, 6.6, 7.1, 7.3, 8.1,
        8.9, 8.8, 8.6, 8.8, 9.3];

var width = 400,
        scaleFactor = width / popData[16];

var barHeight = 20,
        barGap = 5,
        barSpacing = barHeight + barGap;

var barGroup = svg.append("g")
        .attr("transform", "translate(100,30) scale(" + scaleFactor + ",1)"),
        .attr("class", "bar");

barGroup.append("rect")
        .attr("x", 0)
        .attr("y", 0)
        .attr("height", barHeight)
        .attr("width", popData[0]);

barGroup.append("rect")
        .attr("x", 0)
        .attr("y", barSpacing)
        .attr("height", barHeight)
        .attr("width", popData[1]);

barGroup.append("rect")
        .attr("x", 0)
        .attr("y", 2 * barSpacing)
        .attr("height", barHeight)
        .attr("width", popData[2]);

barGroup.append("rect")
        .attr("x", 0)
        .attr("y", 3 * barSpacing)
        .attr("height", barHeight)
        .attr("width", popData[3]);
```

Of course it does! Each of the `barGroup.append("rect")` chains is nearly identical to all the others. We're appending 17 rectangles to barGroup. Each one has the same height and same horizontal position, and the vertical position and the width both depend on where in the order of bars the bar in question happens to be—the first bar, the second bar, or the seventeenth bar.

This is exactly the kind of situation loops were made for. If it's not obvious to you why, don't worry, you'll get a feel for it before long. For now, you might want to take a look at Appendix A again and review the section on loops. To create our 17 bars with a loop, we'll use this basic structure:

```
for (var i = 0; i < 17; i++) {
     // do something
}
```

We have a counter, i, that starts at 0 and is incremented with each iteration, ending at a value of 16 on the last loop. (Recall that a for loop will keep running for as long as the condition is satisfied—in this case, as long as i is less than 17.)

That means we have 17 iterations, which is perfect, because we want to append 17 bars. So, we know that with each iteration we want to do this:

```
for (var i = 0; i < 17; i++) {
     barGroup.append("rect")
}
```

Now, there are some attributes that are the same for all of the bars—namely, x and height. So, we can go ahead and put those in the loop:

```
for (var i = 0; i < 4; i++) {
     barGroup.append("rect")
        .attr("x", 0)
        .attr("height", barHeight)
}
```

For the other two attributes—y and width—we can take advantage of the fact that i changes with each iteration to make those attributes different for each of the bars. To figure out how to do that, we can take a look at each iteration in detail—what i equals and what we want y and width to be.

Iteration	i	y	width
1	0	0	popData[0]
2	1	barSpacing	popData[1]
3	2	2*barSpacing	popData[2]
4	3	3*barSpacing	popData[3]

It's pretty obvious how we should handle the width. Instead of popData[0] or popData[1], we can do popData[i], and the index will change exactly how we want it to with each iteration.

The y attribute is only slightly trickier. If you look at the last two iterations, you can see that y is equal to 2*barSpacing and 3*barSpacing. In these two cases, i*barSpacing would work. But would it work for the others? On the first iteration, i = 0, so i*barSpacing would be 0. Check. And on the second, i = 1, so i*barSpacing would be equal to barSpacing. Check again.

So, we can update our for loop to look like this:

```
for (var i = 0; i < 17; i++) {
      barGroup.append("rect")
             .attr("x", 0)
             .attr("y", i * barSpacing)
             .attr("height", barHeight)
             .attr("width", popData[i]);
}
```

There's one more thing we can do to make this for loop a little more sophisticated. Currently, our loop condition involves a number: i < 17. We are using 17 because we happen to know that our data has 17 data points. But what if we wanted to use a dataset with fewer data points? Say we had a dataset of the age distribution that was broken down into 10-year age groups: 0-9, 10-19, 20-29, etc. In that case, instead of stopping our loop before i gets to 17, we would want to stop it before i gets to, say, 9, or however many data points there are in our new data set.

It would be a pain to have to count those data points every time, and then to have to insert the number into your for loop. So instead, you can use the length property of your data array:

```
for (var i = 0; i < popData.length; i++) {
      barGroup.append("rect")
             .attr("x", 0)
             .attr("y", i * barSpacing)
             .attr("height", barHeight)
             .attr("width", popData[i]);
}
```

Excellent. You'll notice that with the exception of 0—the value of every bar's x attribute—there are no numbers in the for loop. This is a good sign. The more numbers you can take out of the body of your code and put into variables at the top, the better.

Here's the new code for the entire bar section:

```
var popData = [1.6, 1.5, 2.1, 2.6, 3.4, 4.5, 5.1, 6.0, 6.6, 7.1, 7.3, 8.1,
        8.9, 8.8, 8.6, 8.8, 9.3];

var width = 400,
       scaleFactor = width / popData[3];

var barHeight = 20,
       barGap = 5,
       barSpacing = barHeight + barGap;

var barGroup = svg.append("g")
       .attr("transform", "translate(100,30) scale(" + scaleFactor + ",1)"),
       .attr("class", "bar");
```

```
for (var i = 0; i < popData.length; i++) {
    barGroup.append("rect")
            .attr("x", 0)
            .attr("y", i * barSpacing)
            .attr("height", barHeight)
            .attr("width", popData[i]);
}
```

We've just focused on the four rectangles in our chart, but you can, of course, apply all these lessons to the rest of the code. Give it a try! Here's what I came up with:

```
<!DOCTYPE html>
<html>
<head>
<meta charset="utf-8">
<style>
    body {
            font-family: Helvetica;
    }
    svg {
            width:500px;
            height:500px;
    }
    .top-label {
            font-size: 13px;
            font-style: italic;
            text-transform: uppercase;
            float: left;
    }
    .age-label {
            text-align: right;
            font-weight: bold;
            width: 90px;
            padding-right: 10px;
    }
    .clearfix {
            clear: both;
    }
    .bar {
            fill: DarkSlateBlue;
    }
    .bar-label {
            text-anchor: end;
    }
    .axis-label {
            text-anchor: middle;
            font-size: 13px;
    }
```

```
</style>
</head>
<body>
<script src="http://d3js.org/d3.v3.min.js"></script>
<script>
        var popData = [1.6, 1.5, 2.1, 2.6, 3.4, 4.5, 5.1, 6.0, 6.6, 7.1, 7.3, 8.1,
8.9, 8.8, 8.6, 8.8, 9.3],
            axisData = [0, 2.5, 5.0, 7.5],
            barLabels = ["80 and up", "75-79", "70-74", "65-69", "60-64", "55-
59", "50-54", "45-49", "40-44", "35-39", "30-34", "25-29", "20-24", "15-19", "10-
14", "5-9", "0-4"];

    var width = 400,
            leftMargin = 100,
            topMargin = 30,
            barHeight = 20,
            barGap = 5,
            tickGap = 5,
            tickHeight = 10,
            scaleFactor = width / popData[16],
            barSpacing = barHeight + barGap,
            translateText = "translate(" + leftMargin + "," + topMargin + ")",
            scaleText = "scale(" + scaleFactor + ",1)";

    var body = d3.select("body");

    body.append("h2")
            .text("Age distribution of the world, 2010");

    body.append("div")
            .attr("class", "top-label age-label")
      .append("p")
            .text("age group");

    body.append("div")
            .attr("class", "top-label")
      .append("p")
            .text("portion of the population");

    body.append("div")
            .attr("class", "clearfix")

    var svg = body.append("svg");

    var barGroup = svg.append("g")
            .attr("transform", translateText + " " + scaleText)
            .attr("class", "bar");

    for (var i = 0; i < popData.length; i++) {
            barGroup.append("rect")
                    .attr("x", 0)
```

```
                     .attr("y", i * barSpacing)
                     .attr("height", barHeight)
                     .attr("width", popData[i]);
      };

    var barLabelGroup = svg.append("g")
            .attr("transform", translateText)
            .attr("class", "bar-label")

    for (var i = 0; i < barLabels.length; i++) {
            barLabelGroup.append("text")
                    .attr("x", -10)
                    .attr("y", i * barSpacing + barHeight*(2/3))
                    .text(barLabels[i]);
      };

    var axisTickGroup = svg.append("g")
            .attr("transform", translateText)
            .attr("stroke", "black");

    var axisLabelGroup = svg.append("g")
            .attr("transform", "translate(100,30)")
            .attr("class", "axis-label");

    for (var i = 0; i < axisData.length; i++) {
            axisTickGroup.append("line")
                    .attr("x1", axisData[i] * scaleFactor)
                    .attr("x2", axisData[i] * scaleFactor)
                    .attr("y1", 0)
                    .attr("y2", -tickHeight);

            axisLabelGroup.append("text")
                    .attr("x", axisData[i] * scaleFactor)
                    .attr("y", -tickHeight - tickGap)
                    .text(axisData[i] + "%");
      };

</script>
</body>
</html>
</body>
```

Summary

This chapter covered how to get set up using D3 by referencing the library in your HTML. The main focus was on selections and their methods. Selections are D3's way of accessing and changing the elements of a webpage. The key methods that act on selections modify the elements contained within. In this chapter, we used selections and their methods to build a web page from scratch in D3 and to make a bar chart.

5

Data-Joins: Enter

Data-joins are the bread and butter of D3. If you take one thing away from this book, make it understanding how data-joins work and how to use them. Remember that D3 has no basic function for producing charts. Instead, it uses data-joins. This chapter covers how to use data-joins to add elements to a webpage and then manipulate them with data.

What Are Data-Joins?

As the name suggests, data-joins involve joining data with something. That something is an element or a number of elements on a web page—<rect>s, <circles>s, <div>s... all the usual suspects. More specifically, that something is a D3 selection of those elements.

Before we get into all of that, let's take a few steps back. Forget about D3 for a second. Now, imagine an interactive graphic. It could be one you've seen somewhere or made yourself, or it could be one you invent in your mind right now. In this graphic there are shapes on the page that represent data and there are buttons for controlling what data is displayed. When you hit those buttons, the shapes change: their positions shift, they grow or shrink, they change color, or they can even fly off the screen altogether. Make it as crazy as you like.

Now, no matter how complicated or data-rich your graphic is, on a fundamental level, the shapes involved (or the lines, text, colors, or textures) only ever do one of three things:

- **Appear on the page in the first place**—You can't have a data visualization without both data and visuals, so the shapes need to show up.
- **Change**—When you hit a button or adjust a slider, attributes of the shapes update to represent the new data you want to see.
- **Leave the page**—Sometimes a shape or two will leave the page entirely, if the data that it represents is no longer relevant.

That's it. Those three things. An interactive graphic is sort of like theater. During a play, actors enter the stage, they act, and they exit. In a data visualization, shapes, or more broadly, graphical elements, **enter** the page, they **update**, and they **exit**.

Data-joins take full advantage of this rudimentary idea. In using them, you can command graphical elements to enter, update, and exit. (In fact, I took the terms "enter," "update," and "exit" directly from D3.)

What's more, D3 enables you to do all of these things based on data. The way it achieves this is through something called **data binding**. Whenever you perform a data-join, your data is actually connected, or bound, to elements. This is hugely convenient, because D3 gives you easy access to bound data. So you can say, for example, "Okay rectangle, what does your bound data point say? 35? Well, that's what I want your width to be!"

This probably only makes vague sense at this point. Don't worry, we'll go through everything slowly and in detail, using an example as a guide. This chapter will focus just on **enter**, and in Chapter 8, we'll cover **update** and **exit**.

A Conceptual Overview of Data-Joins: Enter

To cover how data-joins work, I'm going to introduce a new example, one that involves all the most fundamental aspects of using data-joins. To build our trusty old age distribution bar chart, we are indeed going to use data-joins, but not all aspects of them. So, although it's a bit of a diversion, introducing a new example will help us cover the entire breadth of what data-joins are about.

This chapter only covers part of what data-joins can do, specifically the **enter** part of their life cycle. But we'll come back to this same example to cover **update** and **exit** in Chapter 8.

Okay, here goes: Say you have a friend named Frank, and Frank has a strange obsession with celebrity gossip magazines and tabloids. *US Weekly*, *People*, the *National Enquirer*...if it's a publication you've ever stared at idly while waiting in the grocery store checkout line, then Frank has a keen interest in it. The thing is, he doesn't really care about the latest updates on Kim and Kanye. He just wants to know one thing: Who's on the cover?

Frank has been taking note of the most prominently featured celebrities on the covers of about 20 different magazines and newspapers—a total of 50 covers a month—for an entire year. Plus, he's done some additional research to figure out who was on those covers during the four years before he started paying attention. "I think the celebrities we are preoccupied with at any given time says a lot about the national psyche," Frank says, a little too often. You have your doubts, but when Frank approaches you and asks if you'll help him visualize all that information, you can't say no.

Frank's idea is to show the five most-featured celebrities every month for all five years of data he's amassed. He wants the visualization to be interactive and animated, but he's not sure what he wants it to look like. You have an idea, though. You scribble

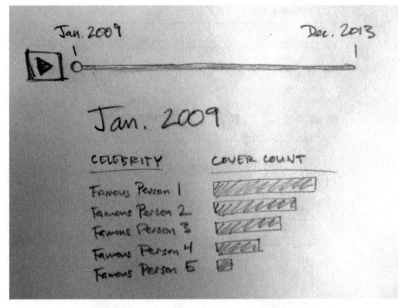

Figure 5.1 The rough sketch we made for Frank

on a notepad for a few minutes, hand Frank a sketch (shown in Figure 5.1), and describe it. The graphic opens on a list of the top-five celebrities by cover count for the oldest month in the set, January 2009, you tell him. Next to each celebrity's name is a bar that represents how many covers he or she appeared on that month, so it's clear if one celebrity has totally dominated. The user will be able to switch to subsequent months in one of two ways: She can press a play button and sit back as the graphic advances through the months on its own, or she can move a slider to navigate to a month of her choosing. When the graphic transitions from one month to another, new celebrity names will **enter** the ranking, others will **exit** it, and still others will move up and down in the list, with their associated bars expanding and contracting to meet the **updated** cover count. "Sweet!" exclaims Frank, and he emails you his 3,000-row spreadsheet.

Enter, update, exit...D3 was made for this.

Enter and Binding Data

Ok, let's check out Frank's data. Say you've already done some number crunching, and you've added up all the covers for each celebrity for every month and sorted them into rankings. Figure 5.2 shows what you found for the first three months, January through March, 2009 (these values are, of course, completely fabricated).

Frank's Data

Jan. 2009		
CELEBRITY NAME	NUMBER OF COVERS	RANK
Angelina Jolie	20	1
Brad Pitt	18	2
Jennifer Aniston	10	3
Britney Spears	8	4

Feb. 2009		
CELEBRITY NAME	NUMBER OF COVERS	RANK
Jennifer Aniston	18	1
Angelina Jolie	15	2
Britney Spears	7	3
Brad Pitt	2	4
"Bat-child"	1	5

Mar. 2009		
CELEBRITY NAME	NUMBER OF COVERS	RANK
The "Octomom"	25	1
Jennifer Aniston	15	2
John Mayer	12	3
Britney Spears	10	4

Figure 5.2   The first three months of Frank's data

Here are a couple of notes concerning the data:

- The number of covers doesn't always add up to 50. This is because sometimes cover shots feature two celebrities together, and in those cases, it counts as a cover for both of them.

- There were only four celebrities total in cover shots in January. A lot of attention was paid to the Brad Pitt/Angelina Jolie saga. (What would Frank say that means about the country?)

- February was similar to January, except that *Weekly World News* provided an update on its famous "bat-child."

- "Octomom" was the nickname given to Nadya Suleman after she successfully gave birth to octuplets in early 2009.

A nice way to structure this data in JavaScript is to create a couple of arrays of objects. For example, for January, we would have:

```
var janData = [
    {name:"Angelina Jolie", covers:20, rank:1},
    {name:"Brad Pitt", covers:18, rank:2},
    {name:"Jennifer Aniston", covers:10, rank:3},
    {name:"Britney Spears", covers:8, rank:4}
];
```

Can you see what makes that structure so nice? The array `janData` contains four objects, and each object contains all of the information for one (and only one) data point. We'll go over data structures more in Chapter 7.

Alright, so first things first: We need to get some graphics on the page. Let's forget about the bars for now and start with just the celebrity names. We could take the approach we used in Chapter 4, in the section "Shaping Web Pages with D3 Selections," using a `for` loop to append one text element for each name. But we aren't going to do that. Forget `for` loops. We're thinking in data-joins now. We want to make text **enter** the page.

Here's how: We're going to create a selection of all the text elements currently on the page, and then we're going to join our data to it. But wait...our page is blank. There are no text elements! So what does it even mean to "select all of them?"

Herein lies the magic of how D3 handles the **enter** phase. You create a selection of elements that don't exist using `d3.selectAll()`. In this case, since we want to make text enter the page, we can select all of the not-yet-existing paragraph elements—`d3.selectAll("p")`. This is shown conceptually in Figure 5.3.

Then you use two methods on that selection: `data()` and `enter()`. This one-two punch does something truly awesome: It creates a new object for every point in your dataset. Yep, that's right—you don't have to tell D3 how large your dataset is. You just join it up with an empty selection, and *it will create the right number of objects for you* (see Figure 5.4).

Those objects are just placeholders to start—no text elements have actually been added to the page yet. To make that happen, we just have to use our trusty old friend, `append()`. We'll append a paragraph element to each of those placeholders (see Figure 5.5).

Now, we've put four text elements on the page, but they don't have any text in them, so our page is still blank. How do we get those celebrity names up there and in the right place? The secret lies in the `data()` method. That method actually performs a data-join, and *when D3 performs a data-join, it binds data to elements*. So, each of those text elements actually has a data point connected, or bound, to it, as shown by the lines in Figure 5.5.

D3 gives us easy access to bound data, so we can use that data to tell the text elements what to say and where to go: "Alright, element, let's look at your data point. Which celebrity do you have? Angelina Jolie? Okay, that's what I want your text to read. And what's the rank? 1? Okay, you're going to the top!"

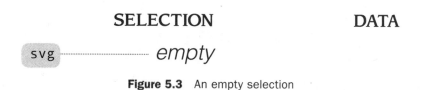

Figure 5.3 An empty selection

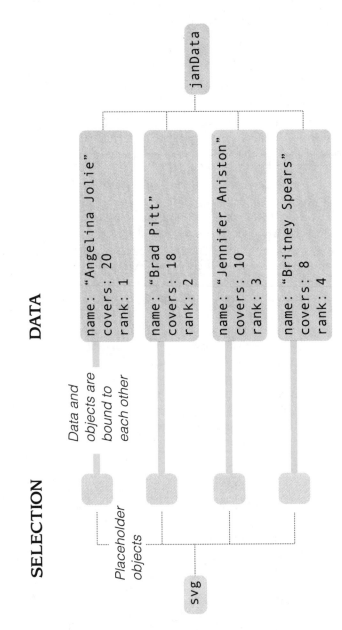

Figure 5.4   The magic of data() and enter()

SELECTION   DATA

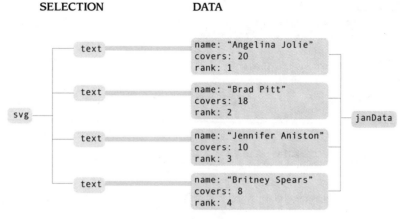

Figure 5.5   Replacing the placeholders with text elements

Using a Data-Join to Make a Bar Chart

In the previous chapter, we remade our global age distribution bar chart in JavaScript, using D3 selections. We put the results in a file called **pop2010–D3.html**, which you should take a moment to review now. For the rest of the chapter, we're going to create that same bar chart again, using a data–join.

To do this, we can use a lot of the same code from **pop2010–D3.html**. Create a new file called **pop2010–data–joins.html** and cut and paste the code in Listing 5.1 from **pop2010–D3.html**:

Listing 5.1   *pop2010-data-joins.html*

```
<!DOCTYPE html>
<html>
<head>
<meta charset="utf-8">
<style>
     body {
          font-family: Helvetica;
     }
     svg {
          width:500px;
          height:500px;
     }
     .top-label {
          font-size: 13px;
          font-style: italic;
          text-transform: uppercase;
          float: left;
     }
```

```
      .age-label {
            text-align: right;
            font-weight: bold;
            width: 90px;
            padding-right: 10px;
      }
      .clearfix {
            clear: both;
      }
      .bar {
             fill: DarkSlateBlue;
      }
      .bar-label {
            text-anchor: end;
      }
      .axis-label {
            text-anchor: middle;
            font-size: 13px;
      }
</style>
</head>
<body>
<script src="http://d3js.org/d3.v3.min.js"></script>
<script>
     var popData = [1.6, 1.5, 2.1, 2.6, 3.4, 4.5, 5.1, 6.0, 6.6, 7.1, 7.3, 8.1,
8.9, 8.8, 8.6, 8.8, 9.3],
         axisData = [0, 2.5, 5.0, 7.5],
         barLabels = ["80 and up", "75-79", "70-74", "65-69", "60-64", "55-59",
"50-54", "45-49", "40-44", "35-39", "30-34", "25-29", "20-24", "15-19", "10-14",
"5-9", "0-4"];

     var width = 400,
                leftMargin = 100,
                topMargin = 30,
                barHeight = 20,
                barGap = 5,
                tickGap = 5,
                tickHeight = 10,
                scaleFactor = width / popData[16],
                barSpacing = barHeight + barGap,
                translateText = "translate(" + leftMargin + "," + topMargin + ")",
                scaleText = "scale(" + scaleFactor + ",1)";

     var body = d3.select("body");

     body.append("h2")
         .text("Age distribution of the world, 2010");
```

```
    body.append("div")
        .attr("class", "top-label age-label")
        .style("width", leftMargin + "px")
      .append("p")
        .text("age group");

    body.append("div")
        .attr("class", "top-label")
      .append("p")
        .text("portion of the population");

    body.append("div")
        .attr("class", "clearfix");

    var svg = body.append("svg");

    var barGroup = svg.append("g")
        .attr("transform", translateText + " " + scaleText)
        .attr("class", "bar");
</script>
</body>
```

This includes everything leading up to the code we used for actually creating the bars of the bar chart, which we did using a for loop. Here's what that code looks like:

```
for (var i = 0; i < popData.length; i++) {
    barGroup.append("rect")
        .attr("x", 0)
        .attr("y", i * barSpacing)
        .attr("height", barHeight)
        .attr("width", popData[i]);
};
```

Recall that popData is an array of our age distribution data, where the first entry is the percentage of people who are 80 years old and older, followed by those between 75 years and 79, then 70 to 74, etc.

In the code above, the for loop goes through one iteration for each value in the popData array—17 in total. With every iteration, it appends a new SVG rectangle to the barGroup group element. To barGroup itself, we've applied a transform attribute designed to position and size the bars correctly: The entire group is shifted to the right 100 pixels to leave a margin for the bar labels and scaled horizontally so the widest bar will be exactly 400 pixels wide.

Good. But what if we wanted to draw those bars using a data–join instead? Let's retrace the same steps we went through with our tabloid covers. Load **pop2010-data-joins.html** in your browser. Figure 5.6 presents what you should see.

Now, we want to make some rectangles enter the page. And, specifically, we want them to be part of the group barGroup (which is shown in the DOM in Figure 5.6). So what we need to do is create a selection out of all of the rectangles in barGroup (of course, there aren't any). Add this line to your code:

```
┌─────────────────────────────────────────────────────────────────┐
│ PAGE                                                              │
│                                                                   │
│ Age distribution of the world, 2010                               │
│                                                                   │
│                                                                   │
│  AGE GROUP  PORTION OF THE POPULATION                             │
│                                                                   │
└─────────────────────────────────────────────────────────────────┘
┌─────────────────────────────────────────────────────────────────┐
│ DOM (this is what you see in your web inspector)                  │
│ <svg>                                                             │
│   <g transform="translate(100,30) scale(43.01075268817204,1)" class="bar"></g> │
│ </svg>                                                            │
└─────────────────────────────────────────────────────────────────┘
```

Figure 5.6   Before the data-join

```
barGroup.selectAll("rect")
```

Then, we use that one-two punch of .data().enter():

```
barGroup.selectAll("rect")
    .data(popData)
  .enter()
```

Neither the page nor the DOM has changed yet, but we have a placeholder object for each of our data points. Let's append some rectangles:

```
barGroup.selectAll("rect")
    .data(popData)
  .enter().append("rect")
```

We have 17 rectangles, and each one has a data point bound to it (see Figure 5.7). We now need to set the attributes of those rectangles. Some attributes will be the same for each rectangle—namely x, which determines where the bars start horizontally (remember, we want all of our bars to be aligned to the left, so x will be equal to 0), and height, because all of our bars will be the same height, a constant that we've called barHeight. Easy. We can go ahead and add those attributes:

```
barGroup.selectAll("rect")
      .data(popData)
  .enter().append("rect")
      .attr("x", 0)
      .attr("height", barHeight)
```

But the other two attributes—width and y—need to be different for each bar:

```
barGroup.selectAll("rect")
      .data(popData)
  .enter().append("rect")
      .attr("x", 0)
      .attr("height", barHeight)
      .attr("width", // What goes here?
      .attr("y", // Or here?);
```

This is where the bound data comes into play. Let's start with the width. When we were relying on a for loop, we iterated through a variable we called i, and set each rectangle's width to popData[i]. We essentially want to do the same thing here—we want the width of each bar to be equal to the associated value in popData. But since popData is bound to our rectangles, we don't need a loop. We can just tell D3, "hey, set the width of each rectangle equal to the data point that it is bound to."

The way we do that is by using something called an **anonymous function**.

Using Anonymous Functions to Access Bound Data

As the name suggests, an anonymous function is a function that doesn't have a name, or technically speaking, it hasn't been bound to an identifier. (What were its parents thinking?!) While a named function might look like this:

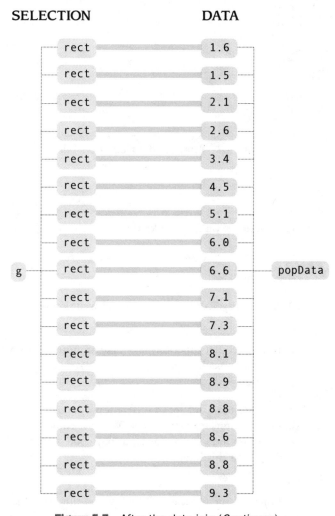

Figure 5.7   After the data-join (*Continues*)

```
PAGE

Age distribution of the world, 2010

AGE GROUP  PORTION OF THE POPULATION
```

```
DOM
<svg>
  <g transform="translate(100,30) scale(43.01075268817204,1)" class="bar">
    <rect></rect>
    <rect></rect>
    <rect></rect>
    <rect></rect>
    <rect></rect>
    <rect></rect>
    <rect></rect>
    <rect></rect>
    <rect></rect>
    <rect></rect>
    <rect></rect>
    <rect></rect>
    <rect></rect>
    <rect></rect>
    <rect></rect>
  </g>
</svg>
```

Figure 5.7 After the data-join (*Continued*)

```
var myFunction = function(){
      return 5;
}
```

a similar anonymous function would look like this:

```
function(){
      return 5;
}
```

or, since it's a small function, we could be concise and write on one line, like this:

```
function(){ return 5; }
```

Anonymous functions, like regular functions, can take arguments. So, you could have an anonymous function that looks like this:

```
function(x){ return x + 5; }
```

Anonymous functions are used in a lot of different programming languages, and there are a lot of different reasons for using them. When it comes to D3, you use them primarily to gain access to bound data. So, as far as our code goes, we are going to replace "What goes here?" on this line:

```
.attr("width", // What goes here?)
```

with an anonymous function, such that it will look something like this:

```
.attr("width", function(){})
```

D3 has a couple of conventions when it comes to using anonymous functions to access bound data. The reasons for these conventions are a little complex, but the good news is, you don't need to know them to use D3. You just need to memorize the conventions themselves.

The first is that the function always takes an argument called d:

```
.attr("width", function(d){})
```

and d has a very specific meaning. For each of the elements in our selection, it represents the bound data point. So, for our first rectangle, the value of d is 1.6. For the second, d is 1.5, and so on.

This is great, because we want to set the widths of our rectangles to be equal to the values in popData. For each rectangle we want the width to be d. How do we do that? Just like with any other function—we tell our anonymous function to return a value of d:

```
.attr("width", function(d){ return d; })
```

Perfect. Now on to the attribute y. We also want to use an anonymous function, something like this:

```
.attr("y", function(d){})
```

Hmm...the problem is that the vertical position, y, doesn't have anything to do with the value of the bound data. Remember that when we used a loop to make the rectangles, we set y equal to our iteration variable, i, times a constant, barSpacing. We never once used any of the data contained in popData. So, we don't need to use d.

Fortunately, D3 gives you access not only to the value of each bound data point, but also to the index of each data point within your data array. How do you access those indices? By introducing another argument to your anonymous function—i.

```
.attr("y", function(d,i){})
```

So, for our first rectangle, i is equal to 0, for the second rectangle, it's equal to 1, and so on.

Just as before, we want y to be equal to the index times our constant, barSpacing. Easy:

```
.attr("y", function(d,i){ return i * barSpacing })
```

And here's the chain in its entirety:

```
barGroup.selectAll("rect")
      .data(popData)
  .enter().append("rect")
      .attr("x", 0)
      .attr("height", barHeight)
      .attr("width", function(d) {return d})
      .attr("y", function(d,i) {return i * barSpacing});
```

which we can rearrange so its ordered in a more sensible way:

```
barGroup.selectAll("rect")
        .data(popData)
    .enter().append("rect")
        .attr("x", 0)
        .attr("y", function(d,i) {return i * barSpacing})
        .attr("width", function(d) {return d})
        .attr("height", barHeight);
```

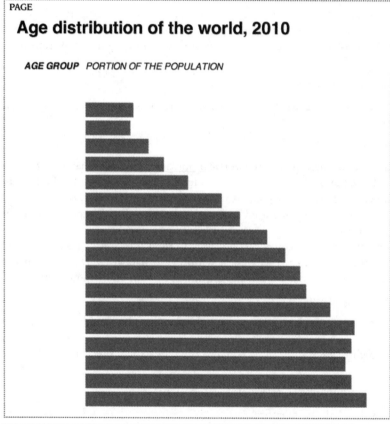

Figure 5.8   Data-driven rectangles

Put that in your code and run it! You should get what you see in Figure 5.8.

A word of congratulations is in order. You have now used all three Ds. You have driven a document with data. Huzzah!

One final note on using anonymous functions in D3 to access bound data. As mentioned, you always need to include d as an argument, no matter what. That's the first convention of using anonymous functions. When we set the value of y above to i * barSpacing, we didn't use d at all. That doesn't matter—we still have to include it as an argument.

The second convention is that you don't need to include i unless you plan on using it. When we set the width attribute above, we didn't need i, and so it appears nowhere in the anonymous function. But if you are going to use i, you have to make sure it is added to your anonymous function as an argument as well as being in the body of your function.

Finishing the Rest of the Chart

As an exercise, you should try finishing the rest of the bar chart on your own using data-joins. I'll include the code here in Listing 5.2 in case you get stuck, but give it a shot on your own:

Listing 5.2 *Building the rest of the chart using a data-join*

```
var barLabelGroup = svg.append("g")
      .attr("transform", translateText)
      .attr("class","bar-label");

barLabelGroup.selectAll("text")
      .data(barLabels)
  .enter().append("text")
      .attr("x",-10)
      .attr("y", function(d,i) {return i * barSpacing + barHeight*(2/3)})
      .text(function(d) {return d});

var axisTickGroup = svg.append("g")
      .attr("transform", translateText)
      .attr("stroke", "black");

axisTickGroup.selectAll("line")
      .data(axisData)
  .enter().append("line")
      .attr("x1", function(d) {return d*scaleFactor})
      .attr("x2", function(d) {return d*scaleFactor})
      .attr("y1", 0)
      .attr("y2", -tickHeight);

var axisLabelGroup = svg.append("g")
      .attr("transform", translateText)
      .attr("class", "axis-label");

axisLabelGroup.selectAll("text")
      .data(axisData)
  .enter().append("text")
```

```
.attr("x", function(d) {return d * scaleFactor})
.attr("y", -tickHeight - tickGap)
.text(function(d) {return d + "%"});
```

Storing Data in Objects

In the tabloid cover example, I mentioned that it helps to structure your data arrays so that each element contains one and only one data point. For our tabloid data for the month of January we have:

```
var janData = [
        {name:"Angelina Jolie", covers:20, rank:1},
        {name:"Brad Pitt", covers:18, rank:2},
        {name:"Jennifer Aniston", covers:10, rank:3},
        {name:"Brittney Spears", covers:8, rank:4}
];
```

Now, let's take a look at our data array for our population bar chart:

```
var popData = [1.6, 1.5, 2.1, 2.6, 3.4, 4.5, 5.1, 6.0, 6.6, 7.1, 7.3, 8.1, 8.9,
8.8, 8.6, 8.8, 9.3];
```

It also has one and only one data point for each entry. But do you notice a difference between the two? In the case of janData, each entry has three pieces of information associated with it: a name, a cover count, and a rank. In popData, on the other hand, each entry only contains a single number. The names of the age groups associated with these values are stored in a separate array:

```
var barLabels = ["80 and up", "75-79", "70-74", "65-69", "60-64", "55-59", "50-
54", "45-49", "40-44", "35-39", "30-34", "25-29", "20-24", "15-19", "10-14",
"5-9", "0-4"];
```

There's something a little dicey about this. We're relying on ourselves to remember that the data starts with the 80 and up age group and gets progressively younger. But what if we were looking at this code months from now and couldn't remember that? Or what if we decided to change the order of the bars and put the 0-4 bar on top? We would either have to flip the arrays around (something we could easily make a mistake doing) or we would have to change the way we set the y attribute of the bars so that the final entry went on top and the first entry went on the bottom. Neither of these methods is ideal.

Instead, we can mimic what we did with janData. We can create an array of objects, where each object has descriptive information about each data point as well as the value:

```
var popData = [
        {age:"80 and up", value:1.6, position:0},
        {age:"75 - 79", value:1.5, position:1},
```

```
    {age:"70 - 74", value:2.1, position:2},
    {age:"65 - 69", value:2.6, position:3},
    {age:"60 - 64", value:3.4, position:4},
    {age:"55 - 59", value:4.5, position:5},
    {age:"50 - 54", value:5.1, position:6},
    {age:"45 - 49", value:6.0, position:7},
    {age:"40 - 44", value:6.6, position:8},
    {age:"35 - 39", value:7.1, position:9},
    {age:"30 - 34", value:7.3, position:10},
    {age:"25 - 29", value:8.1, position:11},
    {age:"20 - 24", value:8.9, position:12},
    {age:"15 - 19", value:8.8, position:13},
    {age:"10 - 14", value:8.6, position:14},
    {age:"5 - 9", value:8.8, position:15},
    {age:"0 - 4", value:9.3, position:16}
]
```

I've included a property called position to indicate where in the chart I want each of the final bars to be displayed (see Figure 5.9).

Here's how it works when we create our rectangles using this new array. We start the same way as we did before:

```
barGroup.selectAll("rect")
        .data(popData)
    .enter().append("rect")
```

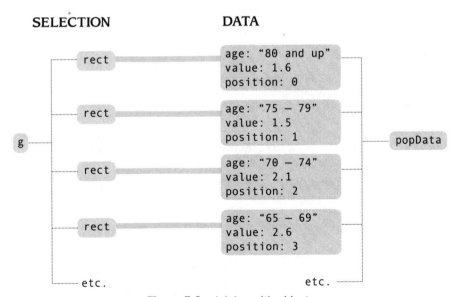

Figure 5.9 Joining with objects

and the x and height attributes still stay the same:

```
barGroup.selectAll("rect")
      .data(popData)
  .enter().append("rect")
      .attr("x", 0)
      .attr("height", barHeight)
```

But when we set the width and y attributes, it works a little differently. Why? Because d is different. Instead of just being equal to a number for each rectangle, d is now equal to an entire object. So, for the first rectangle, d is equal to {age:"80 and up", value:1.6, position:0}, and for the second rectangle, d is equal to {age:"75 - 79", value:1.5, position:1}, and so on.

If you set the width equal to d, D3 doesn't know what to do. But the good news is we can treat d just as we would any other object in JavaScript. If we want to access any of its properties, we just type d followed by a period followed by the property name. So, d.age, or d.value.

That in mind, here's how we can set the width attribute for the rectangles in our bar chart:

```
.attr("width", function(d){ return d.value })
```

And here is how we can set the y attribute:

```
.attr("y", function(d){ return d.position * barSpacing })
```

And here is the whole chain, reordered:

```
barGroup.selectAll("rect")
      .data(popData)
  .enter().append("rect")
      .attr("x", 0)
      .attr("y", function(d){ return d.position * barSpacing })
      .attr("height", barHeight)
      .attr("width", function(d){ return d.value });
```

Now, we can change the order of bars however we like by changing the position property in popData. And we can be sure that the right values will always stay with the right age groups.

Again, I encourage you to try to build the rest of the chart with popData as an array of objects. The entire code is shown in Listing 5.3 in case you get stuck.

Listing 5.3   *Building the chart with our data stored in an array of objects*

```
<!DOCTYPE html>
<html>
<head>
<meta charset="utf-8">
<style>
```

```
        body {
                font-family: Helvetica;
        }
        svg {
                width:500px;
                height:500px;
        }
        .top-label {
                font-size: 13px;
                font-style: italic;
                text-transform: uppercase;
                float: left;
        }
        .age-label {
                text-align: right;
                font-weight: bold;
                width: 90px;
                padding-right: 10px;
        }
        .clearfix {
                clear: both;
        }
        .bar {
                fill: DarkSlateBlue;
        }
        .bar-label {
                text-anchor: end;
        }
        .axis-label {
                text-anchor: middle;
                font-size: 13px;
        }
</style>
</head>
<body>
        <!-- -->
<script src="http://d3js.org/d3.v3.min.js"></script>
<script>
        var popData = [
                {age:"80 and up", value:1.6, position:0},
                {age:"75 - 79", value:1.5, position:1},
                {age:"70 - 74", value:2.1, position:2},
                {age:"65 - 69", value:2.6, position:3},
                {age:"60 - 64", value:3.4, position:4},
                {age:"55 - 59", value:4.5, position:5},
                {age:"50 - 54", value:5.1, position:6},
                {age:"45 - 49", value:6.0, position:7},
```

```
                    {age:"40 - 44", value:6.6, position:8},
                    {age:"35 - 39", value:7.1, position:9},
                    {age:"30 - 34", value:7.3, position:10},
                    {age:"25 - 29", value:8.1, position:11},
                    {age:"20 - 24", value:8.9, position:12},
                    {age:"15 - 19", value:8.8, position:13},
                    {age:"10 - 14", value:8.6, position:14},
                    {age:"5 - 9", value:8.8, position:15},
                    {age:"0 - 4", value:9.3, position:16}
    ];

    var axisData = [0, 2.5, 5.0, 7.5];
    var width = 400,
            leftMargin = 100,
            topMargin = 30,
            barHeight = 20,
            barGap = 5,
            tickGap = 5,
            tickHeight = 10,
            scaleFactor = width / popData[16].value,
            barSpacing = barHeight + barGap,
            translateText = "translate(" + leftMargin + "," + topMargin + ")",
            scaleText = "scale(" + scaleFactor + ",1)";

    var body = d3.select("body");

    body.append("h2")
            .text("Age distribution of the world, 2010");

    body.append("div")
            .attr("class", "top-label age-label")
        .append("p")
            .text("age group");

    body.append("div")
            .attr("class", "top-label")
        .append("p")
            .text("portion of the population");

    body.append("div")
            .attr("class", "clearfix")

    var svg = body.append("svg");

    var barGroup = svg.append("g")
            .attr("transform", translateText + " " + scaleText)
            .attr("class", "bar");

    barGroup.selectAll("rect")
            .data(popData)
        .enter().append("rect")
            .attr("x", 0)
            .attr("y", function(d) {return d.position * barSpacing})
```

```
              .attr("width", function(d) {return d.value})
              .attr("height", barHeight);

        var barLabelGroup = svg.append("g")
              .attr("transform", translateText)
              .attr("class","bar-label");

        barLabelGroup.selectAll("text")
              .data(popData)
          .enter().append("text")
              .attr("x",-10)
              .attr("y", function(d) {return d.position * barSpacing +
barHeight*(2/3)})
              .text(function(d) {return d.age});

        var axisTickGroup = svg.append("g")
              .attr("transform", translateText)
              .attr("stroke", "black");

        axisTickGroup.selectAll("line")
              .data(axisData)
          .enter().append("line")
              .attr("x1", function(d) {return d*scaleFactor})
              .attr("x2", function(d) {return d*scaleFactor})
              .attr("y1", 0)
              .attr("y2", -tickHeight);

        var axisLabelGroup = svg.append("g")
              .attr("transform", translateText)
              .attr("class", "axis-label");

        axisLabelGroup.selectAll("text")
              .data(axisData)
          .enter().append("text")
              .attr("x", function(d) {return d*scaleFactor})
              .attr("y", -tickHeight - tickGap)
              .text(function(d) {return d + "%"});
</script>
</body>
</html>
```

Summary

In this chapter we introduced the concept of using data-joins in D3. A data-join allows you to make elements enter a web page, change, or update, once they are on the page, and exit. And it allows you to do all of those things based on data. This chapter covered in detail how to use a data-join to make elements enter the page. And it also expanded on our population bar chart example, showing how to build the entire thing using data-joins.

6

Sizing Charts and Adding Axes

This chapter covers how to use scales and easily create axes in D3. Scales make it straightforward to translate values in a data set to pixels on a screen. Axis generators make it exceedingly simple to add axes to your charts and customize them. By the end of the chapter, you will have recreated our single-year bar chart example using D3 to its fullest potential.

Linear Scales

In this chapter, instead of starting with general lessons on using D3 and then applying those lessons to our example bar chart, we are going to work on our bar chart from the get-go. Take the most recent version, **pop2010-data-joins.html,** save it as **pop2010-scales.html**, in both your browser and your text editor.

In the chapter on SVG, we covered the transform attribute. Using the transform attribute, you can translate an SVG element from one position to another, you can scale an element in both the horizontal and vertical directions, and you can rotate elements.

In our population bar chart, we are currently using both translate, to create margins for the chart, and scale, to automatically size our bars so they fit in a width we define. Recall also that we created a variable called scaleFactor in which we took the defined width and divided it by the largest value in our data. It's this scaleFactor that we used both to make sure our largest bar fills up the entire width and to place the tick marks of our axis in the right spots.

It all worked just fine, but it's a very laborious way to do things.

D3 makes scaling a lot more convenient by allowing you to set up a function that essentially maps data to pixels. That mapping can be linear—for example, if 0 maps to 0 and 10 maps to 100, then 5 would map to 50—or it can be logarithmic. It can also be ordinal, mapping discrete, non-numeric values to pixels (we'll cover ordinal scales in detail later in this chapter).

You can do most of that with basic JavaScript, just by doing some math, so in a sense, scales aren't totally necessary (we've gotten by so far without them). But scales can make your life a lot easier—for one, they make it insanely easy to create axes. But enough background already, let's get our hands dirty.

Open up the console in **pop2010-data-joins.html**. We aren't going to manipulate anything on the page, we're just going to mess around with D3 in the console, which we can do because **pop-2010-data-joins.html** loads the D3 library.

Let's start by creating a very simple linear scale. Type the following into the console:

```
var scale = d3.scale.linear();
scale.domain([0,10]);
scale.range([0,100]);
```

The variable scale represents a scale function. And specifically, as the code suggests, the scale is linear. Let's play around with it a bit to figure out what it does. Try typing scale(0). You should get 0. Try typing scale(10). You should get 100. What do you think you'll get if you type scale(5)?

Clearly, all our scale function is doing is multiplying our input by 10. Not very interesting. Let's try defining it in a slightly different way:

```
var scale = d3.scale.linear();
scale.domain([0,10]);
scale.range([10,100]);
```

Now, what do you get when you type in scale(0)? You should get 10. And scale(10)? The answer should still be 100. What about scale(5)? This time it's 55, so in this case, scale isn't quite multiplying your input by 10.

Can you guess what it's doing? It is taking the array we've specified inside .domain() and it's **mapping** it to the array we've specified in .range(). And it's doing it in a linear way (see Figure 6.1). In this case, that means multiplying the input by 9 and then adding 10.

Not bad. So how can we use this in our code? We could create a linear scale for our bars: We input a value from our population data, and it spits out the bar width we want. Let's call our scale x, since we'll be using it to size the bars horizontally, or along the x-axis. It will look something like this:

```
var x = d3.scale.linear()
    .domain([])
    .range([]);
```

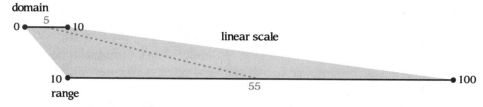

Figure 6.1 How a linear scale works

Note

We can chain the .domain() and .range() methods just as we have been chaining .attr(), .text() and many of the other D3 methods we've been using.

Before we figure out what to put inside those arrays, a brief word on domain versus range. The domain represents the input (your data) and the range represents the output (which is usually how you want to show the data on the page). It's easy to get the two confused, so I like to use a mnemonic device to keep them straight. My psych 101 professor always used to say that, the weirder a mnemonic device is, the easier it is to remember. So here goes:

When you think **range**, you should think **home on the range**, which will make you think **home,** which should make you think **home page**, which you can simplify to just **page**. So, the range is related to the **page**. The range is the output you need to position things correctly on the page. Hope that helps.

Okay, back to our scale. The domain needs to contain our data, and the range needs to contain our charting area. Let's start with the range. The array we use for the range should define our extremes. These should be obvious. For the left extreme, we should have 0 (because our skinniest possible bar has no width), and on the right extreme, we should have the entire width of our charting area (because we still want the largest bar to fill the entire width). Remember, we've already defined the width of our charting area as width:

```
var x = d3.scale.linear()
    .domain([])
    .range([0, width]);
```

Now, what about the domain? For the left extreme we should also have 0, because, if we input a data point of 0, we want it to result in a bar of no width. What about the large extreme? We follow the same logic we did when we set up the scaleFactor variable—we use the largest value in our data set, which we can determine using d3.max().

But instead of just looking at our data and determining the largest value, we can use D3 to do that for us, using the method d3.max():

```
d3.max(popData, function(element) {return element.value})
```

d3.max() works by taking two arguments. The first is an array. The second is an anonymous function you can use to tell d3.max() which values to consider when calculating the maximum. In our case, the array we are interested in is, of course, popData—the array of objects housing our data. But we don't want the maximum value associated with just any property, we only want the maximum value associated with the value property.

That's where the anonymous function comes into play. You'll notice that function takes an argument, element. Inside of the anonymous function, element represents every element of the array that is passed to d3.max(). By telling the anonymous function to return the value element.value, we are telling d3.max() to look at the value property of every element in the array popData.

Let's use d3.max() in our domain().

```
var x = d3.scale.linear()
    .domain([0, d3.max(popData, function(element) {return element.value})])
    .range([0, width]);
```

Enter the above code into your console and play around with x a little bit. x(0) should give you 0, of course, just as x(9.3) should give you 400. Inputting the largest data point gives you the entire width as an output. Perfect.

Let's incorporate this scale function into our code. Go to your editor and slip it into your file near the top, after you've defined both popData and width. Something like this:

```
var width = 400,
    leftMargin = 100,
    topMargin = 30,
    barHeight = 20,
    barGap = 5,
    tickGap = 5,
    tickHeight = 10,
    scaleFactor = width / d3.max(popData, function(element) {return element.
value; }),
    barSpacing = barHeight + barGap,
    translateText = "translate(" + leftMargin + "," + topMargin ")",
    scaleText = "scale(" + scaleFactor + ",1)";

var x = d3.scale.linear()
    .domain([0, d3.max(popData, function(element) {return element.value})])
    .range([0, width]);
```

Now, let's use x to set the widths of our bars. Here's what we have currently:

```
var barGroup = svg.append("g")
    .attr("transform", translateText + " " + scaleText)
    .attr("class", "bar");

barGroup.selectAll("rect")
    .data(popData)
  .enter().append("rect")
    .attr("x", 0)
    .attr("y", function(d) { return d.position * barSpacing})
    .attr("width", function(d) {return d.value})
    .attr("height", barHeight);
```

We are setting the width of the bars equal to the value of the associated data point, but we are doing it by scaling the group the bars are a part of such that the largest one fills the entire width. Now, what we are going to do instead is use x to set the width directly, and get rid of that scale transform:

```
var barGroup = svg.append("g")
    .attr("transform", translateText)
    .attr("class", "bar");
```

```
barGroup.selectAll("rect")
     .data(popData)
  .enter().append("rect")
     .attr("x", 0)
     .attr("y", function(d) { return d.position * barSpacing})
     .attr("width", function(d) {return x(d.value)})
     .attr("height", barHeight);
```

Let's not stop here. We can also use our scale function to set the position of our axis. Again, here's what we have currently:

```
var axisTickGroup = svg.append("g")
     .attr("transform", translateText)
     .attr("stroke", "black");

axisTickGroup.selectAll("line")
     .data(axisData)
  .enter().append("line")
     .attr("x1", function(d) {return d*scaleFactor})
     .attr("x2", function(d) {return d*scaleFactor})
     .attr("y1", 0)
     .attr("y2", -tickHeight);

var axisLabelGroup = svg.append("g")
     .attr("transform", translateText)
     .attr("class", "axis-label");

axisLabelGroup.selectAll("text")
     .data(axisData)
  .enter().append("text")
     .attr("x", function(d) {return d*scaleFactor})
     .attr("y", -tickHeight - tickGap)
     .text(function(d) {return d + "%"});
```

In this case, we can use x in place of that scaleFactor constant:

```
var axisTickGroup = svg.append("g")
     .attr("transform", translateText)
     .attr("stroke", "black");

axisTickGroup.selectAll("line")
     .data(axisData)
  .enter().append("line")
     .attr("x1", function(d) {return x(d)})
     .attr("x2", function(d) {return x(d)})
     .attr("y1", 0)
     .attr("y2", -tickHeight);

var axisLabelGroup = svg.append("g")
     .attr("transform", translateText)
     .attr("class", "axis-label");
```

```
axisLabelGroup.selectAll("text")
    .data(axisData)
  .enter().append("text")
    .attr("x", function(d) {return x(d)})
    .attr("y", -tickHeight - tickGap)
    .text(function(d,i) {return d + "%"});
```

Guess what? Now our code no longer requires two of our constants—scaleText and scaleFactor. Let's go ahead and get rid of those ugly things:

```
var width = 400,
    leftMargin = 100,
    topMargin = 30,
    barHeight = 20,
    barGap = 5,
    barSpacing = barHeight + barGap,
    tickHeight = 10,
    tickGap = 5,
    translateText = "translate(" + leftMargin + "," + topMargin ")";

var x = d3.scale.linear()
    .domain([0,d3.max(popData, function(d) {return d.value})])
    .range([0, width])
```

We're well on our way. The next step is to use D3 to automatically set up an axis for our bars, something that will make our code MUCH simpler. But first, a quick word on how to be smart about setting up your chart margins.

Using Smart Margin Conventions

The way our chart is currently set up, we have what you could call a chart area—where the bars are—and we have a margin on the left where our bar labels are and a margin on the top where our axis is. And we've grouped almost everything in our chart. Our bars are nested inside of an SVG group, as are our axis ticks, our axis labels, and our bar labels.

To each of these groups, we've applied the same transform attribute, described by the constant translateText:

```
translateText = "translate(" + leftMargin + "," + topMargin + ")"
```

What that attribute effectively does is shift the position of each group such that (0,0) is 100 pixels to the right (the size of leftMargin) and 30 pixels down (the size of topMargin). So every group is using the upper left-hand corner of the chart area as its point of origin.

It makes sense to structure things this way, but there's a more elegant way to go about doing it. This comes straight from Mike Bostock, so you know it's good (and you also see it over and over again in his D3 blocks).

First, Bostock uses a JavaScript object to define the margins. For example:

```
var margin = {top: 30, right: 0, bottom: 0, left: 100};
```

So, instead of having separate variables for the top margin and the left margin (or either of the two other margins), we have one object with four properties. Our left margin is now `margin.left` and our top margin is now `margin.top`.

The next thing Bostock does is define `width` and `height` in terms of these margins. In our case:

```
var width = 500 - margin.left - margin.right,
    height = 450 - margin.top - margin.bottom;
```

You're probably wondering where 500 and 450 came from. Those values will be the total width and height of our <svg> element, respectively. So, instead of setting the width of the chart area to 400, as we did before, we're going to set the entire width of the <svg> to 500. And ultimately, instead of setting the height of the bars to 20, we are going to choose a total height, and the bars will fill up the space automatically. Sweet, no?

The reason we do this is because <svg> elements, just like <div>s, will take up all the space they can get on your page. So it's good to keep them contained by defining their proportions.

Now, the next thing Bostock does is when he creates his <svg> element, he immediately appends a group, and he transforms that group such that the point of origin is shifted to the right by an amount equal to `margin.left` and shifted down by an amount equal to `margin.top`. Basically, this is a group within the <svg> that represents the chart area. Everything that follows is appended to that group (and as a result, doesn't need to have its own `transform` attribute):

```
var svg = body.append("svg")
    .attr("width", width + margin.left + margin.right)
    .attr("height", height + margin.top + margin.bottom)
  .append("g")
    .attr("transform", "translate(" + margin.left + "," + margin.top + ")");
```

Notice two things. First, the `width` attribute on the <svg> element is equal to `width + margin.left + margin.right`. In other words, 500. Likewise, the height is 230. Just as planned. The idea is that we can use `width` to refer to the width of the chart area, and `height` to refer to the height.

The second thing is that we've actually defined the variable svg so it refers to a group, not to an <svg> element. This is just for simplicity's sake. We are going to think of our chart area kind of like our core SVG space, even though the actual <svg> element is larger. This might be a little confusing, so take a look at the diagram in Figure 6.2.

Now, let's add this to our code. We can put the `margin` definition up at the top:

```
var margin = {top: 30, right: 0, bottom: 0, left: 100},
    width = 500 - margin.left - margin.right,
    height = 230 - margin.top - margin.bottom;
```

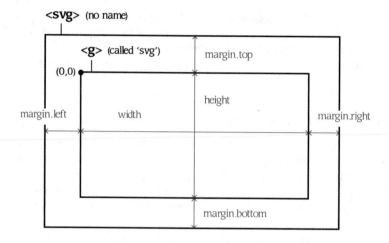

Figure 6.2   Bostock's margin convention

And we can put our svg definition in like so:

```
var svg = chartDiv.append("svg")
    .attr("width", width + margin.left + margin.right)
    .attr("height", height + margin.top + margin.bottom)
  .append("g")
    .attr("transform", "translate(" + margin.left + "," + margintop + ")");
```

Now, we can get rid of all of those `transform` attributes on all of the SVG groups in our code. Here:

```
var barGroup = svg.append("g")
    .attr("class", "bar");
```

And here:

```
var barLabelGroup = svg.append("g")
    .attr("class", "bar-label");
```

Here:

```
var axisTickGroup = svg.append("g")
    .attr("stroke", "black");
```

And here:

```
var axisLabelGroup = svg.append("g")
    .attr("class", "axis-label");
```

And finally, we can get rid of `topMargin`, `leftMargin`, and the dreadful `translateText` altogether:

```
var margin = {top: 30, right: 0, bottom: 0, left: 100};
```

```
        width = 500 - margin.left - margin.right,
        height = 230 - margin.top - margin.bottom;

var barHeight = 45,
    barGap = 5,
    tickHeight = 10,
    tickGap = 5,
    barSpacing = barHeight + barGap;
```

Looking good.

Adding Axes

Scales are cool, but using them to add axes is even cooler. And it's dead simple. Let's start by getting rid of the horizontal axis entirely. All of this code…

```
var axisTickGroup = svg.append("g")
    .attr("stroke", "black");

axisTickGroup.selectAll("line")
    .data(axisData)
  .enter().append("line")
    .attr("x1", function(d) {return x(d)})
    .attr("x2", function(d) {return x(d)})
    .attr("y1", 0)
    .attr("y2", -tickHeight);

var axisLabelGroup = svg.append("g")
    .attr("class", "axis-label");

axisLabelGroup.selectAll("text")
    .data(axisData)
  .enter().append("text")
    .attr("x", function(d) {return x(d)})
    .attr("y", -tickHeight - tickGap)
    .text(function(d) {return d + "%"});
```

…scrap it. We're going to build an axis the D3 way (see Figure 6.3).

The first thing we have to do is create what is called an **axis generator**. Sounds intense, but this is all it is:

```
var xAxis = d3.svg.axis()
    .scale(x)
```

As we did with our scale, we are defining a function, which we initialize with d3.svg.axis() but can then customize. This is the kind of situation in which it often makes sense to consult the D3 API Reference. There's a whole section on creating axes that explains in detail how to customize axis generators (see Figure 6.4).

Age distribution of the world, 2010

AGE GROUP *PORTION OF THE POPULATION*

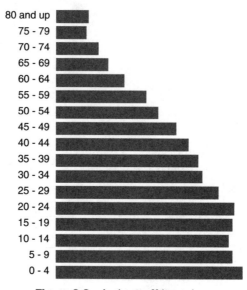

Figure 6.3 A chart off its axis

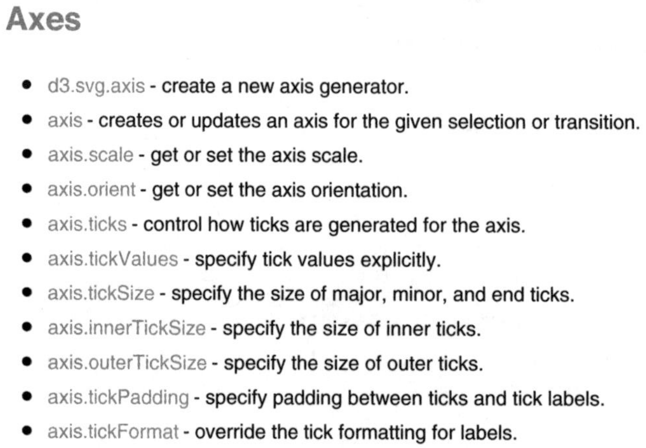

Axes

- d3.svg.axis - create a new axis generator.
- axis - creates or updates an axis for the given selection or transition.
- axis.scale - get or set the axis scale.
- axis.orient - get or set the axis orientation.
- axis.ticks - control how ticks are generated for the axis.
- axis.tickValues - specify tick values explicitly.
- axis.tickSize - specify the size of major, minor, and end ticks.
- axis.innerTickSize - specify the size of inner ticks.
- axis.outerTickSize - specify the size of outer ticks.
- axis.tickPadding - specify padding between ticks and tick labels.
- axis.tickFormat - override the tick formatting for labels.

Figure 6.4 Trust in the API Reference

Here, we've set scale to x. It should be clear what that means. We want the scale of our axis to be x, which, of course, is the linear scale we defined in the first section of this chapter.

Age distribution of the world, 2010

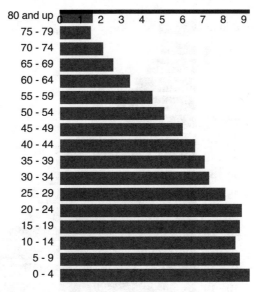

AGE GROUP *PORTION OF THE POPULATION*

Figure 6.5   Defaulting

Adding a new axis to our page is equally simple. All we have to do is append a new group to svg and use a method called call():

```
svg.append("g")
    .call(xAxis)
```

Run that code and you'll get what is shown in Figure 6.5.

It doesn't look very good, but one thing is encouraging—the numbers along the axis do appear to be in the right place.

We can whip this into shape by doing two things: customizing our axis generator and styling our axis group. Let's start with styling the axis group. To do that, we need to add a class:

```
svg.append("g")
    .call(xAxis)
    .attr("class", "axis")
```

As far as styling goes, the first thing we need to attend to is that thick black line. We want tick marks instead. What is that line, anyway? I happen to know from experience that hidden within that thick black line are a few different SVG elements. There is an SVG path that spans the entire width of the chart, and there are a bunch of SVG lines—tick marks. (You could, of course, figure that out by using the Web Inspector.)

Age distribution of the world, 2010

AGE GROUP PORTION OF THE POPULATION

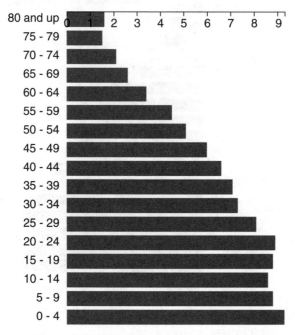

Figure 6.6   The path and lines revealed

Right now, that path has a fill applied to it (by default) and no stroke, and the lines have no stroke. All we can see is the fill on that path. If you put the following CSS into the style tag at the very top of your code, then you'll be able to see both the path and the lines as shown in Figure 6.6.

```
.axis line,
.axis path {
  fill: none;
  stroke: #000;
}
```

Bonus Question: What would happen if you applied these styles to everything with the class "axis"?

As it turns out, we are only interested in the lines, not the path. We just want the tick marks. So let's modify that CSS to look like this:

Age distribution of the world, 2010

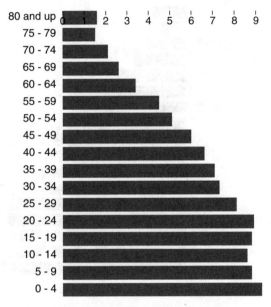

Figure 6.7 Full of ticks, and only ticks

```
.axis line {
    fill: none;
    stroke: #000;
}
.axis path {
    display: none;
}
```

yielding what is shown in Figure 6.7.

And one last thing. We need to set the size of our axis labels to 13px. We can do that like so:

```
.axis text {
    font-size: 13px;
}
```

The result is shown in Figure 6.8.

Excellent. We're getting closer. The rest of the changes we need to make require us to modify the axis generator itself. First, we can shift those numbers and tick marks to the top of the bars by changing the axis **orientation**. By default that orientation is "bottom," but we can change it to "top" (see Figure 6.9):

Age distribution of the world, 2010

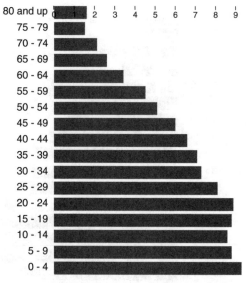

Figure 6.8   Size matters

Age distribution of the world, 2010

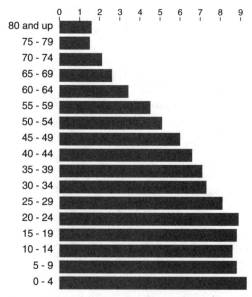

Figure 6.9   Now it's better oriented

```
var xAxis = d3.svg.axis()
    .scale(x)
    .orient("top")
```

We have two things left to do if we want to make the chart look exactly how it did before. We need to decrease the number of tick marks and add percent signs to the end of the tick labels. It turns out we can do that with the same method—.ticks(). Let's start with the number of tick marks.

```
var xAxis = d3.svg.axis()
    .scale(x)
    .orient("top")
    .ticks(5)
```

Figure 6.10 shows the result.

That modifier—axis.ticks()—lets us set the number of tick marks we want. (More or less). If D3 decides the value we put in will result in a scale that doesn't have round numbers, it will override us. Try using 4 instead of 5, for example. With ticks(), we can't get the axis increments we had earlier—0, 2.5, 5, and 7.5. (No matter, let's just roll with D3's recommended number of ticks.) But you can also pass in a second argument to set the format:

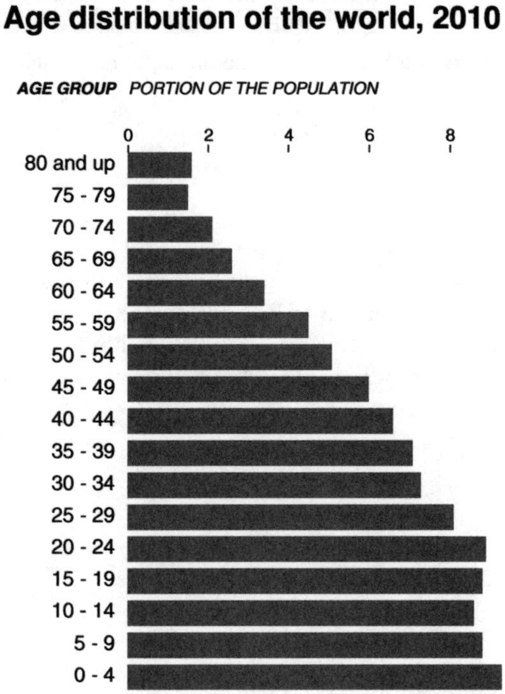

Age distribution of the world, 2010

AGE GROUP *PORTION OF THE POPULATION*

Figure 6.10 Keeping the ticks under control

Age distribution of the world, 2010

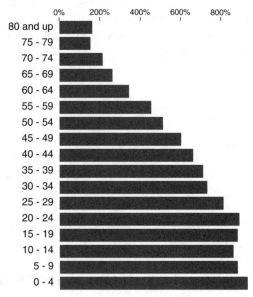

Figure 6.11   Those are some high percentages

```
var xAxis = d3.svg.axis()
    .scale(x)
    .orient("top")
    .ticks(5, "%")
```

Figure 6.11 shows the addition of percentages.

Now we have percent signs, but our values have gone through the roof! Can you guess why? When you format an axis to be a percentage, D3 assumes you are expressing your input values such that 1.0 represents 100%. Behind the scenes, D3 multiplies by 100 before appending that percent sign. To fix the axis, we actually need to move the decimal places in our data:

```
var popData = [
    {age:"80 and up", value:0.016, position:0},
    {age:"75 - 79", value:0.015, position:1},
    {age:"70 - 74", value:0.021, position:2},
    {age:"65 - 69", value:0.026, position:3},
    {age:"60 - 64", value:0.034, position:4},
    {age:"55 - 59", value:0.045, position:5},
    {age:"50 - 54", value:0.051, position:6},
    {age:"45 - 49", value:0.060, position:7},
    {age:"40 - 44", value:0.066, position:8},
```

```
    {age:"35 - 39", value:0.071, position:9},
    {age:"30 - 34", value:0.073, position:10},
    {age:"25 - 29", value:0.081, position:11},
    {age:"20 - 24", value:0.089, position:12},
    {age:"15 - 19", value:0.088, position:13},
    {age:"10 - 14", value:0.086, position:14},
    {age:"5 - 9", value:0.088, position:15},
    {age:"0 - 4", value:0.093, position:16}
];
```

Once we do that we get the chart shown in Figure 6.12.

Voilà! Note that, even though we divided all of the values in our data set by 100, it didn't change anything about the appearance of the chart except the labels on the tick marks. That's a good sign our code is getting pretty robust.

Now that the chart looks like it should, we can prune the code. We no longer have anything on the page with the class axis-label, so we can cut that from our CSS:

```
.axis-label {
    text-anchor: middle;
    font-size: 13px;
}
```

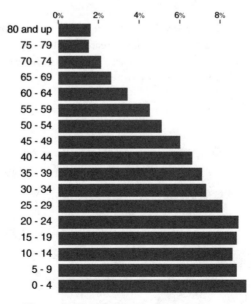

Age distribution of the world, 2010

Figure 6.12 We've seen this before

We also don't need that weird `axisData` array anymore, so we can get rid of that, too:

```
var  axisData = [0, 2.5, 5, 7.5];
```

Ahhh...doesn't that feel better?

Ordinal Scales and Axes

It might not be obvious, but our chart actually has two axes, not just one. We have the x-axis, of course, which is quantitative. Our bars jut out along that axis. But we also have a y-axis, which is qualitative. Along the x-axis, position corresponds to a percentage value. But along the y-axis, position corresponds to an age group (the top of the chart starts with "80 and up" and all the way at the bottom is "0–4").

D3 is also good at creating scales and axes that are qualitative in nature. Such scales, called **nominal** or **ordinal** scales, are good at mapping a set of discrete, often non-numeric inputs to a set of outputs you can easily use to position stuff on the page.

Let's start by getting rid of our axis labels entirely. All this code...

```
var barLabelGroup = svg.append("g")
    .attr("class", "bar-label");

barLabelGroup.selectAll("text")
    .data(popData)
  .enter().append("text")
    .attr("x", -10)
    .attr("y", function(d) {return d.position*barSpacing + barHeight*(2/3)})
    .text(function(d) {return d.age});
```

...scrap it. What is shown in Figure 6.13 is, of course, what you should see.

Now, just as we did with the x-axis, let's create a scale for our y-axis. Since this is an ordinal scale, we won't use `d3.scale.linear()`. Instead, we'll use `d3.scale.ordinal()`. So, we want something like this:

```
var y = d3.scale.ordinal()
    .domain([])
    .range([]);
```

What are our inputs and outputs in this case? Since the y-axis represents age group, we want our inputs to be our age groups. We want an array like this to pass to our domain:

```
["80 and up", "75 - 79", "70 - 74", "65 - 69", "60 - 64", "55 - 59", "50 - 54",
"45 - 49", "40 - 44", "35 - 39", "30 - 34", "25 - 29", "20 - 24", "15 - 19", "10 -
14", "5 - 9", "0 - 4"]
```

But each of those age groups is trapped away inside an object that's part of the popData array. How can we liberate them? Fortunately, JavaScript has a method called map() that acts on arrays and lets you reorganize them or even extract subsets of them with relative ease. Try typing this into your console:

```
popData.map(function(element) {return element.age})
```

Age distribution of the world, 2010

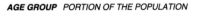

AGE GROUP *PORTION OF THE POPULATION*

Figure 6.13 What does it mean?

In a very general sense, map() works similarly to d3.max(). When you use d3.max(), it goes through every element of your array, extracts the relevant data (based on an anonymous function you define), and then computes the maximum among the values in that relevant pool of data. With map(), the method, similarly, goes through each element of the array and extracting the relevant data (again, which you define using an anonymous function), but instead of computing the maximum, it just throws that data into a new array.

Here's what our scale looks like now:

```
var y = d3.scale.ordinal()
    .domain(popData.map(function(element) {return element.age}))
    .range([]);
```

Note that we don't need brackets, because our map() method returns an array.

Now for the range. There's a question we need to ask ourselves at this point: What do we actually want to use this scale for? To create an axis, sure, but with our x scale we did more than just that—we used it to set the widths of our bars. We used it to turn data into pixels. How can we make our y scale work for us in the same way?

Of course! By using it to set the vertical position of each of our bars! In more technical terms, we pass an age group to the scale function, and it spits out a numerical value we can use to set the y attribute of each of our SVG rectangles.

```
"80 and up" ⟶ 0

  "75 - 79" ⟶ 25    (barSpacing)

  "70 - 74" ⟶ 50    (2*barSpacing)

  "65 - 69" ⟶ 100   (3*barSpacing)
        · · ·
```

Figure 6.14 Nominal and ordinal scales map discrete, sometimes non-numerical values to discrete, numerical values

In our range, we can actually define 17 separate outputs, one for each of our inputs. Remember that our top bar will have a vertical position of 0, the second bar will have a vertical position of 25 (because that's what we've set our bar spacing equal to), and so on. Using that logic, we can set up our scale function like this:

```
var y = d3.scale.ordinal()
    .domain(popData.map(function(element) {return element.age}))
    .range([0, 25, 50, 75, 100, 125, 150, 175, 200, 225, 250, 275, 300, 325, 350,
375, 400]);
```

Better yet, since we've already separately defined barSpacing as a constant, we can use it:

```
var y = d3.scale.ordinal()
    .domain(popData.map(function(element) {return element.age}))
    .range([0, barSpacing, 2*barSpacing, 3*barSpacing, 4*barSpacing,
5*barSpacing, 6*barSpacing, 7*barSpacing, 8*barSpacing, 9*barSpacing,
10*barSpacing, 11*barSpacing, 12*barSpacing, 13*barSpacing, 14*barSpacing,
15*barSpacing, 16*barSpacing]);
```

Now our scale maps each age group to a value, as shown in Figure 6.14.
And we can use the scale to set the y attribute of each of our bars:

```
svg.selectAll("rect")
    .data(popData)
  .enter().append("rect")
    .attr("class","bar")
    .attr("x", 0)
    .attr("y", function(d) { return y(d.age)})
    .attr("width", function(d) {return x(d.value)})
    .attr("height", barHeight);
```

Excellent. And yet, there's something not quite right about this approach. Imagine we had 25 bars instead of 17. It would be a real pain to hard code an array of 25 separate entries to set the range of our scale. True, it's possible to use a loop to make that array, but as with most things in D3, there's a better way.

Instead of specifying a range when we set up our scale, we can tell D3 to create what are called **range bands**. Range bands take an interval for the output (defined by two values) and divide it by the number of inputs to create a series of bands. For example, if we define the scale function like this:

```
var y = d3.scale.ordinal()
    .domain(popData.map(function(element) {return element.age}))
    .rangeBands([0, height]);
```

then the function takes the array [0, height], which represents an interval span-
ning from 0 to 420, and creates 17 equal-sized bands (since we have 17 age groups) as
shown in Figure 6.15.

If we pass each age group to the scale function, we conveniently get the start of the
band as an output. For example, y("80 and up") evaluates to 0, y("75 - 79") evaluates to 24.7, and so on. The result is basically the same as what we had above, but now,
the scale will work equally well if we have 17 bars, 35 bars, or even 8 bars (though
we'd probably want to change the height of the scale). Go ahead and try running your
updated code.

The chart looks indistinguishable from the way it did before, but it's not quite the
same, is it? We have all these weird nonround numbers for our y attributes. Why?
Because we're dividing 420 by 17, and it doesn't divide evenly. But don't worry, you'll
see in a second that we can get back to those nice round numbers really easily.

Another nice thing about using range bands is you can ask the scale for the size of
each band. For example,

```
y.rangeBand();
```

will, in this case, return a value of 24.7. If we want our bars to fill up each band in its
entirety, we can use this to set their height:

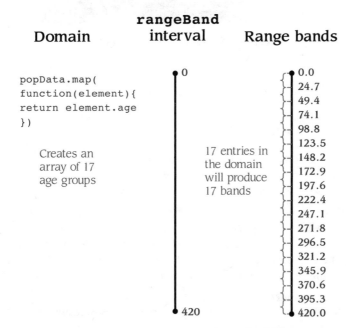

Figure 6.15 Breaking up the bands

Age distribution of the world, 2010

AGE GROUP *PORTION OF THE POPULATION*

Figure 6.16   Home on the `rangeBand`

```
svg.selectAll("rect")
    .data(popData)
  .enter().append("rect")
    .attr("class","bar")
    .attr("x", 0)
    .attr("y", function(d) { return y(d.age)})
    .attr("width", function(d) { return x(d.value); })
    .attr("height", y.rangeBand());
```

Figure 6.16 shows what we get.

But this isn't what we want. All of our bars are 50 pixels in height and butting right up against each other. Fortunately, we can fix that easily, right in our scale definition. Within the `scale.rangeBands()` modifier, it's possible to set what is called **padding**—the amount of space in between the bands:

```
var y = d3.scale.ordinal()
    .domain(popData.map(function(element) {return element.age}))
    .rangeBands([0, height], 0.2);
```

Age distribution of the world, 2010

AGE GROUP *PORTION OF THE POPULATION*

Figure 6.17   Nice pad

The padding yields the result shown in Figure 6.17.

Looks a lot better, but what actually happened here? Figure 6.18 presents a sketch of how padding works, showing a magnified view of the top four bars of our chart.

Play around with the padding and see how it affects the positions of the bars and spacing in between them. You'll notice there's always padding above the top bar and below the bottom bar. By default this so-called outer padding is equal to the padding in between each range band. In some cases this might be desirable, but not in ours. We can get rid of the outer padding by passing a third argument to our `scale.rangeBands()` modifier to tell it how much outer padding we want. In our case, 0:

```
var y = d3.scale.ordinal()
    .domain(popData.map(function(element) {return element.age}))
    .rangeBands([0, height], 0.2, 0);
```

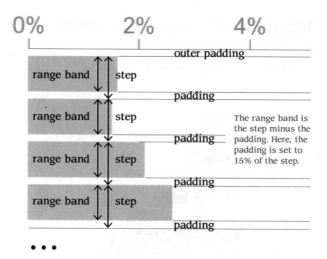

Figure 6.18   Underneath the padding

Great. The only thing we have left at this point is adding the axis. Fortunately, doing this is a lot easier than setting up the scale. It works exactly like it did for the x-axis. First, we have to set up an axis generator. Add the following code to your file, right below where you defined the x-axis generator:

```
var yAxis = d3.svg.axis()
    .scale(y)
    .orient("left");
```

Notice that we are orienting the axis to the left, because we want the labels to be to the left of the bars. Now, again, to draw the axis, you just need to add an SVG group and use .call(). Add this to your code right below where you draw the x-axis:

```
svg.append("g")
    .call(yAxis)
    .attr("class","axis")
```

Figure 6.19 shows what you get.

Now we just have some formatting to do. Since we want our x-axis and y-axis to be formatted a little differently, it makes sense to give them their own classes, in addition to the shared class, axis:

```
svg.append("g")
    .call(xAxis)
    .attr("class","x axis")

svg.append("g")
    .call(yAxis)
    .attr("class","y axis")
```

Age distribution of the world, 2010

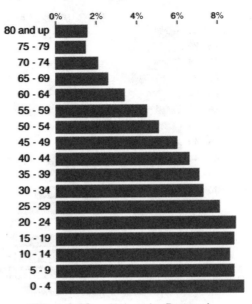

Figure 6.19   Holy axis, Batman!

If we adjust the style rules like so, it'll get rid of the tick marks on the y-axis, format the text how we want it, and keep the path from showing up on either axis:

```
.x.axis line {
  fill: none;
  stroke: #000;
}
.x.axis text {
    font-size: 13px;
}
.axis path {
    display:none;
}
.y.axis line {
    display:none;
}
```

The final result is shown in Figure 6.20.

Now for my favorite part—pruning. We don't have anything with the class bar-label anymore, so we can purge this CSS:

```
.bar-label {
    text-anchor: end;
}
```

Age distribution of the world, 2010

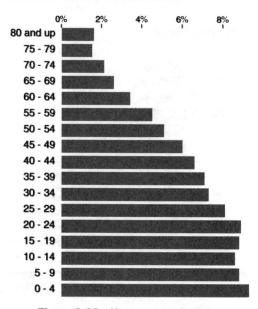

Figure 6.20 Home sweet home

And we also no longer need any of the bar positioning or spacing constants we had defined initially, so we can get rid of this stuff:

```
var barHeight = 45,
    barGap = 5,
    tickGap = 5,
    tickHeight = 10,
    barSpacing = barHeight + barGap;
```

Finally, since we don't need the position property of our data points anymore (because our y scale does all of the vertical positioning for us), we can trash that, too. Change popData to this:

```
var popData = [
    {age:"80 and up", value:0.016},
    {age:"75 - 79", value:0.015},
    {age:"70 - 74", value:0.021},
    {age:"65 - 69", value:0.026},
    {age:"60 - 64", value:0.034},
    {age:"55 - 59", value:0.045},
    {age:"50 - 54", value:0.051},
    {age:"45 - 49", value:0.060},
```

```
    {age:"40 - 44", value:0.066},
    {age:"35 - 39", value:0.071},
    {age:"30 - 34", value:0.073},
    {age:"25 - 29", value:0.081},
    {age:"20 - 24", value:0.089},
    {age:"15 - 19", value:0.088},
    {age:"10 - 14", value:0.086},
    {age:"5 - 9", value:0.088},
    {age:"0 - 4", value:0.093}
];
```

Excellent. Let's take a look at our code in its entirety (Listing 6.1).

Listing 6.1 *The monospace fruits of our labor*

```
<!DOCTYPE html>
<html>
<head>
<meta charset="utf-8">
<style>
    body {
        font-family: Helvetica;
    }
    svg {
        width:500px;
        height:500px;
    }
    .top-label {
        font-size: 13px;
        font-style: italic;
        text-transform: uppercase;
        float: left;
    }
    .age-label {
        text-align: right;
        font-weight: bold;
        width: 90px;
        padding-right: 10px;
    }
    .clearfix {
        clear: both;
    }
    .bar {
        fill: DarkSlateBlue;
    }
    .bar-label {
        text-anchor: end;
    }
    .axis-label {
```

```
        text-anchor: middle;
        font-size: 13px;
    }
    .x.axis line {
      fill: none;
      stroke: #000;
    }
    .x.axis text {
        font-size: 13px;
    }
    .axis path {
        display:none;
    }
    .y.axis line {
        display:none;
    }
</style>
</head>
<body>
    <!-- -->
<script src="http://d3js.org/d3.v3.min.js"></script>
<script>
    var popData = [
        {age:"80 and up", value:0.016},
        {age:"75 - 79", value:0.015},
        {age:"70 - 74", value:0.021},
        {age:"65 - 69", value:0.026},
        {age:"60 - 64", value:0.034},
        {age:"55 - 59", value:0.045},
        {age:"50 - 54", value:0.051},
        {age:"45 - 49", value:0.060},
        {age:"40 - 44", value:0.066},
        {age:"35 - 39", value:0.071},
        {age:"30 - 34", value:0.073},
        {age:"25 - 29", value:0.081},
        {age:"20 - 24", value:0.089},
        {age:"15 - 19", value:0.088},
        {age:"10 - 14", value:0.086},
        {age:"5 - 9", value:0.088},
        {age:"0 - 4", value:0.093}
    ];
    var margin = {top: 30, right: 0, bottom: 0, left: 100},
        width = 500 - margin.left - margin.left,
        height = 450 - margin.top - margin.bottom;

    var x = d3.scale.linear()
        .domain([0, d3.max(popData, function(element) { return element.value;
}}]))
```

```
        .range([0, width]);

var y = d3.scale.ordinal()
        .domain(popData.map(function(element) {return element.age}))
        .rangeBands([0, height], 0.2, 0);

var xAxis = d3.svg.axis()
        .scale(x)
        .orient("top")
        .ticks(5, "%");

var yAxis = d3.svg.axis()
        .scale(y)
        .orient("left");

var body = d3.select("body");

body.append("h2")
        .text("Age distribution of the world, 2010");

body.append("div")
        .attr("class", "top-label age-label")
    .append("p")
        .text("age group");

body.append("div")
        .attr("class", "top-label")
    .append("p")
        .text("portion of the population");

body.append("div")
        .attr("class", "clearfix")

var svg = body.append("svg")
        .attr("width", width + margin.left + margin.right)
        .attr("height", height + margin.top + margin.bottom)
    .append("g")
        .attr("transform", "translate(" + margin.left + "," + margin.top + ")");

var barGroup = svg.append("g")
        .attr("class", "bar");

barGroup.selectAll("rect")
        .data(popData)
    .enter().append("rect")
        .attr("x", 0)
        .attr("y", function(d) {return y(d.age)})
        .attr("width", function(d) {return x(d.value)})
        .attr("height", y.rangeBand());

svg.append("g")
        .call(xAxis)
        .attr("class", "x axis")
```

```
    svg.append("g")
        .call(yAxis)
        .attr("class","y axis")
</script>
</body>
</html>
```

Isn't it elegant? We are finally using D3 to its fullest potential to make this simple bar chart.

Take a moment to compare this code to all of the iterations that came before it. I want you to notice one thing in particular—the evolution of the inputs. We started off doing everything manually in SVG, without even using any math! And now our script has but a few inputs: our data, the size of our SVG element and the margins that define the chart area, how we want our axes to be oriented and how many tick marks our x-axis should have, and how much spacing we want in between our bars.

All of these inputs give us direct control over fairly high-level aspects of the way the chart is designed. And they are all incredibly easy to change. Isn't D3 lovely?

Summary

In this chapter, we covered two major topics: what scales are and how to use them and how to easily create axes. More specifically, we learned about creating and modifying linear scales, setting up an SVG drawing space using a sensible convention for defining margins, adding and formatting axes, and using ordinal scales to handle discrete and non-numerical data.

7

Loading and Filtering External Data

In this chapter, we'll cover how to load data from external data files. A lot of the data you'll find on the web comes in one of a number of standard formats, and it's often way more convenient to use those files directly than it is to hard code the data into your script. By the end of this chapter, you will have made an age distribution bar chart where you can change the year on display simply by changing the value of a single variable in your code.

Building a Graphic that Uses All of the Population Distribution Data

Let's start this chapter with a goal.

Throughout this entire book, we've been working toward an interactive bar chart in D3 that displays the age distribution of the world's population, starting in 1950 and projected through 2050. Right now, we have a static bar chart—made entirely in D3—that displays that distribution for just the year 2010.

As a next step, let's build a graphic that isn't quite interactive, but for which we can show the population distribution for any year in our data set by simply changing a variable in our code. In other words, we're going to have a variable called year in our script:

```
var year = 2010;
```

which we can change (like moving a lever in a factory) to set the year on display.

To make this work, our script is going to need access to our entire data set, not just the data for 2010. When we were working with a single year, it was easy enough to manually type the data out into an array of objects, one for each age group:

```
var popData = [
    {age:"80 and up", value:0.016},
    {age:"75 - 79", value:0.015},
    {age:"70 - 74", value:0.021},
```

```
        {age:"65 - 69", value:0.026},
        {age:"60 - 64", value:0.034},
        {age:"55 - 59", value:0.045},
        {age:"50 - 54", value:0.051},
        {age:"45 - 49", value:0.060},
        {age:"40 - 44", value:0.066},
        {age:"35 - 39", value:0.071},
        {age:"30 - 34", value:0.073},
        {age:"25 - 29", value:0.081},
        {age:"20 - 24", value:0.089},
        {age:"15 - 19", value:0.088},
        {age:"10 - 14", value:0.086},
        {age:"5 - 9", value:0.088},
        {age:"0 - 4", value:0.093}
];
```

But it would be super tedious to do that for all 21 years.

Fortunately, D3 gives us a way to import data from an external data file and automatically turn that data into an array of objects like the one above.

Data Formats You Can Use with D3

As we discussed in Chapter 3, data can be found in a lot of formats on the web. There are the Microsoft-Excel-based spreadsheet formats, like `.xls` and `.xlsx`, the plain text table formats like CSV and TSV, and even JavaScript formats like JSON.

D3 can handle pretty much all of these except the richly formatted spreadsheet files, `.xls` and `.xlsx`. Here's a list of all the external data formats that D3 supports:

Format	Description
.txt	plain text file
.csv	comma-separated values
.tsv	tab-separated values
.json	JSON blob
.html	HTML document
.xml	XML document

For this example, let's start by creating a really simple CSV file. CSVs are ubiquitous, and you can easily create them using freely available tools. We'll use D3 to upload the data in the CSV file we create and then check it out in the console.

Let's start with just a subset of our data—the data from 2010—so we can see how the whole thing works.

In this book's supporting files, you'll find a file called **popData2010.csv** you can use. Alternatively, you can create the file yourself in a text editor or in a Google spreadsheet (see Figure 7.1). If you go the Google spreadsheet route, you can download the file as a CSV by going to File > Download as > Comma-separated values.

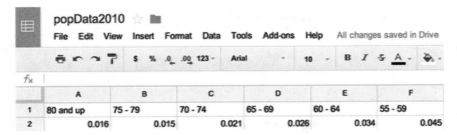

Figure 7.1 popData2010

Note that the first row—the column names—contains the age groups and the second row has the values.

Creating a Server to Upload Your Data

There is a little bit of setup required to use D3 to pull in external data. A lot of browsers will prevent you from accessing files stored locally on your computer when you do the kinds of data requests that D3 does. So you have to set up your own little mini-server. Don't worry, this is dead simple.

You'll need to have Python installed on your computer. It comes preinstalled on Mac OSX, Ubuntu, Fedora, and a few other Linux operating systems. But if you are on a Windows machine, you'll need to download it, which you can do at https://www.python.org/download/.

Initiating a Server on the Command Line

The first thing you need to do is make a directory for this project on your computer. That's just a fancy way of saying create a folder on your desktop called **population**.

Now, open up your terminal emulator (called Terminal on a Mac or a Linux machine, and the DOS window or command line prompt on Windows), and navigate to the folder you just created. You can do that by typing this in the command line:

```
cd ~Desktop/population
```

Now you can set up a server that points to that directory. Type the following into the command line:

```
python -m SimpleHTTPServer 8888 &
```

If you open up your browser and type "localhost:8888" into the address bar, your browser will navigate to your local server—it will show you what's in that **population** folder (see Figure 7.2).

Of course, right now, it's a whole lot of nothing.

Creating an Index File

Loading an HTML file from a local server you've set up is a little different from just opening an HTML file with your browser. I'm assuming you've done some web

Figure 7.2 An empty directory

development before, so you know that when you create a web page, if you want that web page to actually show up when somebody browses to the directory it's in, it has to be called **index.html**. The same is true when you are loading files with your own mini-server.

Let's create a really basic index.html file using the starter snippet we used in Chapter 4:

```
<!DOCTYPE html>
<meta charset="utf-8">
<style></style>
<body>
<script src="http://d3js.org/d3.v3.min.js"></script>
<script>
</script>
</body>
```

Save it in your population folder and then refresh your browser.

Even though you still see a blank page, there's a way to make sure everything is working. How? By trying to use D3 in the console. If you type this into the console:

```
d3.select("body")
```

and you get what is shown in Figure 7.3, you know you're in business.

D3's Functions for Loading Data

Let's upload our simple CSV file. First, we need to put it in our directory so our browser can find it. Add the **popData2010.csv** file to your population folder.

D3 has a small suite of functions for loading data, each of which essentially handles a different data format:

Function	Format
d3.text()	Plain text
d3.csv()	CSV
d3.tsv()	TSV
d3.json()	JSON
d3.html()	HTML
d3.xml()	XML

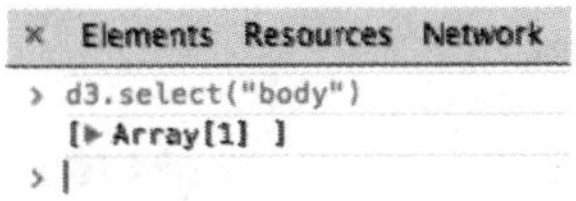

Figure 7.3 Selecting an empty body

Callback Functions

Of course, we're going to use **d3.csv()**. The first argument we pass into **d3.csv()** is the name of our file:

```
d3.csv("popData2010.csv");
```

And the second argument is something known as a callback function. Here's what it looks like:

```
d3.csv("popData2010.csv", function(error, data){});
```

I won't go into too much detail here, but suffice it to say, the callback function helps with problems that arise when you are trying to retrieve data. When you use one of D3's functions for pulling in data, in technical terms, that function is making what is called a *request* for an external resource. In this case, the resource is our CSV file.

The callback function takes two arguments: one associated with success and one associated with failure. In our case, if the callback function succeeds in requesting **popData2010.csv**, then the contents of the file will be stored for use in the success variable, **data**. If the request fails, then the details of the failure will be passed to the **error** variable.

How D3 Interprets CSV Tables

Let's make a request for the data in our CSV file and take a look at the results in the console. Add the following to your **index.html** file, inside the script tag:

```
d3.csv("popData2010.csv", function(error, data){
     console.log(data)
});
```

You should see an array appear in your console. When you expand it, it should look like Figure 7.4.

The console isn't perfectly intuitive, so let's translate what we see into JavaScript. The console is telling us that **data** is an array containing a single object:

```
data = [{}];
```

and that the object has 17 properties, each with a different value:

```
data = [{0 - 4: "0.092849052",
    5 - 9: "0.08782007",
    10 - 14: "0.085697001",
    15 - 19: "0.087628671",
    20 - 24: "0.089268026",
```

```
▼ [Object]
  ▼ 0: Object
      0 - 4: "0.092849052"
      5 - 9: "0.08782007"
     10 - 14: "0.085697001"
     15 - 19: "0.087628671"
     20 - 24: "0.089268026"
     25 - 29: "0.080896946"
     30 - 34: "0.072752538"
     35 - 39: "0.070678427"
     40 - 44: "0.066409696"
     45 - 49: "0.059586949"
     50 - 54: "0.050980812"
     55 - 59: "0.044843055"
     60 - 64: "0.033883539"
     65 - 69: "0.025557823"
     70 - 74: "0.020799846"
     75 - 79: "0.014681544"
     80 and up: "0.015666006"
   ▶ __proto__: Object
   length: 1
 ▶ __proto__: Array[0]

 >
```

Figure 7.4   D3's interpretation of popData2010.csv

```
      25 - 29: "0.080896946",
      30 - 34: "0.072752538",
      35 - 39: "0.070678427",
      40 - 44: "0.066409696",
      45 - 49: "0.059586949",
      50 - 54: "0.050980812",
      55 - 59: "0.044843055",
      60 - 64: "0.033883539",
      65 - 69: "0.025557823",
      70 - 74: "0.020799846",
      75 - 79: "0.014681544",
      80 and up: "0.015666006"
}];
```

Interesting. All of the data is there, but it's not in a very useful structure. Why not?
Think about what would happen if we tried to create a bar chart by joining `data` with
a bunch of rectangles. `data` is an array with only one entry. Remember that when
you carry out a data-join using `data().enter()`, D3 only creates one object for every
entry in your array. So in this case, if you did `data(data).enter().append("rect")`
only one rectangle would be created.

That's no good. We want 17 rectangles, so we need 17 separate entries in our array, one for each age group. What we really want is for popData2010 to look like our old variable, popData:

```
var data = [
    {age:"80 and up", value:0.016},
    {age:"75 - 79", value:0.015},
    {age:"70 - 74", value:0.021},
    {age:"65 - 69", value:0.026},
    {age:"60 - 64", value:0.034},
    {age:"55 - 59", value:0.045},
    {age:"50 - 54", value:0.051},
    {age:"45 - 49", value:0.060},
    {age:"40 - 44", value:0.066},
    {age:"35 - 39", value:0.071},
    {age:"30 - 34", value:0.073},
    {age:"25 - 29", value:0.081},
    {age:"20 - 24", value:0.089},
    {age:"15 - 19", value:0.088},
    {age:"10 - 14", value:0.086},
    {age:"5 - 9", value:0.088},
    {age:"0 - 4", value:0.093}
];
```

Let's take a look at **popData2010.csv** again to see exactly how D3 is interpreting it, and figure out how we need to change it (see Figure 7.5).

Can you see what's happening here? Each entry in that top row—the header row—is becoming a property name, and each entry in the second row is becoming the associated property value (see Figure 7.6).

What do you think we need to do to **popData2010.csv** to get the data variable in the form we want it in? I'll include the answer in Figure 7.7, but I encourage you to try it on your own.

If you save **popData2010.csv** so it looks like Figure 7.7 and then refresh your browser, you should get what is shown in Figure 7.8.

Perfect.

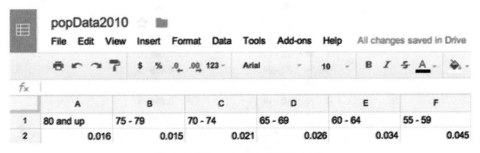

Figure 7.5   popData2010 again

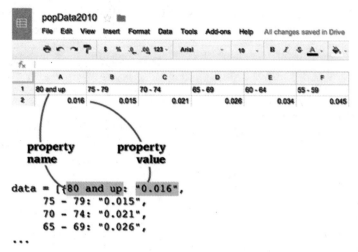

Figure 7.6 How CSV data gets turned into a JavaScript array of objects

	A	B
1	age	value
2	80 and up	0.016
3	75 - 79	0.015
4	70 - 74	0.021
5	65 - 69	0.026
6	60 - 64	0.034
7	55 - 59	0.045
8	50 - 54	0.051
9	45 - 49	0.06
10	40 - 44	0.066
11	35 - 39	0.071
12	30 - 34	0.073
13	25 - 29	0.081
14	20 - 24	0.089
15	15 - 19	0.088
16	10 - 14	0.086
17	5 - 9	0.088
18	0 - 4	0.09

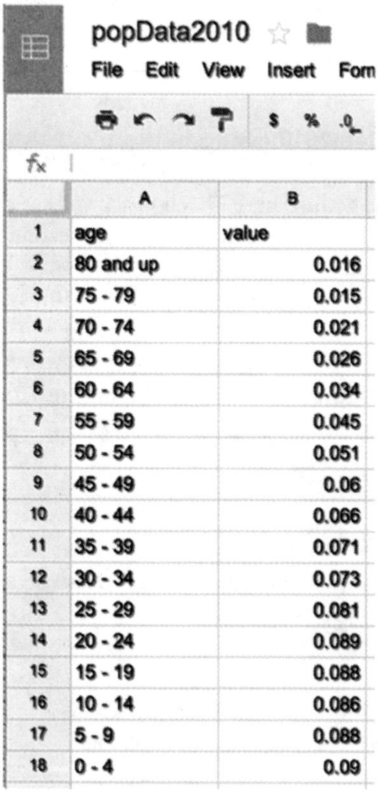

Figure 7.7 Good form

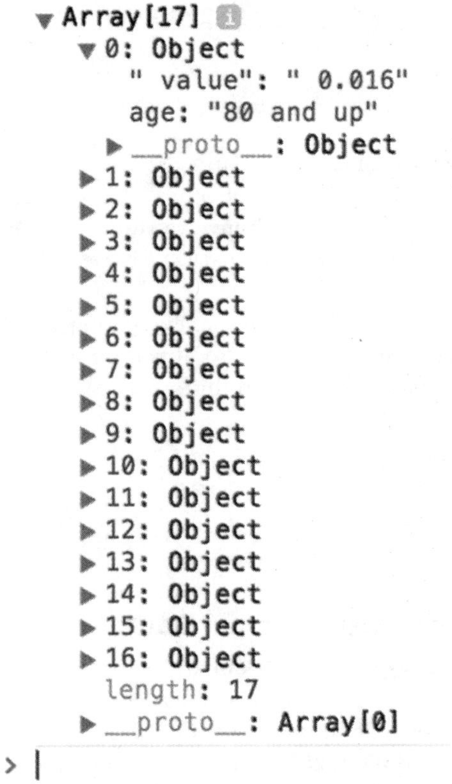

```
▼ Array[17] ℹ
  ▼ 0: Object
      " value": " 0.016"
      age: "80 and up"
    ▶ __proto__: Object
  ▶ 1: Object
  ▶ 2: Object
  ▶ 3: Object
  ▶ 4: Object
  ▶ 5: Object
  ▶ 6: Object
  ▶ 7: Object
  ▶ 8: Object
  ▶ 9: Object
  ▶ 10: Object
  ▶ 11: Object
  ▶ 12: Object
  ▶ 13: Object
  ▶ 14: Object
  ▶ 15: Object
  ▶ 16: Object
    length: 17
  ▶ __proto__: Array[0]
> |
```

Figure 7.8   The old, familiar array

Dealing with Asynchronous Requests

Try the following code in your **index.html** file:

```
var popData;

d3.csv("popData2010.csv", function(error, data){
    popData = data;
});

console.log(popData);
```

The result is probably not quite what you'd expect (see Figure 7.9).

It seems like **popData** should be the old, familiar array we saw above, when **console.log(data)** was part of the callback function. But there's a very good reason why it isn't.

When you use **d3.csv()**, your script doesn't wait for the callback function to finish before it starts running the rest of the code. In technical terms, D3 makes external requests *asynchronously*.

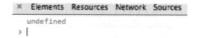

Figure 7.9   Hmm

Here's why: Say you have an especially large data set—one that takes multiple seconds to load. You don't really want all of your code to be held up by that load time. Ideally, everything that doesn't involve your data will run while your data is being pulled in so that all of the non-data-driven stuff on your page can initialize.

Practically speaking, what this means is that everything you do with external data has to happen inside the callback function. So, if you wanted to change the code above so it actually works, you would need to do this:

```
var popData;
d3.csv("popData2010.csv", function(error, data){
    popData = data;
    console.log(popData);
});
```

Creating a Bar Chart with External Data

Now, let's go back to the **pop2010-scales.html** file from Chapter 6. Recall that we used that code to create a bar chart for the population distribution in 2010. We're going to cut and paste that code into our index.html file and do it again, except this time, we're going to use **popData2010.csv** as our data source.

Go ahead and paste all of the **pop2010-scales.html** code into your **index.html** file and put the external data call at the bottom of the script:

```
    svg.append("g")
        .call(xAxis)
        .attr("class", "x axis")
    svg.append("g")
        .call(yAxis)
        .attr("class","y axis")
    d3.csv("popData2010.csv", function(error, data){
    });
</script>
```

Since we're going to be using our CSV file as our data source, we no longer need to define **popData** in the script. So, let's delete this bit of code:

```
var popData = [
    {age:"80 and up", value:0.016},
    {age:"75 - 79", value:0.015},
    {age:"70 - 74", value:0.021},
    {age:"65 - 69", value:0.026},
    {age:"60 - 64", value:0.034},
```

```
    {age:"55 - 59", value:0.045},
    {age:"50 - 54", value:0.051},
    {age:"45 - 49", value:0.060},
    {age:"40 - 44", value:0.066},
    {age:"35 - 39", value:0.071},
    {age:"30 - 34", value:0.073},
    {age:"25 - 29", value:0.081},
    {age:"20 - 24", value:0.089},
    {age:"15 - 19", value:0.088},
    {age:"10 - 14", value:0.086},
    {age:"5 - 9", value:0.088},
    {age:"0 - 4", value:0.093}
];
```

Now, as a first cut, we can put our entire script inside of the callback function. That way, we know our data will always be available:

```
<script>
    d3.csv("popData2010.csv", function(error, data){
        var popData = data;
        var body = d3.select("body");
        var margin = {top: 30, right: 0, bottom: 0, left: 100},
            width = 500 - margin.left - margin.right,
            height = 230 - margin.top - margin.bottom;

    // ... rest of code goes here

        svg.selectAll("rect")
            .data(popData)
          .enter().append("rect")
            .attr("class","bar")
            .attr("x", 0)
            .attr("y", function(d) { return y(d.age)})
            .attr("width", function(d) { return x(d.value); })
            .attr("height", y.rangeBand());
    });
</script>
```

That should produce our bar chart without any problems.

But, obviously, it's not ideal. We're not taking advantage of the asynchronous nature of requests by just throwing everything inside the callback function. So let's pull out the bits that don't require any data.

Listing 7.1 *An asynchronous script*
_____

```
<script>
    var margin = {top: 30, right: 0, bottom: 0, left: 100},
        width = 500 - margin.left - margin.left,
        height = 450 - margin.top - margin.bottom;

    var body = d3.select("body");
```

(Continues)

```
        body.append("h2")
            .text("Age distribution of the world, 2010");
        body.append("div")
            .attr("class", "top-label age-label")
          .append("p")
            .text("age group");
        body.append("div")
            .attr("class", "top-label")
          .append("p")
            .text("portion of the population");
        body.append("div")
            .attr("class", "clearfix")
        d3.csv("popData2010.csv", function(error, data){
            var popData = data;

            var x = d3.scale.linear()
                    .domain([0, d3.max(popData, function(element) { return
element.value; })])
                    .range([0, width]);

            var y = d3.scale.ordinal()
                    .domain(popData.map(function(element) {return
element.age}))
                    .rangeBands([0, height], 0.2, 0);

            var xAxis = d3.svg.axis()
                    .scale(x)
                    .orient("top")
                    .ticks(5, "%");

            var yAxis = d3.svg.axis()
                    .scale(y)
                    .orient("left");

            var svg = body.append("svg")
                    .attr("width", width + margin.left + margin.right)
                    .attr("height", height + margin.top + margin.bottom)
                  .append("g")
                    .attr("transform", "translate(" + margin.left + ","
+ margin.top + ")");

            var barGroup = svg.append("g")
                    .attr("class", "bar");

            barGroup.selectAll("rect")
                    .data(popData)
                  .enter().append("rect")
                    .attr("x", 0)
                    .attr("y", function(d) {return y(d.age)})
                    .attr("width", function(d) {return x(d.value)})
                    .attr("height", y.rangeBand());
```

(Continues)

```
    svg.append("g")
        .call(xAxis)
        .attr("class", "x axis")

    svg.append("g")
        .call(yAxis)
        .attr("class","y axis")

    });
</script>
```

Excellent. But we can go further. For both of our scales—x and y—only the domain depends on data. The range does not. Turns out, it's actually possible to define a scale in a couple of steps, like so:

```
var x = d3.scale.linear()
    .domain([0,d3.max(popData, function(element) {return
element.value})]);

x.range([0, width]);
```

It's also possible to set the range before you set the domain:

```
var x = d3.scale.linear()
    .range([0, width]);

x.domain([0,d3.max(popData, function(element) {return element.value})]);
```

So, we can set the ranges for each of our scales outside of the callback function, and set the domains inside.

But wait, there's more! We can also set up our axis generators outside of the callback function. They don't depend directly on our data, but rather, on our scales. Does it matter that the domains of our scales aren't set until we're inside of our callback function? Nah. By the time we actually use the call() method to create our axes, those domains will have been defined.

Here's what the code should look like, with only the truly necessary stuff inside the callback function:

Listing 7.2 *Doing asynchronous right*

```
<script>
    var margin = {top: 30, right: 0, bottom: 0, left: 100},
        width = 500 - margin.left - margin.left,
        height = 450 - margin.top - margin.bottom;

    var body = d3.select("body");

    var x = d3.scale.linear()
        .range([0, width]);

    var y = d3.scale.ordinal()
        .rangeBands([0, height], 0.2, 0);

    var xAxis = d3.svg.axis()
        .scale(x)
```

(Continues)

```
            .orient("top")
            .ticks(5, "%");
    var yAxis = d3.svg.axis()
            .scale(y)
            .orient("left");
    body.append("h2")
            .text("Age distribution of the world, 2010");
    body.append("div")
            .attr("class", "top-label age-label")
        .append("p")
            .text("age group");
    body.append("div")
            .attr("class", "top-label")
        .append("p")
            .text("portion of the population");
    body.append("div")
            .attr("class", "clearfix")
    d3.csv("popData2010.csv", function(error, data){
            var popData = data;
            x.domain([0, d3.max(popData, function(element) { return
element.value; })]);
            y.domain(popData.map(function(element) {return element.age}));
            var svg = body.append("svg")
                    .attr("width", width + margin.left + margin.right)
                    .attr("height", height + margin.top + margin.bottom)
                .append("g")
                    .attr("transform", "translate(" + margin.left + "," +
margin.top + ")");
            var barGroup = svg.append("g")
                    .attr("class", "bar");
            barGroup.selectAll("rect")
                    .data(popData)
                .enter().append("rect")
                    .attr("x", 0)
                    .attr("y", function(d) {return y(d.age)})
                    .attr("width", function(d) {return x(d.value)})
                    .attr("height", y.rangeBand());
            svg.append("g")
                    .call(xAxis)
                    .attr("class", "x axis")
            svg.append("g")
                    .call(yAxis)
                    .attr("class","y axis")
        });
    </script>
```

	A	B	C
1	year	age	value
2	1950	80 and up	0.006
3	1955	80 and up	0.006
4	1960	80 and up	0.006
5	1965	80 and up	0.006
6	1970	80 and up	0.007
7	1975	80 and up	0.008
8	1980	80 and up	0.009
9	1985	80 and up	0.010
10	1990	80 and up	0.011
11	1995	80 and up	0.012
12	2000	80 and up	0.012
13	2005	80 and up	0.014
14	2010	80 and up	0.016
15	2015	80 and up	0.017
16	2020	80 and up	0.019

Figure 7.10   allData.csv

Loading and Filtering a Large(r) Data Set

Now for the fun stuff. We're going to pull in all of our population data and then selectively choose specific years.

It'll be easier to follow if we go back to using a stripped down index file. Take everything you currently have in **index.html** and save it in a separate file, called **index2.html**. We're just going to put it aside for a moment while we play with our full data set.

The first thing we need is a CSV file for all of our data. There are instructions for how to make one from scratch in Appendix B, but I've already done it for you. It's the file called **allData.csv** in the supplementary materials. Make sure to put that file in your **population** folder.

Figure 7.10 presents a screenshot of what it looks like. Notice that now we have a third column—**year**—that lets us know which year each of those data points belongs to.

```
▼ [Object, Object, Object, Object, Object, Object, Object, Object, Object, Object, Object,
   Object, Object, Object, Object, Object, Object, Object, Object, Object, Object, Object,
   Object, Object, Object, Object, Object, Object, Object, Object, Object, Object, Object,
   Object, Object, Object, Object, Object, Object, Object, Object, Object, Object, Object,
   Object, Object, Object, Object, Object, Object, Object, Object, Object, Object, Object,
   Object, Object, Object, Object, Object, Object, Object, Object, Object, Object, Object,
   Object, Object, Object, Object, Object, Object, Object, Object, Object, Object, Object,
   Object, Object, Object, Object, Object, Object, Object, Object, Object, Object, Object,
   Object…]
   ▶ [0 … 99]
   ▶ [100 … 199]
   ▶ [200 … 299]
   ▶ [300 … 356]
     length: 357
   ▶ __proto__: Array[0]
```

Figure 7.11 A sea of objects

Now put this basic snippet into your **index.html** file and refresh your browser:

```
<!DOCTYPE html>
<meta charset="utf-8">
<style></style>
<body>

<script src="http://d3js.org/d3.v3.min.js"></script>

<script>
    d3.csv("allData.csv", function(error, data){
      console.log(data)
    });
</script>

</body>
```

Let's check out the console (see Figure 7.11). We have an array with a bunch of objects—should be 357 in all, since our data covers 21 different years and 17 age groups for each year.

So far, so good. Now we need to learn how we can winnow that large array down to only the objects for a specified year. Let's start with the obvious. We need to set the year we're interested in:

```
var year = 2010;

d3.csv("allData.csv", function(error, data){
    // do something here to filter data based on year
});
```

As it turns out, JavaScript arrays have a method, filter(), we can use here. It works in a similar way to d3.max() or map(), in that you pass in an anonymous function to tell the method which parts of your array elements to focus on. So, if we want to use filter() to pull out a specific year, here's what it would look like:

```
var year = 2010;

d3.csv("allData.csv", function(error, data){
    var popData = data.filter(function(element) {return element.year == year});
    console.log(popData);
});
```

```
▼ [Object, Object, Object, Object, Object, Object, Object, Object, Object, Object, Object,
   Object, Object, Object, Object, Object, Object]
  ▼ 0: Object
      age: "80 and up"
      value: "0.0156660059"
      year: "2010"
    ▶ __proto__: Object
  ▼ 1: Object
      age: "75 - 79"
      value: "0.0146815437"
      year: "2010"
    ▶ __proto__: Object
  ▶ 2: Object
```

Figure 7.12   What a year, 2010

And that's all there is to it. We tell `filter()` to only return objects where the "year" property is equal to our variable **year**, and it does just that (see Figure 7.12).

Putting It All Together

We're finally ready to create an HTML file that will let us easily create an age distribution bar chart for whatever year we want. We just need to combine our **index. html** and **index2.html** files. Let's modify our **index2.html** file and then cut and paste the entire thing into **index.html**.

First, we need to add the **year** variable. We can slip it in right above where we define our margins:

```
var year = 2010;

var margin = {top: 30, right: 0, bottom: 0, left: 100};
        width = 500 - margin.left - margin.right,
        height = 450 - margin.top - margin.bottom;
```

Then, we need to change the filename we pass to d3.csv() from **popData2010. csv** to **allData.csv**:

```
d3.csv("allData.csv", function(error, data){
    var popData = data;
    x.domain([0,d3.max(popData, function(d) {return d.value})]);
    y.domain(popData.map(function(element) {return element.age}));
    // ... rest of code here
});
```

And finally, instead of simply setting `popData` equal to `data`, we want to use that nifty filtering trick from the last section:

```
d3.csv("allData.csv", function(error, data){
    var popData = data.filter(function(element) {return element.year == year});
    x.domain([0,d3.max(popData, function(d) {return d.value})]);
    y.domain(popData.map(function(element) {return element.age}));
    // ... rest of code here
});
```

Age distribution of the world, 1950

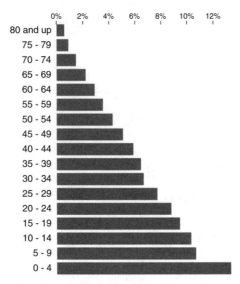

Figure 7.13   The age distribution of yore

If you copy and paste the code from **index2.html** to **index.html** and then reload your local server, you should see that old familiar bar chart.

Now, let's look at some other years. You can pull up the age distribution for any year in our data set simply by changing the value of the **year** variable. To make things a little more sophisticated, we can also use the **year** variable to set the title at the top of the page:

```
body.append("h2")
    .text("Age distribution of the world, " + year);
```

Let's try the extremes. Figure 7.13 shows 1950.

And Figure 7.14 shows the projection for 2050.

Those two charts look vastly different—the world certainly is getting older. But they are also a little hard to compare because the scales aren't the same. The scale on the chart for 1950 extends past 12%, while the scale on the chart for 2050 only extends a little beyond 6%.

This makes sense given how we define the domain for our **x** scale:

```
var popData = data.filter(function(element) {return element.year == year});

x.domain([0,d3.max(popData, function(d) {return d.value})]);
```

To set the upper end of the domain, we use the maximum value in the **popData** array, the array that we've filtered to only include the year of interest. That maximum, of course, changes depending on the year we choose.

Age distribution of the world, 2050

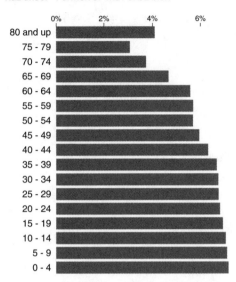

Figure 7.14 The age distribution of the future

But what if we want to keep the scale the same for all of the charts, so they're easier to compare? All we have to do is set the upper limit of our **x** scale to the largest value in our entire data set. That way, we can be certain the bars for every single year will fit comfortably. Doing this is easy. We just have to change our scale definition to use the maximum value in **data** instead of just in **popData**. Here's what the code looks like:

```
var popData = data.filter(function(element) {return element.year == year});

x.domain([0,d3.max(data, function(element) {return element.value})]);
```

Summary

In this chapter, we covered how to request and use external data in D3. We started with how to set up a local server to access data in a tabular format like CSV. Then we discussed how D3 interprets that data, and what it means that D3 processes requests asynchronously. Finally, we covered some basic data filtering.

8

Making Charts Interactive and Animated

In this chapter, we will cover the update and exit phases of the data-join. I'll explain them first on a conceptual level, using the fanciful example of Frank's tabloid cover data. Then, we'll learn how to apply these concepts to make the age distribution bar chart interactive.

Data-Joins: Update and Exit

In Chapter 5, we covered the **enter** phase of the data-join. In this chapter, we're going to cover both **update** and **exit** phases.

Let's go back to that tabloid cover data set you got from that quirky buddy of yours, Frank. Now might be a good time to take a look back at Chapter 5 and review the first three months of Frank's data and what we've done with it so far. Here, we're going to pick up where we left off.

So far, we've made the data from January **enter** the page and we've turned it into a bunch of text elements. We didn't actually walk through how to set the text or the position of those elements in Chapter 5, but you should have an idea of how to do that now based on what we've done with our age distribution bar chart. As we walk through **update** and **exit** we're going to leave that part out again just to simplify things.

Figure 8.1 presents a diagram of where we left off.

There are text elements on the page, one for each of the data points in janData. Now say we want to update the page so that it shows the data for February. Just as with **enter**, we select the text elements on the page and then use data() to perform a data-join. The difference is, this time there are already text elements on the page. So, instead of creating all new elements, we are going to bind some of our data to elements that are already there (see Figure 8.2).

This is **update**. We are updating the elements on the page with new data. Now we can tell the text at the top to read "Jennifer Aniston" instead of "Angelina Jolie"

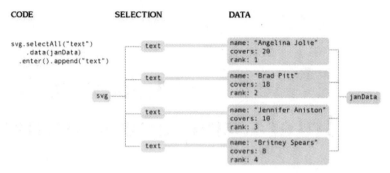

Figure 8.1 Making text enter the page

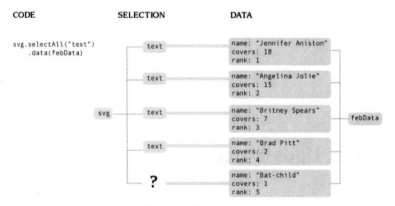

Figure 8.2 Update

because we've bound new data to that element. (We'll cover how to do this later in this chapter.)

Note that there is no update() method. With the enter() method, you create a special selection of placeholder objects, one for each point in your data set that is not already bound. But to update the elements already on the page, you don't need to do that. You can just create a selection of those elements. And then you can tell them what to do based on their newly bound data.

There's a glaring question mark in the diagram in Figure 8.2 you are probably wondering about. The reason it's there is that we have five data points for February, whereas we only had four for January. So what do we do with that fifth data point, which doesn't have an element to bind to?

If you guessed that we make it enter the page, bravo! You are dead on. We can use enter() just as before (see Figure 8.3). But instead of creating five entirely new placeholder elements, the method will just create one for the data point that has no element to bind to. D3 is very good at responding to your needs.

Now, again, just as we did before, we can append a text element. Now our data and our page mirror each other once again (see Figure 8.4).

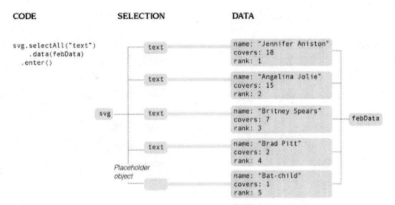

Figure 8.3 Update plus enter

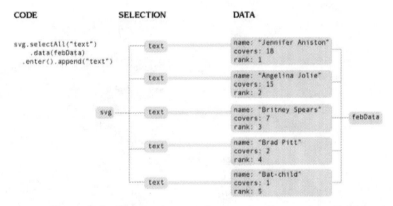

Figure 8.4 Data and page mirror each other once again

Great, let's move on to March. Again, what we want to do is select all of the text elements on the page and then join the March data to them (see Figure 8.5).

But hmm…this time, since there are only four data points for March, we actually have fewer data points than we do elements. The elements that actually have an incoming data point to bind to can simply be updated. But what about the element that doesn't? This is where **exit** comes in. We need to get rid of that fifth text element (time for that actor to leave the stage!), and the exit() method can help. Generally speaking, after we've carried out a data-join, we can use exit() to select any element that no longer has a data point bound to it. And then we can use another method— remove()—to get rid of it (see Figure 8.6).

And that's it. We've covered all phases of the data-join—**enter**, **update**, and **exit**. The foundation of data-joins is simple: Graphics are always appearing on the page, changing, or leaving the page, just as actors in a play are always entering the stage, acting, or exiting. The way D3 handles these three phases of existence is by joining

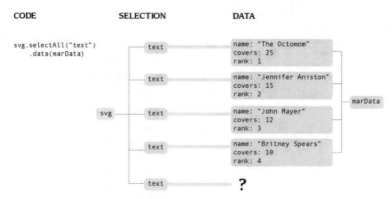

Figure 8.5   Update again

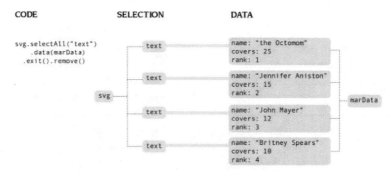

Figure 8.6   Exit

data points up with elements, then comparing their numbers.[1] There are only three possible outcomes:

1. There are more data points than there are elements. This triggers the enter phase (and possibly the update phase).

2. There are the same number of elements and data points. This triggers the update phase.

3. There are more elements than data points. This triggers the exit phase (and possibly the update phase).

But here's where data joins depart from the theater analogy: In a play, the actors have to enter, act, and exit, but when you use D3, you don't always have to use all three phases of the data join. Sometimes, you'll use D3 to make static graphics, and all you'll need is enter(). In other cases, every time you update, the number of data

---

1. Only generally speaking. It's possible to use something called keys in D3 to link specific data points to specific objects, in which case data joins don't just involve comparing the numbers of data points and elements. We'll cover keys at the end of this chapter.

points will be the same, so you'll never need to use exit() (in fact, this is the case with our age distribution bar chart).

Of course, every time a data join is computed, data is bound to elements. And D3 gives us easy access to bound data, which is especially useful for updating, as we'll see below.

Interactive Buttons

In this chapter, we're going to make our bar chart interactive and animated, relying heavily on the update phase of the data-join to make it all work. We won't need to use exit() because for every year in our data set, there is the same number of data points.

At the end of the last chapter, we got our age distribution bar chart to the point where we could choose a year to display. All we had to do was specify that year in our code. That's a neat trick, but only the person writing the code can use it. The code itself is flexible, but there's no way for the user to interact with it. Now we're going to set things up so anybody can select the year directly from the browser and change the data that's displayed.

First, we'll need something the user can click on to select the year she wants to see. We need some buttons. Figure 8.7 is a screenshot of what we might want the page to look like after we put some buttons on it.

Making Buttons Using a Data Join

We could write those buttons in HTML, hard coding a <div> for each one. But why do that, when we can use a data-join to make the buttons enter the page?

To use a data-join, we, of course, need some data. In this case, it makes sense for our data to be an array of every year for which we want a button. Let's make one for every year in our data set. So, our array should look like this:

```
var buttonYears = [1950, 1955, 1960, 1965, 1970, 1975, 1980, 1985, 1990, 1995,
2000, 2005, 2010, 2015, 2020, 2025, 2030, 2035, 2040, 2045, 2050];
```

You can put that array right into your script at the very top. Now, according to good HTML practice, we want to put all of these buttons inside of a large container <div>, so we should create that first. Let's put it right after the title of the page (from which we can delete the year) and give it a class "buttons-container."

```
body.append("h2")
    .text("Age distribution of the world");

body.append("div")
    .attr("class", "buttons-container")
```

Now we can add those buttons. Currently, there is nothing inside of the container <div> we just made. But we want to fill it with <div>s, one for each button, using a data join. The first thing to do is select all of the <div>s inside of our container <div>. (Of course, there aren't any, but that's how enter() works.)

Age distribution of the world, 2010

1950 1955 1960 1965 1970 1975 1980 1985 1990 1995 2000
2005 **2010** 2015 2020 2025 2030 2035 2040 2045 2050

AGE GROUP   *PORTION OF THE POPULATION*

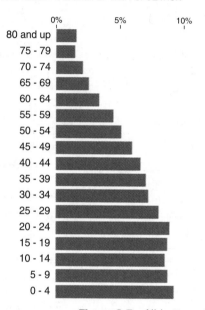

Figure 8.7   All buttoned up

```
body.append("div")
    .attr("class", "buttons-container")
    .selectAll("div")
```

Now we can compute a data-join using data():

```
body.append("div")
    .attr("class", "buttons-container")
    .selectAll("div").data(buttonYears)
```

And then use enter().append("div") to add those <div>s:

```
body.append("div")
    .attr("class","years-div")
    .selectAll("div").data(buttonYears)
  .enter().append("div")
```

Run that code. You won't see a difference on the page, but if you open up the Web Inspector and expand the container <div>, you should see 21 new <div>s inside (see Figure 8.8).

```
▼<div class="buttons-container">
    <div></div>
    <div></div>
    <div></div>
    <div></div>
    <div></div>
    <div></div>
    <div></div>
    <div></div>
    <div></div>
    <div></div>
    <div></div>
    <div></div>
    <div></div>
    <div></div>
    <div></div>
    <div></div>
    <div></div>
    <div></div>
    <div></div>
    <div></div>
</div>
```

Figure 8.8 All divvied up

Now we need to add some text. For each of our button <div>s we want the text to be the year itself. That's easy enough, because each <div> is bound to the year it represents:

```
body.append("div")
    .attr("class", "buttons-container")
    .selectAll("div").data(buttonYears)
  .enter().append("div")
    .text(function(d) { return d; });
```

Now let's take a look at what we have (see Figure 8.9).

Ah, we need to float those button <div>s to the left so each one doesn't start on a new line. First, let's give them a class:

```
body.append("div")
    .attr("class", "buttons-container")
    .selectAll("div").data(buttonYears)
  .enter().append("div")
    .text(function(d) { return d; })
    .attr("class", "button");
```

And then let's change the float for that class:

```
.button {
    float: left;
}
```

And we get what is shown in Figure 8.10.

Okay, okay. Clearly, there's some formatting we need to tweak here. First of all, our container <div> needs to have a width so the buttons don't spill over to the right way beyond the edge of the chart. Also, the buttons themselves need to be spaced apart. We can fix both of these easily in our CSS:

```
.buttons-container {
    width: 520px;
    margin-bottom: 15px;
}
.button {
    float: left;
    margin-left: 10px;
}
```

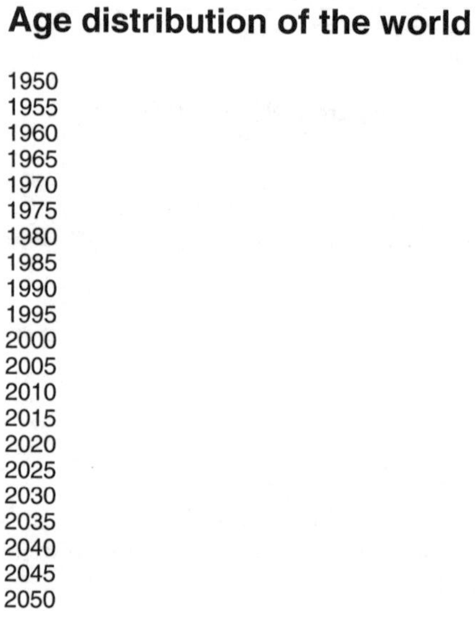

Age distribution of the world

```
1950
1955
1960
1965
1970
1975
1980
1985
1990
1995
2000
2005
2010
2015
2020
2025
2030
2035
2040
2045
2050
```

Figure 8.9   A long column of years

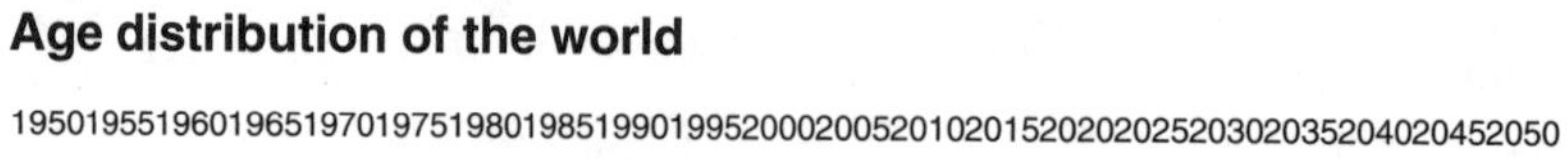

Age distribution of the world

19501955196019651970197519801985199019952000200520102015202020252030203520402045 2050

Figure 8.10   A long row of years

(I went ahead and added a bottom margin to the container <div> just to keep things looking nice). Let's take a look now (see Figure 8.11).

So now those two labels at the top are off—"age group" and "portion of the population." We can fix this by inserting a <div> in between the buttons and giving it the class "clearfix," which will clear the float property:

```
body.append("div")
    .attr("class", "buttons-container")
    .selectAll("div").data(buttonYears)
  .enter().append("div")
    .text(function(d) { return d; })
    .attr("class", "button");

body.append("div")
    .attr("class", "clearfix")
body.append("div")
    .attr("class", "top-label age-label")
  .append("p")
    .text("age group");
```

One last thing: We want to distinguish the year on display from the rest of the years so the user knows what she's looking at. A pretty standard way of doing this is to make the year bold.

Age distribution of the world

| 1950 | 1955 | 1960 | 1965 | 1970 | 1975 | 1980 | 1985 | 1990 | 1995 | 2000 |
| 2005 | 2010 | 2015 | 2020 | 2025 | 2030 | 2035 | 2040 | 2045 | 2050 | **AGE GROUP** PORTION OF THE POPULATION |

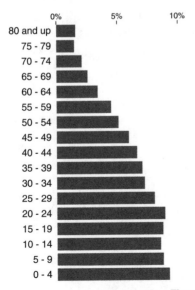

Figure 8.11   Float on

Let's do that by creating a new class called `selected` (the next section will clarify why it makes sense to take this approach).

```
.selected {
    font-weight: bold;
}
```

When we set the class for the buttons, we don't want them all to just have the class buttons. We also want the button corresponding to the year on display to have the class `selected`. So we need to set the class using an anonymous function:

```
body.append("div")
    .attr("class", "buttons-container")
    .selectAll("div").data(buttonYears)
  .enter().append("div")
    .text(function(d) { return d; })
    .attr("class", function(d) {});
```

What should we put inside that function? (I encourage you to figure it out on your own.) We still have that year variable at the top of our script that we used to set the year at the end of the previous chapter. (Currently, mine is set back to 2010.) We can use that variable to keep track of which year is selected (and to set a default year the user will see when the page loads) and style the buttons accordingly. To do this, inside our anonymous function, we can test to see if d is equal to year. If it is, we'll give it both the class `button` and the class `selected`; if it's not, we'll just give it the class `button`.

```
body.append("div")
    .attr("class", "buttons-container")
    .selectAll("div").data(buttonYears)
  .enter().append("div")
    .text(function(d) { return d; })
    .attr("class", function(d) {
        if(d == year)
            return "button selected";
        else
            return "button";
    });
```

The result is shown in Figure 8.12.

I don't know about you, but to my eyes, the selected year—2010—doesn't quite pop enough. One way to further distinguish it is to decrease the weight of the other buttons. We can do that in CSS:

```
.button {
    float: left;
    margin-left: 10px;
    font-weight: lighter;
}
```

Age distribution of the world

1950 1955 1960 1965 1970 1975 1980 1985 1990 1995 2000
2005 **2010** 2015 2020 2025 2030 2035 2040 2045 2050

AGE GROUP   *PORTION OF THE POPULATION*

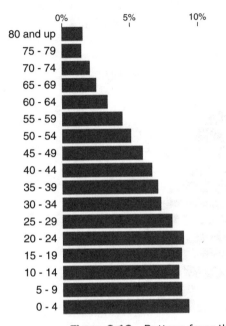

Figure 8.12   Buttons favor the bold

```
.selected {
    font-weight: bold;
}
```

Figure 8.13 shows the result.

Making the Buttons Clickable

Now that we have the buttons on the page, we need to make them functional. How do you tell a button to do something when it is clicked? By using an **event handler**.

As the name suggests, an event handler handles events, or actions, on the part of the user. It listens for an event, and when that event happens, it tells the browser to do something. Clicking is an event. So is hovering the cursor over an element. In our case, we are interested in clicking.

To set up an event listener for a given element, D3 has the method on(). If we want to use on() to set up an event listener for our buttons, this is what it would look like:

```
body.append("div")
    .attr("class", "buttons-container")
    .selectAll("div").data(buttonYears)
```

Age distribution of the world

1950	1955	1960	1965	1970	1975	1980	1985	1990	1995	2000
2005	**2010**	2015	2020	2025	2030	2035	2040	2045	2050	

AGE GROUP PORTION OF THE POPULATION

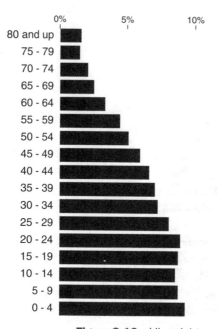

Figure 8.13   Like night and day

```
.enter().append("div")
   .text(function(d) { return d; })
   .attr("class", function(d) {
       if(d == year)
           return "button selected";
       else
           return "button";
   })
   .on("click", function(d) {});
```

So what do we want to happen when a button gets clicked? For now, a good goal would be for the button to become bold, which we can do by giving it the class `selected`. All we have to do is create a selection out of the button you clicked and add that class to it.

But wait...how do we do that? The easiest way is to employ a bit of JavaScript magic. JavaScript has a self-referential variable called `this` that can be both very easy to use and very confusing. All the ins and outs of `this` are beyond the scope of this book, but fortunately, in our case, `this` is easy to use. We're defining a function that is triggered when we click something, and inside of that function, this is the element that we clicked. We can create a D3 selection out of this like so: d3.select(this). Easy.

Once we've selected this we need to add the class selected. We can use attr() to do that, but D3 also has a method classed() you can use to essentially turn a class on and off:

```
body.append("div")
    .attr("class", "buttons-container")
    .selectAll("div").data(buttonYears)
  .enter().append("div")
    .text(function(d) { return d; })
    .attr("class", function(d) {
        if(d == year)
            return "button selected";
        else
            return "button";
    })
    .on("click", function(d) {
        d3.select(this)
            .classed("selected", true);
    });
```

The true means that yes, we want our selection to have the class selected.

Give it a shot. You will notice that although the years you click become bold without a problem, the other years that have been selected before stay bold (see Figure 8.14).

This is clearly not what we want. So, in addition, inside of our on() method, we need to remove the class selected from the button that is currently bold before adding it to the button we clicked:

```
body.append("div")
    .attr("class", "buttons-container")
    .selectAll("div").data(buttonYears)
  .enter().append("div")
    .text(function(d) { return d; })
    .attr("class", function(d) {
        if(d == year)
            return "button selected";
        else
            return "button";
    })
    .on("click", function(d) {
        d3.select(".selected")
            .classed("selected", false);

        d3.select(this)
            .classed("selected", true);
    });
```

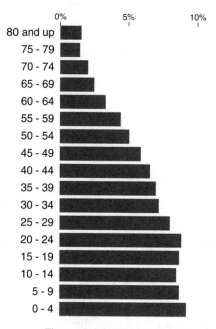

Age distribution of the world

1950 1955 1960 1965 **1970** 1975 1980 1985 1990 1995 2000
2005 **2010 2015 2020** 2025 **2030** 2035 2040 2045 2050

AGE GROUP *PORTION OF THE POPULATION*

Figure 8.14 Emboldened to stay that way

One last thing: If somebody were to come across our page the way it is now, they would have no way of knowing the years are actually clickable. Why? Because when you hover the cursor over them, it just turns into a text selector instead of a little pointing hand. You can change that in CSS:

```
.button {
    float: left;
    margin-left: 10px;
    font-weight: lighter;
    cursor: pointer;
}
```

Updating Charts

It's great that we have buttons that become bold when you click them. But we also want those buttons to actually do something. When we click 1950, we want the bars on the page to update so they show the data for 1950.

How can we do that? Well, we already have an event handler applied to our buttons that tells each button to become bold when clicked and tells all the others to stop being bold. Now, we need to put some additional commands inside of that event handler to update the data.

The first, and most obvious thing to do, is to change the variable year:

```
body.append("div")
    .attr("class", "buttons-container")
    .selectAll("div").data(buttonYears)
  .enter().append("div")
    .text(function(d) { return d; })
    .attr("class", function(d) {
        if(d == year)
            return "button selected";
        else
            return "button";
    })
    .on("click", function(d) {
        d3.select(".selected")
            .classed("selected", false);

        d3.select(this)
            .classed("selected", true);

        year = d;
    });
```

Recall that in this case, d represents each of the values in our array, buttonYears. By setting year equal to d, we are setting it to whichever year has just been clicked.

The next step is filtering the data. We want to grab only the data corresponding to our newly chosen year. Then we'll join that data to our bars to update their widths.

Because we want to manipulate data inside of our event handler, we actually need to put that event handler inside of our d3.csv() function. Remember: The data will load *asynchronously*, so everything you do involving external data needs to happen inside of that function. We don't need external data to create the buttons in the first place—we still want to do that outside of d3.csv(). How do we pull that off? We can assign those buttons to a variable up top, and then reference the variable inside of our d3.csv() call:

```
// The code up top:

var buttons = body.append("div")
    .attr("class", "buttons-container")
    .selectAll("div").data(buttonYears)
  .enter().append("div")
    .text(function(d) { return d; })
    .attr("class", function(d) {
        if(d == year)
            return "button selected";
        else
            return "button";
    });
```

```
// ...
// And inside of d3.csv():

svg.append("g")
    .call(yAxis)
    .attr("class","y axis")

buttons.on("click", function(d) {
    d3.select(".selected")
        .classed("selected", false);

    d3.select(this)
        .classed("selected", true);

    year = d;
});
```

Great. Now we need to filter the data so we only have our selected year. Easy enough—we've already made that filter. We just need to use it again and redefine our data variable, popData:

```
buttons.on("click", function(d) {
    d3.select(".selected")
        .classed("selected", false);

    d3.select(this)
        .classed("selected", true);

    year = d;

    popData = data.filter(function(element) {return element.year == year});
});
```

Now to update, we need to join our new popData array with our rectangles. This has to happen inside of our event listener, so we need a way to refer to those rectangles. Again, we can solve this problem by using a variable:

```
var bars = barGroup.selectAll("rect")
    .data(popData)
  .enter().append("rect")
    .attr("x", 0)
    .attr("y", function(d) {return y(d.age)})
    .attr("width", function(d) {return x(d.value)})
    .attr("height", y.rangeBand());

// ...

buttons.on("click", function(d) {
    d3.select(".selected")
        .classed("selected", false);

    d3.select(this)
        .classed("selected", true);
```

```
        year = d;

        popData = data.filter(function(element) {return element.year == year});

        bars.data(popData)
});
```

Now to update. D3 makes this super easy. Remember, there is no update() method. After we compute the data-join—bars.data(popData)—our selection is still bars. We can apply new attributes directly to that selection and it will update.

In this case, the only thing we need to update is the width. We want the rectangles to stay in the same position, have the same height, and remain the same color. We can update those widths like so:

```
bars.data(popData)
    .attr("width", function(d){});
```

What should go in that function? Exactly what went inside it before— return x(d.value). The thing is, d.value is different now, since we've joined new data to our rectangles.

```
bars.data(popData)
    .attr("width", function(d) { return x(d.value); });
```

Run that code in your browser and play around with it a bit. You should see the bars update when you click the buttons. Again, Figure 8.15 and Figure 8.16 show what the extremes should look like.

Congratulations! You have made an interactive graphic!

Adding Transitions

As is, the graphic is perfectly functional. With a click of the mouse, you can see a bar chart for any year in our data set. But the transition in between years is totally jerky. Wouldn't it be nice if the bars actually animated to their new values every time you clicked a year?

Again, D3 makes this painfully easy to do. All you have to do is use a D3 method—transition()—to make it happen:

```
bars.data(popData)
    .transition()
    .attr("width", function(d) { return x(d.value); });
```

Note: For it to work, you have to insert the transition() method before applying the change. Play around with the page a little more and watch the bars shrink and grow. Pretty fun, eh?

There are ways to customize transitions. You might be thinking that our bars are currently growing and shrinking a little faster than is ideal. The default duration of a transition is 250 milliseconds, or one quarter of a second. You can make that duration

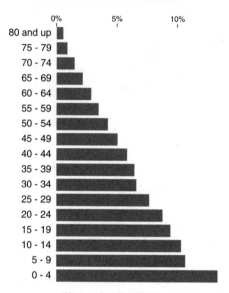

Age distribution of the world

1950 1955 1960 1965 1970 1975 1980 1985 1990 1995 2000
2005 2010 2015 2020 2025 2030 2035 2040 2045 2050

AGE GROUP PORTION OF THE POPULATION

Figure 8.15 The good old days

longer or shorter by using the duration() method, which takes as an argument the number of milliseconds for which you want the transition to last:

```
bars.data(popData)
    .transition()
    .duration(500)
    .attr("width", function(d) { return x(d.value); });
```

Play around with that 500-millisecond transition. I don't know about you, but that looks a lot better to me.

You can also add a delay to a transition, so that it doesn't start right away, but instead waits for a specified amount of time (again, given in milliseconds) to begin. Try this:

```
bars.data(popData)
    .transition()
    .delay(500)
    .duration(500)
    .attr("width", function(d) { return x(d.value); });
```

Hmm...not very useful in this case. But imagine you wanted a couple of different transitions to happen in a sequence. If the first one takes 500 milliseconds, then you might want to use a delay to tell the second transition to hold off until the first one is done.

Age distribution of the world

1950 1955 1960 1965 1970 1975 1980 1985 1990 1995 2000
2005 2010 2015 2020 2025 2030 2035 2040 2045 **2050**

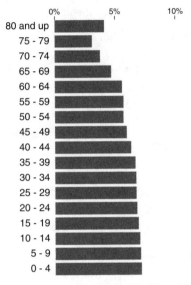

AGE GROUP PORTION OF THE POPULATION

Figure 8.16   The old days

You'll notice that with our current transition, the bars seem to accelerate at first and then slow down as they reach the target width. The way an object eases into and out of a transition like this is called easing, and it can be mathematically described by what is called an easing function. D3 let's you customize that easing function to your heart's content, but it also has a few presets you can use to create certain kinds of animations.

For example, instead of D3's default acceleration and deceleration, you can make our bars grow and shrink at a constant speed by specifying that the easing function be linear:

```
bars.data(popData)
    .transition()
    .duration(500)
    .ease("linear")
    .attr("width", function(d) { return x(d.value); });
```

Or you can make them pull back and slingshot forward by using the "back" preset:

```
bars.data(popData)
    .transition()
    .duration(500)
    .ease("back")
    .attr("width", function(d) { return x(d.value); });
```

You can even make the transitions super wacky using the `"bounce"` preset:

```
bars.data(popData)
    .transition()
    .duration(500)
    .ease("bounce")
    .attr("width", function(d) { return x(d.value); });
```

But I would definitely caution against using either `"back"` or `"bounce."` Although they are both really fun, they're super distracting. If we were to use them with our age distribution chart, it's likely that the person looking at the graphic would just start clicking years at random to see the bars spring forward or bounce a couple times when they come to a stop. The graphic would cease to be about age distribution at all and be purely about how the easing function itself looks.

It's best to stick with the default transition in almost every case, unless changing the easing function somehow helps the clarity of the interactive.

Using Keys

One final note on how to use data-joins the right way. Let's say that for some reason, our data set is out of order. That is, in the CSV file, for some years, the first age group is "0 - 4" but for others, it's either "80 and up" or one of the other age groups. Currently, when we compute the data-join to update our bars, the first data point is always joined to the first bar, the second data point to the second bar, and so on. If the data is out of order, this is a real problem.

The solution is to use what are called *keys*. A key is a way of identifying an object based on the data it is joined to. If you join new data, then D3 matches up the keys so the right data always gets paired up with the object it belongs to.

In our case, we want the key to be the age group. Here's how it works. First, we have to define a helper function to grab the key we want:

```
function keys(d) {
    return d.age;
}
```

When the function `keys()` is passed one of our data points, it will return the age group (which we've called "age"). We can add it to our code, outside of the `d3.csv()` function call:

```
var yAxis = d3.svg.axis()
    .scale(y)
    .orient("left");

function keys(d) {
    return d.age;
}
```

Now, all we have to do is use keys as a second argument in the method `data()`:

```
var bars = barGroup.selectAll("rect")
    .data(popData, keys)
```

```
  .enter().append("rect")
    .attr("x", 0)
    .attr("y", function(d) {return y(d.age)})
    .attr("width", function(d) {return x(d.value)})
    .attr("height", y.rangeBand());
// ...
buttons.on("click",function(d) {
    // ...

    bars.data(popData, keys)
        .transition()
        .duration(500)
        .attr("width", function(d) { return x(d.value); });
});
```

And that's it! Now, our data can be completely out of order and it won't matter in the slightest. Phew!

But keys can do a lot more than help you avoid getting burned when your data is dirty. They help transitions work the way you want them to. Think about Frank's data again for a second. Between February and March, Jennifer Aniston goes from being the most featured celebrity on tabloid covers to the second most (the "Octomom" edges her out in March). If you updated the data from February to March without using keys, then the text object in the number one spot would actually change from reading "Jennifer Aniston" to "Octomom." If you do use a key, then you can simply update the position of the "Jennifer Aniston" text object from the top spot to the second spot—you can make it slide seamlessly down in the ranking.

The difference is one between object constancy and object inconstancy. Using a key, you can locate the "Jennifer Aniston" text object and update it with new data. As an object, it will always be the "Jennifer Aniston" object. It's constant. But if you don't use a key, then the "Jennifer Aniston" object will become the "Octomom" object as you switch from February to March. It's inconstant.

Object constancy is a good thing. Think about it in terms of the theater metaphor. You want a given actor to keep playing the same role even as he or she moves about the stage.

Summary

In this chapter, we opened with a conceptual introduction to the update and exit phases of the data-join and then applied those concepts to our age distribution bar chart. The goal was to make it interactive. We added a series of buttons, one for each year, and then made them clickable. Then we made the chart update with new data every time one of the buttons was clicked. We added an animated transition to make the chart flow seamlessly from one year to another. Finally, we used keys to ensure the object constancy of the bars on our page.

9

Adding a Play Button

In this chapter, we'll be taking things up a notch by adding a play button to our bar chart. We'll start by making a generalized update function we can use to tell our bar chart to update to any given input year. Then we'll actually add a play button to our page. And finally, we'll make the whole thing work.

Wrapping the Update Phase in a Function

Think of this chapter as kind of like a bonus chapter. You've already learned everything you know to be well on your way to creating awesome graphics in D3. In this chapter, we're just going to make that bar chart we've been working on slightly more sophisticated by adding a play button.

What will that play button do, exactly? When the user clicks on it, the chart will first be set to the earliest year, 1950. The button for 1950 will turn bold and black and the bars will grow or shrink to the levels associated with that year. Then the chart will automatically step through each subsequent year in order, advancing from one to the next at a fixed pace. The idea is that the user can click the play button, sit back, and watch the shape of the world's age distribution change over time.

So how do we go about making this thing? Before we add an actual button to our page, let's think a little bit about what needs to happen under the hood.

As the chart plays through all the years, it will involve a series of updates—in the D3 sense of the word. Each update will be equivalent to the user clicking whichever year comes next. In other words, the same sequence of code that is triggered when a user clicks a year button needs to be triggered when a user clicks the play button.

```
buttons.on("click", function(d) {
    d3.select(".selected")
        .classed("selected", false);

    d3.select(this)
        .classed("selected", true);
```

```
    year = d;

    popData = data.filter(function(element) {return element.year == year});

    bars.data(popData, keys)
        .transition()
        .duration(500)
        .attr("width", function(d) { return x(d.value); });
});
```

The code above is the code we'll need to *reuse* for our play button. Fortunately, we won't need to write it in our script twice. All programming languages have a basic, built-in mechanism that helps you reuse code easily: the ability to define functions. Anytime you're programming and you realize there is a sequence of code you want to reuse, your first thought should be: I should put that code in a function!

So let's define a function—call it update—we can use both to tell the chart to update once when a user clicks a year button and to tell the chart to update 21 times in a row when a user clicks the play button. This will really help simplify things when we actually start to build the play button.

```
function update() {
};
```

What should this function contain? Or better yet, what should it do? The thing is, it has to be general—it needs to be able to update the chart both when a user clicks a year button and when a user clicks the play button. Hmm...so how can we make it general? What about this: What if we could give our function a year, say 2035, and then it would update the chart to that year?

```
function update(updateYear) {
}
```

Okay, so what should go inside? For starters, let's add everything that's inside of our event handler for buttons, shown above.

```
function update(updateYear) {
    d3.select(".selected")
        .classed("selected", false);

    d3.select(this)
        .classed("selected", true);

    year = d;

    popData = data.filter(function(element) {return element.year == year});

    bars.data(popData, keys)
        .transition()
        .duration(500)
        .attr("width", function(d) { return x(d.value); });
};
```

Now let's step through what we have piece-by-piece. The first little bit of code is perfect:

```
d3.select(".selected")
    .classed("selected", false);
```

Every time the chart updates, we want to remove the class selected from whatever the currently selected year button is. Great. What about this next bit?

```
d3.select(this)
    .classed("selected", true);
```

It's a little problematic. Can you see why? This code is designed to create a selection out of a year button so we can add the selected class to it. Right now, it relies on this to create that selection. That is totally fine when a user has just clicked a year button—this refers to the year button clicked. But we want our update function to be general. We want to pass in a year (updateYear) and have it update, and we can't rely on this to do that.

So how can we use updateYear to create a selection out of the right button? It turns out that D3 has a filter method you can use to take a selection of multiple elements and winnow it down to only the elements you want. It works a lot like the array method filter, but there's one major difference: Since it's designed to work on selections, you can use it to filter based on bound data.

This helps, because we already have a selection of all of the buttons, stored in a variable called buttons. We can use filter to winnow it down to only the button that is bound to updateYear.

```
buttons
    .filter(function(d) { return d == updateYear; })
    .classed("selected", true)
```

Great, let's move on to the next bit of code.

```
year = d;

popData = data.filter(function(element) {return element.year == year});
```

This is close. We just need to change two things. First, the variable d doesn't exist within our update function. But that's an easy fix—we can just set year equal to updateYear.

Actually, on second thought, why bother? We don't need to worry about changing the year variable. Instead, we can just use updateYear where we had previously been using year.

```
popData = data.filter(function(element) {return element.year ==
    updateYear});
```

Finally, let's look at our last bit of code.

```
bars.data(popData, keys)
    .transition()
```

```
        .duration(500)
        .attr("width", function(d) { return x(d.value); }); );
```

Everything in there is perfect. We don't need to change a thing. Okay, so let's look at our entire update function.

```
function update(updateYear) {

    d3.select(".selected")
        .classed("selected", false);

    buttons
        .filter(function(d) { return d == updateYear; })
        .classed("selected", true)

    popData = data.filter(function(element) {return element.year ==
        updateYear});

    bars.data(popData, keys)
        .transition()
        .duration(500)
        .attr("width", function(d) { return x(d.value); }); );
};
```

Now, where in our code should that function go? Because it relies on our array, data, it needs to go inside that d3.csv() callback function. We can slip it in there right at the end. Why don't we also go ahead and change the event handler on our buttons so it takes advantage of the update function we've just defined.

```
buttons.on("click", function(d) {
    update(d);
});

function update(updateYear) {

    d3.select(".selected")
        .classed("selected", false);

    buttons
        .filter(function(d) { return d == updateYear; })
        .classed("selected", true)

    popData = data.filter(function(element) {return element.year ==
        updateYear});

    bars.data(popData, keys)
        .transition()
        .duration(500)
        .attr("width", function(d) { return x(d.value); }); );
};
```

Does it matter that the event handler, which now calls the function update, is defined before the update function in our code? Nah. Whenever you use a function in JavaScript, the compiler (generally a browser) combs through your entire script to see if that function is defined anywhere.

Adding a Play Button to the Page

Now that we have a reusable function that will take any year and update the chart to that year, we can start making a play button. It's pretty easy to see how this will play out (as it were). We create some code that will cycle through all of the years and then pass each of those years in sequence to our update function. But before we do that, let's put a play button on our page. That way, we'll be able to easily test whether or not things are working—all we'll have to do is click and see what happens.

Let's insert a play button right after our title:

```
body.append("h2")
    .text("Age distribution of the world");

var playAll = body.append("div")
    .attr("class", "play-button")
    .text("▶ PLAY ALL YEARS");

var buttons = body.append("div")
    .attr("class", "buttons-container")
    .selectAll("div").data(buttonYears)
  .enter().append("div")
    .text(function(d) { return d; })
    .attr("class", function(d) {
        if(d == year)
            return "button selected";
        else
            return "button";
    });
```

A couple of notes. First, I'm using the Unicode black right-pointing triangle ("U+25B6") here to denote that this is a play button. It's not the sleekest solution, so if you want to jazz it up a bit, go for it! Second, I went ahead and assigned the play button to a variable, playAll. I'm just thinking ahead here. I know that ultimately, we'll be creating an event handler for this play button (so that clicking it will actually prompt the chart to cycle through all of the years). I also know the event handler will need to be defined inside of our d3.csv() callback function, because the play sequence will depend on our data. By assigning the play button to a variable, we'll be able to refer to it lower down inside of that callback function.

Figure 9.1 shows what our page looks like with the play button.

Clearly, this play button lacks style. Let's fix that with some CSS.

```
.play-button {
    margin-left: 10px;
    margin-bottom: 15px;
    font-style: italic;
```

Age distribution of the world

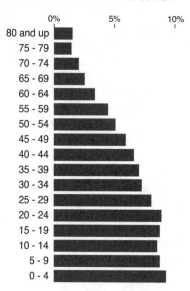

▶ PLAY ALL YEARS

1950 1955 1960 1965 1970 1975 1980 1985 1990 1995 2000
2005 **2010** 2015 2020 2025 2030 2035 2040 2045 2050

AGE GROUP *PORTION OF THE POPULATION*

Figure 9.1 With a play button

```
    cursor: pointer;
    color: grey;
}
.play-button:hover {
    color: black;
}
```

Figure 9.2 shows the result.

Making the Play Button Go

Now that we have a clickable play button, we can tell our program what to do when
that click happens. Let's go ahead and set up an event handler. Again, this has to
go inside of the callback function within d3.csv(). Let's put it right after the event
handler for our year buttons.

```
buttons.on("click", function(d) {
    update(d);
});

playAll.on("click", function() {
});
```

Age distribution of the world

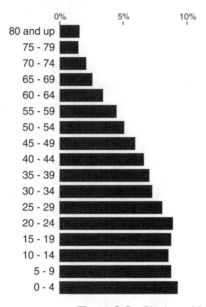

Figure 9.2   Playing with style

When that play button gets clicked, we want the chart to cycle through all the years. How can we do that? Let's try using a `for` loop.

```
playAll.on("click", function() {
    for (var i = 0; i < buttonYears.length; i++) {
        update(buttonYears[i]);
    };
});
```

What do you see when you run that code and click the play button? The chart immediately jumps to 2050, right? Do you know why? It's because the `for` loop runs through all of its iterations very quickly and doesn't pause along the way to let the chart update. So we need to use something different, something that will behave like a `for` loop, but will take a breather after each iteration instead of just rushing through them all.

I happen to know of such a function—it's called `setInterval()`. It basically takes two arguments. The first is a function and the second is an amount of time, in milliseconds. What `setInterval()` does is take that function in the first argument and run it over and over, with a period equal to the number of milliseconds specified in the second argument. For example, if you pass setInterval() a function that creates a pop-up window reading "Hello," and a time of 1000 milliseconds, then setInterval() will keep producing a new pop-up window every second. Forever! Or until you turn it off using a function called clearInterval().

Okay, so how might this work in our case?

```
playAll.on("click", function() {
    setInterval(function() {}, 700);
});
```

I went ahead and picked a time for us: 700 milliseconds. Remember that it takes our bars 500 milliseconds to update. That extra 200 milliseconds will give us a little bit of a pause in between each year, which is a good thing. We don't want our animation going too fast.

But choosing a time is the easy part. What goes inside of that anonymous function? Just like with the for loop, we want our setInterval() function to iterate through all of our years, or equivalently, all of the values in our buttonYears array. How can we do that? We can follow the conventions of a for loop and set up a loop counter (i) that gets incremented every time the setInterval() function completes an iteration.

```
playAll.on("click", function() {

    var i = 0;

    setInterval(function() {

        update(buttonYears[i]);

        i++;

    }, 700);
});
```

Note that we initialize that loop counter outside of our setInterval() function. Why? Because otherwise, the counter would be set back to 0 with each iteration, and the chart would always display the first year, 1950. Try running the code above and then clicking on the play button. It works, right? Huzzah!

Well, it doesn't totally work. We never shut off that setInterval() function. It just keeps running and running. (Don't believe me? Add a console.log() statement to the inside of the setInterval() function and watch it continue to get repeated after the play sequence makes it to 2050.)

That is bad enough in and of itself. There's no reason to make somebody's browser do useless work. But not shutting off that loop also creates a couple of visible problems. When the play sequence gets to 2050, the button for 2050 becomes bold, but then that boldness goes away (because the first thing our update() function does is remove it, and in this case, update() continues to get called after the sequence has reached 2050). This leaves us with a chart that has no indication of which year it is showing. Also, if you click on one of the year buttons, say 1960, after the play sequence has blown past 2050, the chart will update to 1960, and the button will momentarily turn bold, but then that boldness will go away (again, because the loop counter is still ticking higher and higher and the update() function is still being called).

Clearly, we need to bring that loop to a stop when it reaches 2050. We can do that using the function clearInterval().

```
setInterval(function() {

    update(buttonYears[i]);

    i++;

    if(i > buttonYears.length - 1) {
        clearInterval();
    }
}, 700);
```

Hmm...but as you'll notice, the code above doesn't do what we want it to. The reason is that the clearInterval() function needs to know what interval you're talking about. Assigning our setInterval() call to a variable and then passing that variable to clearInterval() will do the trick:

```
var playInterval = setInterval(function() {
    update(buttonYears[i]);

    i++;

    if(i > buttonYears.length - 1) {
        clearInterval(playInterval);
    }
}, 700);
```

Allowing the User to Interrupt the Play Sequence

There's one more minor issue we should take care of. Click the play button. Then while the sequence is running, click one of the year buttons. You'll notice that the chart updates to the year you clicked, but then the play sequence picks right back up where it left off.

This is not ideal. We should give the user a way to interrupt the interval. What if she had clicked the play button by accident? Or what if she wanted to stop on a year partway into the sequence? Not every user will feel the need to interrupt the interval, of course, but some users might. It's something worth accommodating.

And doing so is relatively easy. (I encourage you to try it on your own.) All we have to do is add a clearInterval() function call to the event handler that is triggered when any of the year buttons is clicked.

```
buttons.on("click", function(d) {
    update(d);
    clearInterval(playInterval);
});
```

But, of course, that `playInterval` variable is currently only defined inside of the play button's event handler. The year button's event handler has no access to it. That's an easy fix. All we have to do is declare the variable `playInterval` outside of the play button's event handler.

```
buttons.on("click", function(d) {
    update(d);
    clearInterval(playInterval);
});

var playInterval;

playAll.on("click", function() {

    var i = 0;

    playInterval = setInterval(function() {
        update(buttonYears[i]);

        i++;

        if(i > buttonYears.length - 1) {
            clearInterval(playInterval);
        }

    }, 700);
});
```

And that's it! Listing 9.1 shows our code in its entirety.

Listing 9.1 **An asynchronous script.**

```
<!DOCTYPE html>
<html>
<head>
<meta charset="utf-8">
<style>
    body {
        font-family: Helvetica;
    }
    svg {
        width: 500px;
        height: 500px;
    }
    .play-button {
        margin-left: 10px;
```

```css
    margin-bottom: 15px;
    font-style: italic;
    cursor: pointer;
    color: grey;
}
.play-button:hover {
    color: black;
}
.buttons-container {
    width: 520px;
    margin-bottom: 25px;
}
.button {
    float: left;
    margin-left: 10px;
    font-weight: lighter;
    cursor: pointer;
}
.selected {
    font-weight: bold;
}
.top-label {
    font-size: 13px;
    font-style: italic;
    text-transform: uppercase;
    float: left;
}
.age-label {
    text-align: right;
    font-weight: bold;
    width: 90px;
    padding-right: 10px;
}
.clearfix {
    clear: both;
}
.bar {
    fill: DarkSlateBlue;
}
.bar-label {
    text-anchor: end;
}
.axis-label {
    text-anchor: middle;
    font-size: 13px;
}
.x.axis line {
```

```
        fill: none;
        stroke: #000;
    }
    .x.axis text {
        font-size: 13px;
    }
    .axis path {
        display:none;
    }
    .y.axis line {
        display:none;
    }
</style>
</head>
<body>
    <!-- -->
<script src="http://d3js.org/d3.v3.min.js"></script>
<script>

    var year = 2010;

    var buttonYears = [1950, 1955, 1960, 1965, 1970, 1975, 1980, 1985, 1990,
1995, 2000, 2005, 2010, 2015, 2020, 2025, 2030, 2035, 2040, 2045, 2050];

    var margin = {top: 30, right: 0, bottom: 0, left: 100},
        width = 500 - margin.left - margin.left,
        height = 450 - margin.top - margin.bottom;

    var body = d3.select("body");

    var x = d3.scale.linear()
        .range([0, width]);

    var y = d3.scale.ordinal()
        .rangeBands([0, height], 0.2, 0);

    var xAxis = d3.svg.axis()
        .scale(x)
        .orient("top")
        .ticks(5, "%");

    var yAxis = d3.svg.axis()
        .scale(y)
        .orient("left");

    function keys(d) {
        return d.age;
    }
```

```
body.append("h2")
    .text("Age distribution of the world");

var playAll = body.append("div")
    .attr("class", "play-button")
    .text("▶ PLAY ALL YEARS");

var buttons = body.append("div")
    .attr("class", "buttons-container")
    .selectAll("div").data(buttonYears)
  .enter().append("div")
    .text(function(d) { return d; })
    .attr("class", function(d) {
        if(d == year)
            return "button selected";
        else
            return "button";
    });

body.append("div")
    .attr("class", "clearfix")

body.append("div")
    .attr("class", "top-label age-label")
  .append("p")
    .text("age group");

body.append("div")
    .attr("class", "top-label")
  .append("p")
    .text("portion of the population");

body.append("div")
    .attr("class", "clearfix")

d3.csv("allData.csv", function(error, data){

    var popData = data.filter(function(element) {return element.year ==
year});

    x.domain([0, d3.max(data, function(element) { return element.value;
})]);

    y.domain(popData.map(function(element) {return element.age}));

    var svg = body.append("svg")
        .attr("width", width + margin.left + margin.right)
        .attr("height", height + margin.top + margin.bottom)
      .append("g")
        .attr("transform", "translate(" + margin.left + "," + margin.top +
")");
```

```
var barGroup = svg.append("g")
    .attr("class", "bar");

var bars = barGroup.selectAll("rect")
      .data(popData, keys)
  .enter().append("rect")
      .attr("x", 0)
      .attr("y", function(d) {return y(d.age)})
      .attr("width", function(d) {return x(d.value)})
      .attr("height", y.rangeBand());

svg.append("g")
    .call(xAxis)
    .attr("class", "x axis")

svg.append("g")
    .call(yAxis)
    .attr("class","y axis")

buttons.on("click", function(d) {
    update(d);
    clearInterval(playInterval);
});

var playInterval;

playAll.on("click", function() {

    var i = 0;

    playInterval = setInterval(function() {
        update(buttonYears[i]);

        i++;

        if(i > buttonYears.length - 1) {
            clearInterval(playInterval);
        }
    }, 700);
});

function update(updateYear) {

    d3.select(".selected")
        .classed("selected", false);

    buttons
        .filter(function(d) { return d == updateYear; })
        .classed("selected", true)
    popData = data.filter(function(element) {return element.year ==
updateYear});
```

```
              bars.data(popData, keys)
                  .transition()
                  .duration(500)
                  .attr("width", function(d) { return x(d.value); });

          };
      });
</script>
</body>
</html>
```

Summary

In this chapter we created a generalized update() function that takes a year as input and updates the bar chart to display that year. This allowed us to reuse a sequence of code both for our play button and for our individual year buttons. Then we created a play button using a Unicode triangle character. We used the setInterval() function to make the play button go. Finally, we added a clearInterval() function call to the year button event listeners so users can interrupt the play sequence by clicking any of the years.

10

Striking Out on Your Own

The intention of this book was to provide a springboard to help you dive right in to D3. But all of the learning you do will happen as you try to build stuff. The goal of this chapter is to give you some pointers for how to move forward with D3.

This Book Is a Foundation for Learning D3

You could say this book has only scratched the surface. D3 can easily produce a multitude of chart forms that animate in a variety of ways, and we've only made a fairly basic bar chart that grows and shrinks. D3 offers other kinds of scales besides linear and ordinal, other types of user interactions besides just clicking, and a whole host of premade layouts for making more complex graphics such as chord diagrams, treemaps, and dendrograms. Oh yeah, and you can use D3 to make geographic maps.

But scratching the surface isn't really the right metaphor. Hopefully, what this book has done is laid a foundation. No matter what you end up using D3 for—to make a map of US counties shaded according to population density, or to visualize your network of friends on Facebook—you'll almost certainly be using data-joins. Understanding what data-joins are and how to use them is core to programming with D3.

To take your understanding of selections and data-joins to the next level, there is an excellent intermediate tutorial written by Mike Bostock you should read, called "How Selections Work."[1] It covers a lot of the same ground covered in Chapters 5 and 8 of this book, but it goes a little deeper and gets a little more technical. It will definitely come in handy, especially if you ever want to create multiple charts on the same page.

How to Get Unstuck

As with any programming language or library, the best way to learn D3 is to build stuff. But, of course, as you build stuff you are inevitably going to get stuck. So, how do you get unstuck?

---

1. The tutorial can be found at http://bost.ocks.org/mike/selection/

First and foremost, you should go to D3's API Reference, which I've mentioned throughout this book.[2] It is filled with excellent, though necessarily very technical, descriptions of all of D3's functions and methods (which include many, many more than were covered in this book). Consulting the API Reference isn't always the fastest way to get things done—oftentimes you can just copy a snippet of code from an example online—but it's the best way to make sure you fully understand what you are doing. In the long run, reading the API Reference is worth the investment, because doing so will help you master D3.

But if reading the Reference doesn't shed any light on the problem you are trying to solve (or if you just aren't even sure where to begin), then there are tons and tons of examples online, covering almost any chart type and any interaction you could dream of. The best place to look for examples is in the D3 examples gallery.[3]

Mike Bostock, in addition to bestowing the gift of D3 on the world, has also built an online interface that allows people to easily share D3 examples. It's called **bl.ocks** and it's built on top of GitHub's quick code-sharing service, Gist. There are tons and tons of bl.ocks out there, and Bostock himself has written hundreds (which you should definitely spend some time browsing through).[4]

Figure 10.1 shows an example of a bl.ock that I made.

Bl.ocks are structured like this: Whatever the code does is shown in a box at the top. Then there is a read-in, which most people use to describe what the code does or where the data come from. Then the code itself (always written in a single **index. html** file) is shown, with the syntax highlighted. And finally, if there is an external data file used in the code, that data is shown in full. (Figure 10.1 is not long enough to show the data file I used in that example.)

A JavaScript developer named Irene Ros at Bocoup has made an excellent tool for exploring blocks called Blocksplorer (http://bl.ocksplorer.org/). You can type a function or method into the search bar, and Blocksplorer will show you all of the existing blocks that use that function or method. It's really helpful if you know what you want to use but aren't totally sure how to use it.

Of course, there won't always be a bl.ock to help you troubleshoot a specific problem. So where to next?

Message boards. There is a D3 Google group, and there are thousands of D3-related threads on StackOverflow. If you encounter some weirdness, chances are, somebody else has encountered similar weirdness and has asked people about it on one of those two forums. If you can't find it anywhere, then post a question yourself! These forums only get better as the number of threads grows, so long as the questions aren't easily answered by reading the D3 documentation. (For example, "How do I reference the D3 library in my HTML file?" is a bad question to ask, because the answer is right on the home page of the D3 wiki).

---

2. https://github.com/mbostock/d3/wiki/API-Reference
3. https://github.com/mbostock/d3/wiki/Gallery
4. http://bl.ocks.org/mbostock

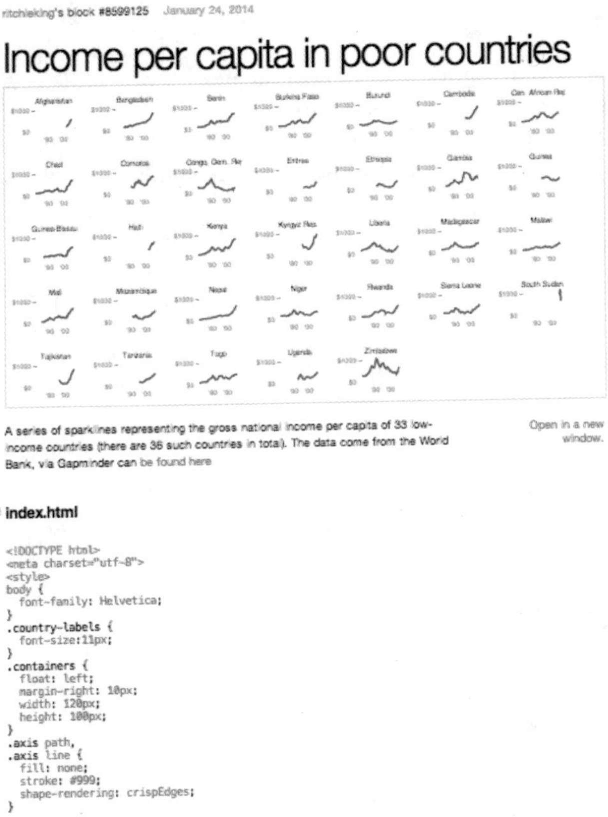

ritchieking's block #8599125   January 24, 2014

Income per capita in poor countries

A series of sparklines representing the gross national income per capita of 33 low-income countries (there are 36 such countries in total). The data come from the World Bank, via Gapminder can be found here

Open in a new
window.

index.html

```
<!DOCTYPE html>
<meta charset="utf-8">
<style>
body {
    font-family: Helvetica;
}
.country-labels {
    font-size:11px;
}
.containers {
    float: left;
    margin-right: 10px;
    width: 120px;
    height: 100px;
}
.axis path,
.axis line {
    fill: none;
    stroke: #999;
    shape-rendering: crispEdges;
}
```

Figure 10.1   A chip off the old bl.ock

Always Be Coding

They call it the ABCs of programming: Always Be Coding.

Coding is not like riding a bike; it's more like playing a musical instrument. If you only pick up your guitar once every month or two, you're going to spend most of your practice time reminding yourself of the stuff you've already learned. Coding is very much the same way.

So if you don't use D3 much at work, try to set aside some extracurricular time to practice.

A good way to get some D3 coding in is to build your own bl.ocks, giving yourself a fresh challenge with each one. It's a nice, closed-ended assignment. Building bl.ocks is also a good way to contribute to the D3 ecosystem. Finally, if you want to show off your D3 skills—say, to a potential employer—then having a repertoire of bl.ocks is a great idea. Plus, it's a lot of fun!

Summary

This final chapter covered how you can take the next steps with D3. Whenever you get stuck on a problem, there are three main sources you can consult: the D3 API Reference, examples on the web (especially D3 bl.ocks), and message boards. Learning D3 is challenging, and it takes practice and patience. Remember: Always Be Coding!

A

JavaScript for Beginners

This JavaScript primer is designed for people who have little or no experience with JavaScript. It covers everything you need to know to get up and running with D3.

JavaScript In Brief

JavaScript is a native of the web. It's a programming language that was created to run in web browsers so web pages can respond to input from users. JavaScript can take most of the credit for making websites interactive.

Remember that when you go to a website, all that is really happening is that your browser is opening up an HTML file (unless the website is in a different format, like PHP). So if a website involves JavaScript, the HTML file has to tell the browser somehow. It does this in one of two ways:

- The HTML file itself can contain JavaScript. If you add a `<script>` tag to your markup, you can insert JavaScript directly into it.
- The HTML file can call in an external JavaScript file (don't worry: if you've never done this before, we'll go over how to do it later in this chapter).

Unlike HTML, JavaScript is not a markup language. HTML is very specifically a way of applying structure to the elements of a webpage. But JavaScript is a full-fledged programming language. You can write reusable functions in JavaScript, you can define variables, or you can use it to do basic math. Though it began as a liaison between users and the web pages they were using, JavaScript has since come to be used in building non-web applications and video games as well.

Your Browser's JavaScript Console

Every modern browser has a built-in JavaScript console. The true purpose of the console is for debugging a web page's JavaScript. If you fire up the console with a web page open, it will tell you, for one, if the page's JavaScript has any bad syntax and couldn't be interpreted by the browser.

But you can also use the console as a JavaScript command line. In other words, you can key lines of JavaScript into the console and hit enter, and it will execute that code. Later, we'll go over how to use the console to inspect your JavaScript, but first, let's go over some basics using the console as a command line.

Basic Math, Variables, and Data Types

Launch your browser, if you haven't already. To access the console in Chrome you can click on the so-called hamburger menu (see Figure A.1), then go to Tools > JavaScript Console. The keyboard shortcut for Windows is Ctrl + Shift + J and on a Mac it's ⌥-⌘-J (Option + Command + J). You should see the window shown in Figure A.2 pop up.

Now key in 1 + 1 and hit enter. The console will automatically print the answer. If it's not 2, then I suggest you go lie down for a quick nap. If that was the first time you ever coded in JavaScript, congratulations! Basic math is a breeze in JavaScript. In addition to addition, you can do subtraction (using the - operator), multiplication (*), and division (/), and you can use parentheses to dictate the order of operations. There is also an operator (%) for calculating the remainder (long division, whoa!) you would get if you divided two numbers. For example, 12 % 10 = 2.

In JavaScript, you can store a value in a variable, which is handy if you want to use that value more than once. JavaScript variables work sort of like algebra in reverse. In algebra, you are usually trying to figure out what x is, but in JavaScript, you set x equal to whatever you want.

To create a variable, you first have to do what is called declaring it. Listing A.1 shows some examples (which you should type into the console as you go):

Figure A.1   The hamburger menu

Elements   Resources   Network   Sources   Timeline   Profiles   Audits   Console
> |

Figure A.2   The console

Listing A.1   *Declaring variables in JavaScript.*

```
var x;
var y = 10;
var z = 5 + 2;
var MyVariable, myVariable = 2, myvariable = 2 - 2;
```

You declare a variable by typing var followed by a space followed by the variable name. You finish declaring with a semicolon. (Important: It's best practice to end every JavaScript statement with a semicolon. JavaScript is a very forgiving programming language, and it will usually work if you don't include semicolons, but not always.) In the example above, x is declared as a variable but not defined, y is declared and set equal to 10 in a single statement, and z is declared and set equal to the result of 5 + 2 in a single statement. Also, MyVariable, myVariable, and myvariable are declared and varyingly defined or not in a single statement, separated by commas. Note that var only has to be typed once per statement.

Now that we have some variables, we can use them (see Listing A.2).

Listing A.2 *Performing operations with variables.*

```
myVariable + y;
myVariable + myVariable;
var newVariable = myVariable;
myVariable = 4;
newVariable;
```

As I'm sure you've noticed, variable names are case-sensitive. It's also the case that you can't start a variable name with a number, and you can't include operators in a variable name. (For example, my-variable would be read as subtracting variable from my. Use my_variable or myVariable instead.)

Variables can contain more than just numbers. They can also contain a range of other data types, arrays, objects, and even functions (see Listing A.3). In some programming languages, you have to declare the data type when you declare a new variable, but in JavaScript you don't. Furthermore, you can change a variable's type: You can declare a variable and set it equal to a number, only to later set that same variable equal to, say, a string.

> **Note**
>
> In JavaScript, the sequence // initiates a comment; everything after // on a line will not be interpreted as part of your code.

Listing A.3 *Basic data types in JavaScript.*

```
// Numbers
var myWholeNumber = 5;
var myFractionalNumber = 5.1;
var myDividedNumber = myWholeNumber / myFractionalNumber;

// Strings
var myString = "Hello";
var myStringSingle = 'Hello';
var myStringQuotes = '"Hello," she said.';
myWholeNumber = "Now I'm a string";
```

```
// Booleans (true or false)
5 > 4;
5 == 4;
var myBoolean = (4 > 5);
```

Booleans might be a little confusing if you're a programming newbie. What's the value in all this true or false business? You'll find that it's useful to set up conditionals in your JavaScript—to only run a snippet of code if some condition is true, say if a variable is larger than 5. We'll go over how to do that using an if statement later in this chapter.

It's not that common, at least in my experience, to store a Boolean value in a variable; it's far more common to just type out a Boolean expression inside of an if statement. To use Booleans effectively, you need to be familiar with a few comparison operators and a few logical operators (see Table A.1).

Table A.1   **Operators**

Comparison Operators

Operator	*Definition*
==	is equal to
!=	is not equal to
>	is greater than
<	is less than
>=	is greater than or equal to
<=	is less than or equal to

Logical operators

Operator	*Definition*
&&	And
||	or
!	Not

Listing A.4 presents some examples of Boolean expressions

Listing A.4   *Examples of Boolean expressions.*

```
5.1 >= 5;
3 != 3;
5.1 >= 5 && 3 != 3;
5.1 >= 5 || 3 != 3;
!(5.1 >= 5 && 3 != 3);
"Hello" == 'Hello';
```

One final note on data types and operations. JavaScript will do what is called automatic type conversion (see Listing A.5). Recall that the + operator means addition when you're dealing with numbers. When you're dealing with strings, it means concatenation. So, "concat" + "enation" will evaluate to "concatenation." If you try adding a number to a string, then JavaScript will convert the number into a string and then concatenate the two. But if you try multiplying a number and a string, JavaScript will try to convert the string into a number before completing the operation.

Listing A.5   *Examples of automatic type conversion.*

```
"I have " + 5 + " dogs";
"5" + 5;
"5" * 5;
5 * "dogs";
```

Note

NaN means "Not a Number."

We went through these basics pretty quickly. There are a lot of lessons hidden in the examples that weren't spelled out explicitly, so it's worth spending some time with them. JavaScript is a truly quirky language. Sometimes those quirks make it simpler to use than other languages, but other times they can lead to copious head scratching. If you want to learn more, Marijn Haverbeke has written an excellent book on the weirdness that is JavaScript called *Eloquent JavaScript*. The full text is available online at http://eloquentjavascript.net/.

Writing JavaScript in Markup and .js Files

So far, we've been doing all of our JavaScript coding in the browser's console. But, of course, when you design a web page for somebody else to look at, you won't have access to that person's console, and you'll need the browser to load all of the page's JavaScript with the page itself. As mentioned, there are two ways to do that: You can put JavaScript directly into the markup, and you can create a separate JavaScript file.

To put JavaScript in your markup, you need to use a `<script>` tag. Let's create a new HTML document and call it **js-basics.html** (see Listing A.6).

Listing A.6   *Writing script directly in your markup.*

```
<!DOCTYPE html>
<meta charset="utf-8">
<body>
<script>
        var myVar = "Voila! It worked!";
</script>
</body>
```

Open **js-basics.html** in your browser. Not a whole lot to look at. Now open up the console. If all went well, you should be able to access all of your variables from the console's command line. Type myVar and hit enter. Voila! It worked!

The other way to add JavaScript to a web page is to call in an external JavaScript (.js) file. Go to the directory on your computer where **js-basics.html** lives and create a folder called script. Now create a new file in your text editor and type in var myVar = "Voila! It worked!"; at the top. Save that file as **js-basics-script.js** in the script folder you just created. Finally, change your markup to look like Listing A.7.

Listing A.7   *Calling in an external JavaScript file.*

```
<!DOCTYPE html>
<meta charset="utf-8">
<body>
<script src="script/js-basics-script.js"></script>
</body>
```

Now open the console back up and type in myVar. Note: Just to be clear, the JavaScript file doesn't have to live in a folder called script. The folder could be called anything. Or **js-basics-script.js** could be in the same directory as **js-basics.html**. In that case, when you call in the script, you would write:

```
<script src="js-basics-script.js"></script>
```

As long as your markup knows how to find the JavaScript file, everything will be dandy. (Personally, I like to store my .js files in a separate folder to keep things organized.)

Arrays and Objects

In addition to the basic data types we covered above, JavaScript has a couple of special varieties that are capable of containing multiple values at once.

One of these is called an array. The values in an array are enclosed within square brackets and separated by commas. Open up **js-basics-script.js** and insert the following statement to create an array:

```
var myArray = [1,2,3,4,5];
```

Go back into your browser and open up the console. Type in myArray and hit enter. There it is. Now, it's possible to access any one of the values in myArray individually (also known as indexing into the array) by typing myArray[i] where i is the position of the value within the array (or its index). So, if we want to access the first value, we might try typing myArray[1] (see Figure A.3).

Hmm...so we're clearly getting the value in the second position in myArray, not the first. The reason is that in JavaScript the first position of an array has an index of 0, not 1. Try myArray[0]. Perfect.

Arrays can hold multiple data types. You can even nest an array inside of an array or put objects into an array. Listing A.8 presents some examples of valid arrays.

Listing A.8   *Examples of arrays.*

```
var myArray = [1,2,3,4,5];
var textArray = ["one","two","three","four"];
var mixedArray = [1,true,"three"];
var nestedArray = [1,[2,3,4],5];
```

Let's play with nestedArray in the console for a second. After you've defined it, type nestedArray, hit enter, and behold (see Figure A.4).

You can see that in between the 1 and the 5 is something that says Array[3] with a dropdown arrow to the left of it. The [3] in this case refers to the number of values in the array, or its length. Now click on that dropdown arrow to expand it (see Figure A.5).

There are the values, 2, 3, and 4, sitting in the 0, 1, and 2 positions, respectively. The length is also shown. Length is a property of an array; you can ask JavaScript for the length of an array by typing, for example, nestedArray.length. Try it. (Don't worry about __proto__ for the time being; it's just a list of standard methods you can use to analyze and manipulate arrays.)

So, in the case of nestedArray, there is an array smack dab in the middle of an array. How do you access the values of the inner array? You first have to access the array itself—nestedArray[1]. Now, since nestedArray[1] is just like any other array,

```
> myArray
  [1, 2, 3, 4, 5]
> myArray[1]
  2
>
```

Figure A.3   Indexing into an array

```
> nestedArray
  [1, ▶ Array[3] , 5]
>
```

Figure A.4   An array within an array

```
> nestedArray
  [1, ▼ Array[3] ▣          , 5]
      0: 2
      1: 3
      2: 4
      length: 3
    ▶ __proto__: Array[0]
>
```

Figure A.5   The inner array

you can access its values using the index. Thus, `nestedArray[1] [0]` will give you the 0 position value of the array being stored in the 1 position of `nestedArray` (see Figure A.6).

The other kind of data type that can hold multiple values is an object. Listing A.9 shows what an object looks like.

Listing A.9   *An example of an object.*

```
var myCar = {
        make: "Nissan",
        model: "Sentra",
        color: "silver",
        year: 2004,
        new: false,
        gears: [1,2,3,4,5,"R"]
};
```

> **Note**
>
> The line breaks in Listing A.9 have no significance in JavaScript; they are neither necessary nor do they change the way the code is interpreted. I've inserted them just to make the object more readable.

Like arrays, objects can hold multiple data types, including arrays (and yes, other objects). Each value in an object is assigned to a property. In `myCar`, the properties are make, model, color, year, new, and gears. Let's take a look at `myCar` in the console (see Figure A.7).

After expanding `myCar` in the console, you'll notice a couple of things. First, it has no length property. Objects generally do not. Second, the order of the properties has been rearranged alphabetically. Don't worry! Unlike with arrays, the values in objects don't have positions or indices; the order doesn't matter.

> **Note**
>
> There are ways to insert line breaks when entering code in the console, but I would suggest just sticking the code into **js-basics-script.js** or **js-basics.html**.

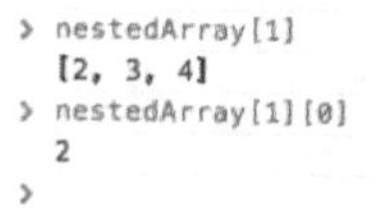

```
> nestedArray[1]
  [2, 3, 4]
> nestedArray[1][0]
  2
>
```

Figure A.6   Indexing all the way in

```
> myCar
  ▼ Object {make: "Nissan", model: "Sentra", color: "silver", year: 2004, new: false...} ▣
      color: "silver"
    ▶ gears: Array[6]
      make: "Nissan"
      model: "Sentra"
      new: false
      year: 2004
    ▶ __proto__: Object
> |
```

Figure A.7   A closer look at `myCar`

The way you access values in an object is by using the property name itself. For example, typing in `myCar.make` will return `"Nissan"`, `myCar.model` will return `"Sentra"`, and `myCar.gears[5]` will return `"R"`.

Methods and Functions

In programming in general, if you want to perform a sequence of operations over and over again, then you can save that sequence into a packet of instructions called a function. This is a weird example, but say you wanted to take a number, square it, add 7, and then divide by 2. You could type out all of those commands by hand, but if you were doing it a bunch of times, it could quickly get pretty tedious. Listing A.10 shows how you would store those operations in a function.

Listing A.10   *An example of a function.*

```
function myMath(num) {
        return (num * num + 7)/2
}
```

When you define a function, you declare that you are defining a function with the word function (just like you declare variables with var). In Listing 6.10, `myMath` is the name of the function, and num is what's called an argument. Arguments are necessary if you want your function to perform a series of commands on a value or values of your choosing—but not all functions have arguments. In the function definition, arguments are treated as dummy variables: For example, `myMath` is saying, "I don't know what num is, but when you tell me, I'll know what to do with it!" The expression return is needed in `myMath` so that when you run the function, it actually spits out the solution to (num * num + 7)/2.

Okay, so go ahead and put the definition of `myMath` into your js or HTML file, save it, and go back to your browser. Now that the browser has run that definition, `myMath` is a function that is available to that web page. Open the console and type `myMath(5)`. Then try `myMath(myArray[2])`.

JavaScript has a ton of built-in functions. `alert()`, for instance, will tell your browser to open up an alert box and display any string that is passed to it as an argument. Try `alert("Eureka!")`.

Methods are like functions, but they only work on a particular data type. Arrays have methods and objects have methods. The syntax for methods is a little different from that of functions. The variable you want to perform the method on isn't passed in as an argument, but rather proceeds the method name. For example, `myArray.indexOf(3)` performs the method `indexOf()` on the array `myArray`. What `indexOf` does is it takes the array and looks for the value that is passed in as an argument—in this case 3—and then returns the position, or index, within the array where that value is located. `myArray.indexOf(3)` should return an index of 2.

A JavaScript library, like D3, is merely a bunch of functions and methods. D3 is really just a .js file full of function and method definitions, not unlike the definition for `myMath`, sitting on the Internet waiting for you to run it.

`If` **Statements and** `for` **Loops**

Let's create an array of objects called `myCars` (see Listing A.11).

Listing A.11   *An array of objects,* `myCars`.

```
var myCars = [{
        make: "Nissan",
        model: "Sentra",
        color: "silver",
        year: 2004,
        used: true,
        gears: [1,2,3,4,5,"R"]
        },
        {
        make: "Ford",
        model: "Taurus",
        color: "champagne",
        year: 2001,
        used: true,
        gears: ["automatic"]
        },
        make: "Porsche",
        model: "911 Turbo",
        color: "black",
        year: 2013,
        used: false,
        gears: [1,2,3,4,5,6,"R"]
        }
];
```

Now, let's say we want to build a function that will tell us how old a car is. What would that function look like? Well, for starters, you would want to pass it an object as an argument, and it would return a value with the age of the car. Or better yet, a sentence that says "That car is x years old." Or even better, "That [make] [model] is x years old." I'll put the answer in Listing A.12, but try to see if you can come up with it on your own.

Listing A.12   *A function for determining a car's age.*

```
function carAge(obj) {
        var name = obj.make + " " + obj.model;
        var age = 2013 - obj.year;
        return "That " + name + " is " + age + " years old.";
};
```

If you run carAge() on each of the objects in the myCars array, then you'll get what is shown in Figure A.8.

Brilliant. But I think we could make one tiny improvement. Nobody would ever say that a car is 0 years old; somebody would say that it's brand new. Also, if a car was made in 2012, then carAge() would say that it is 1 years old...perfectly comprehensible, but utterly ungrammatical.

To fix these issues, we need some way of telling carAge() to return one thing if the car is new, something else if the car is a year old, and a third thing if the car is two years old or older. We can do that using what's called a conditional statement. I'll give you the syntax (see Listing A.13) and then explain it.

Listing A.13   *Determining a car's age in plain English.*

```
function carAge(obj) {
        var name = obj.make + " " + obj.model;
        var age = 2013 - obj.year;
        if (age == 0) {
                return "That " + name + " is brand new!";
        }
        else if (age == 1) {
                return "That " + name + " is only a year old.";
        }
        else {
                return "That " + name + " is " + age + " years old.";
        }
};
```

```
> carAge(myCars[0])
  "That Nissan Sentra is 9 years old."
> carAge(myCars[1])
  "That Ford Taurus is 12 years old."
> carAge(myCars[2])
  "That Porsche 911 Turbo is 0 years old."
>
```

Figure A.8   Revealing the ages of the cars

The code should be fairly readable, I hope. It employs what is called an `if` statement, or technically, a series of `if…else` statements. It starts at the top. If the variable age is equal to 0, then it executes return `"That " + name + " is brand new!"`. And then it stops. Whenever a function reaches a return statement, it returns the value and then ignores the rest of the code.

If age is not equal to 0, then `carAge()` checks to see if it is equal to 1, and if so it returns `"That " + name + " is only a year old."`. If not, then it returns `"That " + name + " is " + age + " years old."`. Simple.

It would be good to check `carAge()` to make sure everything is working as it should be. Our array, `myCars`, contains two cars that are older than 2 years old and one car that is brand new. That covers two of the three cases in our `if…else` statements. Let's add a car that was made in 2012. First, we need to define it.

```
var jeep = {
      make: "Jeep",
      model: "Wrangler",
      color: "forest green",
      year: 2012,
      used: false,
      gears: [1,2,3,4,5,"R"]
};
```

We can add `Jeep` to `myCars` using an array method called `push()`. The `push()` simply takes whatever is passed in as an argument and tacks it onto the end of the array on which it's operating. Type in `myCars.push(jeep)`—that should do the trick.

Now, if we call `carAge()` on each of the objects in `myCars` in turn, what is shown in Figure A.9 is what we get.

Perfect.

One last exercise. Say we wanted to create a function that would take an array of car objects, like `myCars`, and compute the average age of all of the cars. What we would need is a way to go through every object in the array, calculate the age, tally all those ages up, and then divide that tally by the number of objects. We can do this using a loop.

In programming, loops are designed to repeat a series of commands over and over again, for as long as a specified condition is true. You've probably heard the term "infinite loop." An infinite loop never gets to the point where the specified condition

```
> carAge(myCars[0])
  "That Nissan Sentra is 9 years old."
> carAge(myCars[1])
  "That Ford Taurus is 12 years old."
> carAge(myCars[2])
  "That Porsche 911 Turbo is brand new!"
> carAge(myCars[3])
  "That Jeep Wrangler is only a year old."
> |
```

Figure A.9 With natural language

is false; thus it keeps looping and looping through the commands forever. It's a cool term, but something you should try to avoid when you're coding.

There are a couple of different kinds of loops, but we're going to use a for loop, probably the most common. Simply speaking, for loops use a counter to keep track of the number of times the commands in the loop have been executed (in programming-speak, each cycle through the sequence of commands is called an iteration). When that number exceeds a specified value, the loop stops. (A for loop doesn't have to be set up exactly this way, but it's often the most straightforward way to do it.) Here is an example of a basic for loop:

```
for (var i = 0; i < 10; i++) {
    1+1;
};
```

Every for loop has three statements. The first statement is a definition of the loop counter. In the code above, the loop counter is a variable called i that we initially set equal to 0. The second statement is the condition that must be satisfied for the loop to keep looping. Before each iteration, the for loop looks at that condition—in our example, i < 10—and checks to see if it's true. If it's true, then it proceeds. The third and final statement increments the loop counter, or adds 1 to i, at the end of every iteration.

Okay, now put that basic for loop into **js-basics-script.js** and run it. Hmm…not a lot to look at. The reason is that, yes the loop is running through 10 iterations and adding 1 and 1 each time, but it doesn't do anything with the result—it doesn't store it in a variable, and it doesn't print it out on the console. To do the latter, you can use a function called console.log():

```
for (var i = 0; i < 10; i++) {
    console.log(1+1);
};
```

You should see something like Figure A.10.

The 2 on the right is the output…but since the for loop printed the exact same thing (the number 2) a total of 10 times, it just indicates the number of times that output has been printed (the 10 on the left).

Doing the same thing for every iteration is pretty boring. But how can you tell the for loop to do something different each time through? Well, there is a variable that changes predictably with each iteration: i. You can actually incorporate i into the sequence of commands within a for loop:

```
for (var i = 0; i < 10; i++) {
    console.log(i);
};
```

10 2
>

Figure A.10 Logging the iterations

Now, here's where it gets interesting. We can actually use i as a way of indexing into an array:

```
for (var i = 0; i < myCars.length; i++) {
    console.log(myCars[i]);
};
```

This loop will log every object in the myCars array to the console. Note that in the second statement in the for loop, the conditional statement, myCars.length is used instead of a number. This is a handy way to do it, because you don't have to know how long myCars is—regardless of the length, the for loop will run through exactly as many iterations.

Okay, now back to the exercise at hand—how can we build a function that will take an array like myCars and tell us the average age of the cars contained within? You should have all the tools you need to do it, so I won't go through all the steps involved. But you should try to solve it on your own before looking at the solution shown in Listing A.14.

Listing A.14   **A function for finding the average car age.**

```
function carAvgAge(obj) {
    var age,
        ageTotal = 0;
    for (var i = 0; i < obj.length; i++) {
        age = 2013 - obj[i].year;
        ageTotal = ageTotal + age;
    };
    return ageTotal / obj.length;
};
```

Debugging

As mentioned, the main purpose of your browser's JavaScript console is for debugging. If your JavaScript syntax has an error, then the console will alert you to that error and even let you know which line in your code the error appears in. Say you were defining the object Jeep and you forgot the closing bracket:

```
var jeep = {
    make: "Jeep",
    model: "Wrangler",
    color: "forest green",
    year: 2012,
    used: false,
    gears: [1,2,3,4,5,"R"]
;
```

When you load **js-basics.html** and open up the console, you should see something like Figure A.11.

⊗ Uncaught SyntaxError: Unexpected token ;   script/js-basics-script.js:63
> |

Figure A.11 Syntax error

There is a syntax problem: The browser found an unexpected semicolon in the file inside of the folder `script` called **js-basics-script.js** in line 63 (at least in my version of the file; your line number may be different).

Sometimes your code doesn't work the way you want it to, but there isn't actually a problem with the syntax. For example, here's a slightly modified version of `carAvgAge()`:

```
function carAvgAge2(obj) {
      var age,
            ageTotal;
      for (var i = 0; i < obj.length; i++) {
            age = 2013 - obj[i].year;
            ageTotal = ageTotal + age;
      };
      return ageTotal / obj.length;
};
```

If you try calling this version of the function on `myCars` to compute the average age, you get `NaN`, which stands for "not a number." Something is going awry somewhere in the code. Time to put on your Sherlock Holmes deerstalker.

The value that `carAvgAge2` is returning is `ageTotal / obj.length`. That expression will only return `NaN` if one of the two values involved is `NaN`. We can use `console.log()` to determine which. Let's start with `obj.length`. Insert `console.log(obj.length)` into the code before the return statement, like so...

```
console.log(obj.length)
return ageTotal / obj.length;
```

...and then run the code. Now, try calling the function on `myCars` again. Doesn't appear to be the problem—`obj.length` is equal to 4 just as we would expect it to be. So something must be up with `ageTotal`. Let's look at the `for` loop above. With each iteration, `ageTotal` is defined recursively: The new value is set equal to the current value plus age. Let's try the `console.log()` trick on age to see if it's the culprit:

```
for (var i = 0; i < obj.length; i++) {
      age = 2013 - obj[i].year;
      console.log(age);
      ageTotal = ageTotal + age;
};
```

Nope, again, the console is printing exactly what you would expect: The age of each of the cars individually as it goes through each iteration. So something is wrong with ageTotal itself. Let's try simulating just one iteration of the for loop to see what's going on with ageTotal. Type the following into the console:

```
var ageTotal;
var age = 12;
ageTotal = ageTotal + age;
```

I've set age to 12 arbitrarily, but it doesn't actually matter what the value is. We're just trying to understand why ageTotal is NaN when you set its new value equal to its current value plus something that we know for sure is a number. When you run the lines of code above, you can see that ageTotal is still NaN. Drill down further. Type in the following (you'll want to reset the variables):

```
var ageTotal;
var age = 12;
ageTotal + age;
ageTotal;
```

Ah, so things are starting to make a little sense. When you declare ageTotal without defining it, it exists as a variable but has no data type: It is undefined. And then, when you add something that is undefined to something else that is defined and is a number, you get a third thing that is not a number. How do we solve this problem? By setting ageTotal equal to 0 initially instead of leaving it undefined, just as we did in the first version of carAvgAge().

B

Cleaning the Population Distribution Data

This appendix will cover how to find and clean the raw data used for the interactive population distribution bar chart built throughout the course of this book.

All of the data comes from the United Nations Population Division. And all of the cleaning can be done with two pieces of free software—Open Office and the statistical programming language, R. If you're planning on following along, you should go ahead and install those programs on your computer (if you have Microsoft Excel, you don't need Open Office). You can find Open Office at https://www.openoffice.org/ and R at http://www.r-project.org/.

Start by going to the UN Population Division's homepage: http://www.un.org/en/development/desa/population/. From there you can navigate to its population data portal by clicking on "Estimates and Projections" in the sidebar. If you're having trouble finding it, the full link for that page is http://esa.un.org/unpd/wpp/index.htm. Then, click on "Data in EXCEL format." Again, here is the full link if you need it: http://esa.un.org/unpd/wpp/Excel-Data/population.htm. Don't worry that all the data on this page is in Excel format—Open Office can handle .xls files.

The dataset you want is under the "Age composition" topic, and it's called "Population by Age Groups - Both Sexes." Click on that link, and the spreadsheet will start downloading. Once it's finished, open it up in Open Office (or Excel). Your file should look like the one in Figure B.1.

There are multiple worksheets in the file. The first is called "ESTIMATES," followed by "MEDIUM FERTILITY," "HIGH FERTILITY," and so on. We are only interested in two of them: ESTIMATES (data from years past) and MEDIUM FERTILITY (the middle of the road projections).

Let's take a closer look at the ESTIMATES sheet. All of the data for the entire world is conveniently right there at the top. (If the values are appearing as a few hash marks—like "###"—don't worry. That just means the columns aren't wide enough for the numbers to be displayed. You can make a column wider by scrolling over the boundary between

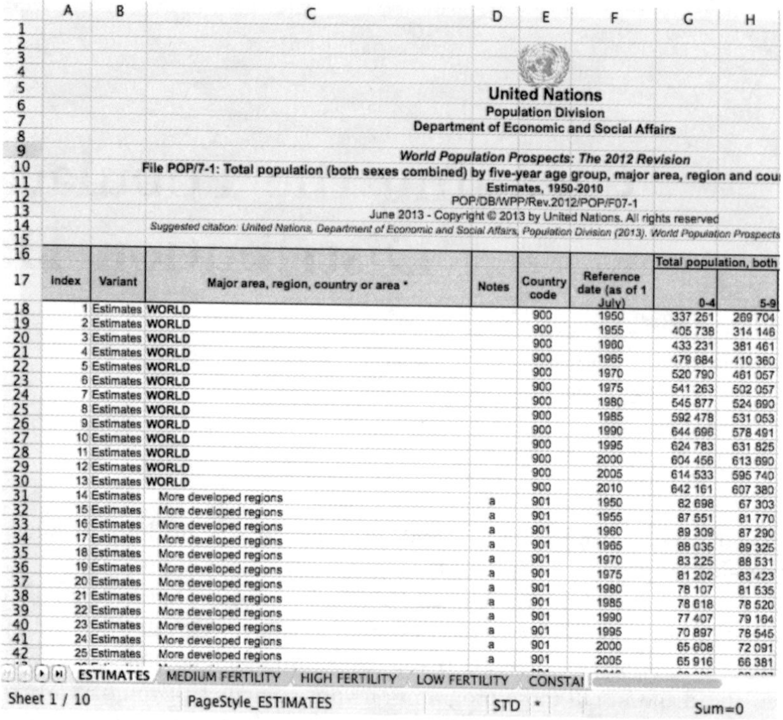

Figure B.1   The raw data

column letters at the top until your cursor turns into a vertical line with two arrows pointing out of the sides in either direction. Then just click and drag.)

The first step is to go ahead and delete all of the data that doesn't pertain to the entire world. There are a lot of ways to do this, but one way is to start by selecting the first cell of the first row that doesn't contain world-level data—cell A31, shown in Figure B.2—and then scroll all the way down to the last row in the spreadsheet and all the way over to the last column. While holding down shift, click on that very last cell—AB3085, shown in Figure B.3. Then hit backspace.

Now, there's some junk at the top of the worksheet to get rid of. Every row from row 1 through row 16 is unnecessary. You can select an entire row by clicking on that row's number on the left, and you can select multiple, subsequent rows by clicking on the first row you want, then holding down shift and clicking on the last row you want. Do that now—click on row 1, then hold down shift and click on row 16. Once you've done that, you can right-click with your cursor over the row numbers and choose "Delete Rows," as shown in Figure B.4.

Next, get rid of that UN logo at the top, shown in Figure B.5, by just selecting it and hitting backspace.

Looking better. There are also some columns you can get rid of. That index value is meaningless, so you can get rid of column A, and we don't need to keep track of the

16			
17	Index	Variant	Major area, region, country or area *
18	1	Estimates	WORLD
19	2	Estimates	WORLD
20	3	Estimates	WORLD
21	4	Estimates	WORLD
22	5	Estimates	WORLD
23	6	Estimates	WORLD
24	7	Estimates	WORLD
25	8	Estimates	WORLD
26	9	Estimates	WORLD
27	10	Estimates	WORLD
28	11	Estimates	WORLD
29	12	Estimates	WORLD
30	13	Estimates	WORLD
31	14	Estimates	More developed regions
32	15	Estimates	More developed regions
33	16	Estimates	More developed regions
34	17	Estimates	More developed regions
35	18	Estimates	More developed regions

Figure B.2 The first cell that contains irrelevant data

	V	W	X	Y	Z	AA	AB
3072	2	...	1	0	0	0	0
3073	0	0	...	...	...	...	...
3074	0	0	...	...	...	...	...
3075	0	0	...	...	...	...	...
3076	0	0	...	...	...	...	...
3077	0	0	...	...	...	...	...
3078	0	0	...	...	...	...	...
3079	1	0	...	...	...	...	...
3080	1	1	...	...	...	...	...
3081	1	...	0	0	0	0	0
3082	1	...	0	0	0	0	0
3083	1	...	1	0	0	0	0
3084	1	...	1	0	0	0	0
3085	1	...	1	0	0	0	0

Figure B.3 The last cell with irrelevant data

Figure B.4 Deleting the header rows

D	E	F
Notes		**Reference date (as of 1 July)**
	900	1950
	900	1955
	900	1960
	900	1965
	900	1970
	900	1975
	900	1980
	900	1985
	900	1990
	900	1995
	900	2000
	900	2005
	900	2010

Figure B.5   Get rid of that logo

	F	G	H	I	J
16		**Total population, both sexes combined, by fi**			
17	**Reference date (as of 1 July)**	**0-4**	**5-9**	**10-14**	**15-19**
18	2015	666 097	634 175	603 817	589 119
19	2020	668 233	658 727	630 771	600 313
20	2025	664 093	661 608	655 969	627 849
21	2030	663 764	658 124	659 148	653 250
22	2035	669 455	658 403	655 909	656 644
23	2040	677 340	664 644	656 412	653 602
24	2045	682 671	673 035	662 847	654 269
25	2050	684 194	678 836	671 418	660 852

Figure B.6   Grab the projections

variant because we know that everything for years past is an estimate and that every projection we'll use is going to be a medium fertility projection. We can also get rid of columns C, D, and E. Delete those in the exact same way you deleted rows 1 to 16 earlier.

Looking good. Now we just need to bring in the projection data from the MEDIUM FERTILITY sheet (Figure B.6). Go to that worksheet and select everything from cell F18 through cell AA25, and copy it.

Then paste it into the ESTIMATES worksheet (Figure B.7).

Now, scroll all the way to the right, to the last columns. You'll notice that the data you've just pasted doesn't quite line up with the data that is already there (Figure B.8).

What's going on here? Go back to the MEDIUM FERTILITY worksheet for a second and take a look at the older age groups.

Ah, as Figure B.9 shows, there is no "80+" column on this worksheet. So, currently, for the data that you just pasted into the ESTIMATES sheet, the values that are in the 80+ column should be in the 80-84 column, and the values that are in the 80-84 column should be in the 85-89 column. In other words, they need to be shifted

	A	B	C	D	E
1	Reference date (as of 1 July)	0-4	5-9	10-14	15-19
2	1950	337 251	269 704	260 697	238 747
3	1955	405 738	314 146	263 500	254 932
4	1960	433 231	381 461	308 046	258 324
5	1965	479 684	410 360	373 429	302 363
6	1970	520 790	461 057	405 234	368 391
7	1975	541 263	502 057	455 229	399 769
8	1980	545 877	524 690	497 005	450 683
9	1985	592 478	531 053	520 141	492 895
10	1990	644 696	578 491	527 461	516 614
11	1995	624 783	631 825	575 497	523 100
12	2000	604 456	613 690	628 646	571 501
13	2005	614 533	595 740	611 503	624 735
14	2010	642 161	607 380	592 696	606 056
15	2015	666 097	634 175	603 817	589 119
16	2020	668 233	658 727	630 771	600 313
17	2025	664 093	661 608	655 969	627 849
18	2030	663 764	658 124	659 148	653 250
19	2035	669 455	658 403	655 909	656 644
20	2040	677 340	664 644	656 412	653 602
21	2045	682 671	673 035	662 847	654 269
22	2050	684 194	678 836	671 418	660 852

Figure B.7   Combine all the data in one sheet

R	S	T	U	V	W
80+	80-84	85-89	90-94	95-99	100+
14 136	...	...	...	...	...
16 086	...	...	...	...	...
18 597	...	...	...	...	...
21 479	...	...	...	...	...
25 730	...	...	...	...	...
31 046	...	...	...	...	...
37 994	...	...	...	...	...
46 931	...	...	...	...	...
...	36 279	15 389	4 463	862	107
...	41 209	18 810	5 778	1 102	140
...	42 328	21 799	7 229	1 443	181
...	54 048	23 517	8 803	1 882	246
...	64 356	31 200	9 975	2 464	353
70 765	36 926	13 504	2 929	499	
80 376	41 403	16 394	4 164	639	
87 600	47 779	18 895	5 253	926	
109 250	53 317	22 289	6 285	1 241	
137 984	67 705	25 674	7 632	1 575	
155 248	85 737	33 324	9 156	1 987	
182 874	98 066	42 225	12 205	2 499	
206 325	116 872	49 475	15 513	3 392	

Figure B.8   The data doesn't quite align

over to the right. You can do that by selecting cells R15 through V22, cutting them, and pasting them into cell S15. The result is shown in Figure B.10.

Now, the thing is, we want to be able to compare all of these years. Currently, for every year from 1950 to 1985, the oldest age group is 80+. There is no breakdown beyond that. We have to put the other years in those terms, too, to make them

V	W	X	Y	Z	AA
75-79	**80-84**	**85-89**	**90-94**	**95-99**	**100+**
113 975	70 765	36 926	13 504	2 929	499
122 123	80 376	41 403	16 394	4 164	639
150 106	87 600	47 779	18 895	5 253	926
188 842	109 250	53 317	22 289	6 285	1 241
210 089	137 984	67 705	25 674	7 632	1 575
245 042	155 248	85 737	33 324	9 156	1 987
274 220	182 874	98 066	42 225	12 205	2 499
292 863	206 325	116 872	49 475	15 513	3 392
301 484	222 527	133 247	59 807	18 784	4 447
339 704	230 979	145 707	68 967	23 098	5 646
381 111	262 396	153 265	76 897	26 995	7 154
377 296	296 494	175 875	82 675	30 902	8 684
371 873	296 016	200 104	95 931	34 207	10 356
385 771	293 747	202 434	109 458	40 142	11 979
412 377	306 872	203 134	113 193	45 662	14 200
438 578	330 618	214 234	115 805	48 761	16 351
449 010	354 608	233 058	123 711	51 351	18 279
454 244	365 766	252 715	135 971	55 687	20 109

Figure B.9 Inspecting the older age groups

R	S	T	U	V	W
80+	**80-84**	**85-89**	**90-94**	**95-99**	**100+**
14 136	...	...	...	...	...
16 086	...	...	...	...	...
18 597	...	...	...	...	...
21 479	...	...	...	...	...
25 730	...	...	...	...	...
31 046	...	...	...	...	...
37 994	...	...	...	...	...
46 931	...	...	...	...	...
...	36 279	15 389	4 463	862	107
...	41 209	18 810	5 778	1 102	140
...	42 328	21 799	7 229	1 443	181
...	54 048	23 517	8 803	1 882	246
...	64 356	31 200	9 975	2 464	353
	70 765	36 926	13 504	2 929	499
	80 376	41 403	16 394	4 164	639
	87 600	47 779	18 895	5 253	926
	109 250	53 317	22 289	6 285	1 241
	137 984	67 705	25 674	7 632	1 575
	155 248	85 737	33 324	9 156	1 987
	182 874	98 066	42 225	12 205	2 499
	206 325	116 872	49 475	15 513	3 392

Figure B.10 Shifting the cells over

comparable. Starting with 1990, we have to compute the number of people who are 80 years old or older.

You can do this using the "sum" formula. Go to cell R10 (the 80+ column for 1990) and start typing "=sum(". Once you've started to type the formula like this, including adding that parenthesis, you can select the cells you want to sum. Do that by using a combination of the arrow keys and the shift key. Use the right arrow to navigate to cell S10, then hold down shift and keep pressing the right arrow key until you get to cell W10. This will select all of those cells. Then close the parentheses and hit enter. The result is shown in Figure B.11.

Now, you need to repeat this formula for all of the other rows. But don't just go through them one by one, entering in the formula. That would be super tedious, and there's a much better way. If you select cell R10 (the cell where you just entered the formula), you'll notice that the selection box has a solid square in the bottom-right corner, as shown in Figure B.12.

If you hover your cursor over that square (which is called the fill handle), you'll get a little crosshairs. Double-click and the formula will automatically fill in for the rest of the rows, as shown in Figure B.13. Neat, eh?

Now you can get rid of those columns at the end—columns 80 to 84 through 100+. We won't need those anymore. But wait! Not so fast. Remember, we have formulas in the 80+ column that depend on those other columns at the end. If we

Q	R	S	T	U	V	W
75-79	**80+**	**80-84**	**85-89**	**90-94**	**95-99**	**100+**
21 846	14 136	...	...	...	...	...
23 995	16 086	...	...	...	...	...
26 681	18 597	...	...	...	...	...
30 058	21 479	...	...	...	...	...
33 566	25 730	...	...	...	...	...
40 151	31 046	...	...	...	...	...
48 655	37 994	...	...	...	...	...
56 550	46 931	...	...	...	...	...
63 531	57 100	36 279	15 389	4 463	862	107
64 473	...	41 209	18 810	5 778	1 102	140
79 044	...	42 328	21 799	7 229	1 443	181
91 600	...	54 048	23 517	8 803	1 882	246
101 540	...	64 356	31 200	9 975	2 464	353
113 975		70 765	36 926	13 504	2 929	499
122 123		80 376	41 403	16 394	4 164	639
150 106		87 600	47 779	18 895	5 253	926
188 842		109 250	53 317	22 289	6 285	1 241
210 089		137 984	67 705	25 674	7 632	1 575
245 042		155 248	85 737	33 324	9 156	1 987
274 220		182 874	98 066	42 225	12 205	2 499
292 863		206 325	116 872	49 475	15 513	3 392

Figure B.11   Adding up all the 80+ age groups

57 100

Figure B.12   Finding an easier way to copy formulas

just delete them, we'll get an error. So first we have to copy those computed cells and repaste them, as the numbers they are now, not as the formulas.

To do that, select all of those cells in the 80+ column that contain a "sum" formula—cells R10 through R22. Copy. To paste, go to Edit > Paste Special and then check "Numbers" (see Figure B.14).

Now you can chop off those columns on the end as in Figure B.15.

	R	S	T	U	V	W
9	**80+**	**80-84**	**85-89**	**90-94**	**95-99**	**100+**
6	14 136	...	...	...	...	...
5	16 086	...	...	...	...	...
1	18 597	...	...	...	...	...
8	21 479	...	...	...	...	...
6	25 730	...	...	...	...	...
1	31 046	...	...	...	...	...
5	37 994	...	...	...	...	...
0	46 931	...	...	...	...	...
1	57 100	36 279	15 389	4 463	862	107
3	67 040	41 209	18 810	5 778	1 102	140
4	72 980	42 328	21 799	7 229	1 443	181
0	88 496	54 048	23 517	8 803	1 882	246
0	108 349	64 356	31 200	9 975	2 464	353
5	124 622	70 765	36 926	13 504	2 929	499
3	142 975	80 376	41 403	16 394	4 164	639
6	160 453	87 600	47 779	18 895	5 253	926
2	192 382	109 250	53 317	22 289	6 285	1 241
9	240 570	137 984	67 705	25 674	7 632	1 575
2	285 453	155 248	85 737	33 324	9 156	1 987
0	337 870	182 874	98 066	42 225	12 205	2 499
3	391 578	206 325	116 872	49 475	15 513	3 392

Figure B.13   The beauty of auto-fill

Selection
- ☐ Paste all
- ☐ Text
- ☑ Numbers
- ☐ Date & time
- ☐ Formulas
- ☐ Comments
- ☐ Formats
- ☐ Objects

Options
- ☐ Skip empty cells
- ☐ Transpose
- ☐ Link

Operations
- ⦿ None
- ☐ Add
- ☐ Subtract
- ☐ Multiply
- ☐ Divide

Shift cells
- ⦿ Don't shift
- ☐ Down
- ☐ Right

[OK]
[Cancel]
[Help]

Figure B.14   Paste everything back as raw values

Great. Now we need to get those population numbers into percentages. How do we do that? By finding the total population for each year and then dividing the values for each age group by that total population. Easy enough. First, create a new column for the totals and use the "sum" formula to compute them. The result is shown in Figure B.16.

N	O	P	Q	R
60-64	**65-69**	**70-74**	**75-79**	**80+**
73 348	55 075	37 370	21 846	14 136
76 988	59 465	40 474	23 995	16 086
85 598	63 339	44 695	26 681	18 597
95 795	70 864	48 199	30 058	21 479
107 974	82 362	56 068	33 566	25 730
117 564	93 786	66 144	40 151	31 046
118 393	103 190	76 472	48 655	37 994
140 566	103 976	84 634	56 550	46 931
159 575	124 412	85 650	63 531	57 100
171 014	141 395	103 480	64 473	67 040
187 315	152 398	118 139	79 044	72 980
195 182	168 016	129 177	91 600	88 496
234 345	176 763	143 856	101 540	108 349
291 342	213 077	152 312	113 975	124 622
318 764	265 858	185 101	122 123	142 975
364 891	291 963	231 883	150 106	160 453
402 028	335 850	256 020	188 842	192 382
423 726	371 511	296 296	210 089	240 570
432 060	392 664	329 387	245 042	285 453
479 928	401 092	349 626	274 220	337 870
530 790	446 986	358 142	292 863	391 578

Figure B.15   Don't need those columns anymore

P	Q	R	S
70-74	**75-79**	**80+**	total
37 370	21 846	14 136	2525779
40 474	23 995	16 086	2761651
44 695	26 681	18 597	3026003
48 199	30 058	21 479	3329122
56 068	33 566	25 730	3691173
66 144	40 151	31 046	4071020
76 472	48 655	37 994	4449049
84 634	56 550	46 931	4863602
85 650	63 531	57 100	5320817
103 480	64 473	67 040	5741822
118 139	79 044	72 980	6127700
129 177	91 600	88 496	6514095
143 856	101 540	108 349	6916183
152 312	113 975	124 622	7324782
185 101	122 123	142 975	7715749
231 883	150 106	160 453	8083413
256 020	188 842	192 382	8424937
296 296	210 089	240 570	8743447
329 387	245 042	285 453	9038687
349 626	274 220	337 870	9308438
358 142	292 863	391 578	9550945

Figure B.16   Find the total population

Now, dividing each value by the total for its year involves a little trickery. Why? Because you can't compute a new value for a cell in a self-referential way. In other words, you can't replace the value in cell B2 by dividing cell B2 by the total for 1950 (the value in cell S2). So, you have to create what is essentially a new table where you'll compute the percentages. The first step is to copy the headers over again, next to column S, where you have the population totals (see Figure B.17).

Then, starting with cell T2, you can do some division. You want to divide cell B2 by cell S2, so enter =B2/S2. The result is shown in Figure B.18.

Now, you want to do that division over and over again for all of the values in the table. It would, of course, be really tedious to type a formula in every time. But don't worry—you can use those crosshairs again to copy formulas over to other cells. Select cell T2, hover over the fill handle, and then click with the crosshairs and drag over to cell U2. See Figure B.19.

Hmm...that number seems pretty large. What's going on? If you look at the formula bar just above the column letters, you can see cell C2 is being divided by cell T2. Ah, so when we dragged the formula over both the numerator and the denominator shifted. But

S	T	U	V	W	X	Y
total	0-4	5-9	10-14	15-19	20-24	25-29
2525779						
2761651						
3026003						
3329122						
3691173						
4071020						
4449049						
4863602						
5320817						
5741822						
6127700						
6514095						
6916183						
7324782						
7716749						
8083413						
8424937						
8743447						
9038687						
9308438						
9550945						

Figure B.17 Create a new table

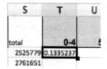

Figure B.18 Calculate a percentage

we only want the numerator to shift. As it turns out, there's a way to lock columns and rows in a formula, so that when you copy it to other cells they don't change. You do that by inserting a dollar sign before either the column letter or the row number in the formula.

Try typing the following formula into cell T2: =B2/$S2. Then drag that formula over with the crosshairs to cell U2. The result is shown in Figure B.20.

That looks better. Now drag the formula all the way to cell AJ2, and then with cells T2 through AJ2 selected, double-click on the fill handle with the crosshairs to fill the formula all the way down, as in Figure B.21.

Great, this part is almost done. Now that you have the percentages, you don't need the absolute values anymore. But you can't just delete the columns that contain those

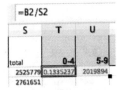

Figure B.19 Dragging the formula over

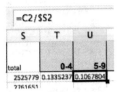

Figure B.20 Locking the denominator

T	U	V	W	X	Y
0-4	5-9	10-14	15-19	20-24	25-29
0.1335237	0.1067804	0.1032144	0.094524	0.0878956	0.0769092
0.1469186	0.1137531	0.0954141	0.0923115	0.0839142	0.0778625
0.1431693	0.1260611	0.1017997	0.085368	0.0820528	0.0746395
0.1440871	0.1232636	0.1121704	0.0908237	0.0756989	0.0728072
0.1410907	0.1249081	0.1097846	0.0998032	0.0802686	0.0668583
0.1329551	0.1233247	0.1118219	0.0981986	0.0890458	0.0717858
0.1226953	0.1179331	0.1117104	0.1012988	0.0886304	0.0802902
0.1218189	0.1091893	0.1069456	0.1013436	0.0915371	0.0800075
0.1211648	0.1087222	0.0991316	0.097093	0.0914997	0.0825222
0.1088128	0.1100391	0.100229	0.0911035	0.0886488	0.0836642
0.0986432	0.1001502	0.1025908	0.0932652	0.0842241	0.0819565
0.094339	0.0914541	0.0938739	0.0959052	0.086583	0.0781855
0.0928491	0.0878201	0.085697	0.0876287	0.089268	0.0808969
0.0909374	0.0865794	0.0824348	0.0804282	0.0821087	0.0836141
0.0865951	0.0853632	0.0817405	0.0777935	0.0757683	0.0773363
0.082155	0.0818477	0.08115	0.0776713	0.0737556	0.0717961
0.0787856	0.0781162	0.0782377	0.0775377	0.0740299	0.0702332
0.0765665	0.0753025	0.0750172	0.0751013	0.0742608	0.0708406
0.0749379	0.0735332	0.0726225	0.0723116	0.0722391	0.0713819
0.0733389	0.0723037	0.0712093	0.0702877	0.0698424	0.0697329
0.0716362	0.0710752	0.0702986	0.0691923	0.0681602	0.067693

Figure B.21 Calculating all the percentages

values, because the percentages are computed from them. First, you have to copy all of
the percentages and paste them back as numbers, like you did for the sum formulas in the
80+ column before. Then you can delete columns B through S. The last step is to change
that first column heading to something simpler. Let's call it "year" (see Figure B.22).

The last step is to save this worksheet as a CSV file so we can pull it into R. Go to
File > Save As... and choose "Text CSV" under file type. Then call the file **rawData**,
as in Figure B.23.

Click OK on all of the boxes that pop up. And then close the file.

Now, open up R. There's a lot to know about R, too much to go into a whole lot
of detail here, but I will walk through how to do what we need to do with this data.

So, what is that exactly? In Chapter 7, we covered how D3 takes data from a CSV
file and converts it into an array of JavaScript objects. Recall that every row in a CSV

	A	B	C	D	E	F
1	year	0-4	5-9	10-14	15-19	20-24
2	1950	0.1335237	0.1067804	0.1032144	0.094524	0.0878956
3	1955	0.1469186	0.1137531	0.0954141	0.0923115	0.0839142
4	1960	0.1431693	0.1260611	0.1017997	0.085368	0.0820528
5	1965	0.1440871	0.1232636	0.1121704	0.0908237	0.0756989
6	1970	0.1410907	0.1249081	0.1097846	0.0998032	0.0802686
7	1975	0.1329551	0.1233247	0.1118219	0.0981986	0.0890458
8	1980	0.1226953	0.1179331	0.1117104	0.1012988	0.0886304
9	1985	0.1218189	0.1091893	0.1069456	0.1013436	0.0915371
10	1990	0.1211648	0.1087222	0.0991316	0.097093	0.0914997
11	1995	0.1088128	0.1100391	0.100229	0.0911035	0.0886488
12	2000	0.0986432	0.1001502	0.1025908	0.0932652	0.0842241
13	2005	0.094339	0.0914541	0.0938739	0.0959052	0.086583
14	2010	0.0928491	0.0878201	0.085697	0.0876287	0.089268
15	2015	0.0909374	0.0865794	0.0824348	0.0804282	0.0821087
16	2020	0.0865951	0.0853632	0.0817405	0.0777935	0.0757683
17	2025	0.082155	0.0818477	0.08115	0.0776713	0.0737556
18	2030	0.0787856	0.0781162	0.0782377	0.0775377	0.0740299
19	2035	0.0765665	0.0753025	0.0750172	0.0751013	0.0742608
20	2040	0.0749379	0.0735332	0.0726225	0.0723116	0.0722391
21	2045	0.0733389	0.0723037	0.0712093	0.0702877	0.0698424
22	2050	0.0716362	0.0710752	0.0702986	0.0691923	0.0681602

Figure B.22   Simplify, simplify

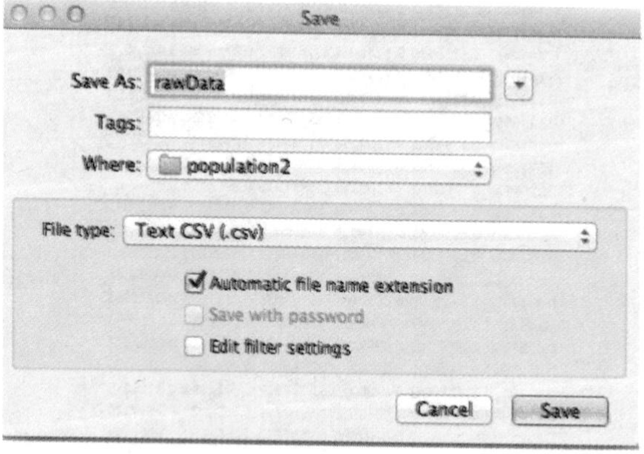

Figure B.23   Save the file

file ends up as its own JavaScript object. And to be able to use data-joins in the way we would like to, it makes sense for each object to only contain one data point. Thus, every row in our CSV file should only have one data point. This is not the case in **rawData.csv**—currently, each row contains 17 data points. So we need to massage the data a bit to get it in the right form.

A note about what I mean by "one data point." A data point can (and should) be more than just a single value—it can also have descriptive information associated with it. For example, the portion of the population between 0 and 4 in 2010 was 9.3%. That value—0.093—is the data point, but there are also two pieces of associated descriptive information: the year (2010) and the age group (0-4). In our ideal CSV file, that descriptive information belongs on the same row as its data point. Why? Because you want it to be part of the same JavaScript object when it is interpreted by D3. Then you can use it for, say, creating scales, positioning bars in a bar chart, or using keys when you compute a data-join, as we did in this book.

As it turns out, there is a package in R (you can think of R packages as being like JavaScript libraries) that has a function that takes a table like the one in **rawData.csv** and melts it down so that every data point is on its own row. In fact, the function is called "melt" and the package is called "reshape2."

Open up R. The interface, shown in Figure B.24, is a console into which you type code in the R language. (Your console is probably white. I've customized the colors on mine.)

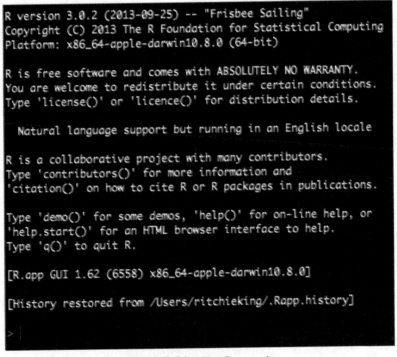

```
R version 3.0.2 (2013-09-25) -- "Frisbee Sailing"
Copyright (C) 2013 The R Foundation for Statistical Computing
Platform: x86_64-apple-darwin10.8.0 (64-bit)

R is free software and comes with ABSOLUTELY NO WARRANTY.
You are welcome to redistribute it under certain conditions.
Type 'license()' or 'licence()' for distribution details.

  Natural language support but running in an English locale

R is a collaborative project with many contributors.
Type 'contributors()' for more information and
'citation()' on how to cite R or R packages in publications.

Type 'demo()' for some demos, 'help()' for on-line help, or
'help.start()' for an HTML browser interface to help.
Type 'q()' to quit R.

[R.app GUI 1.62 (6558) x86_64-apple-darwin10.8.0]

[History restored from /Users/ritchieking/.Rapp.history]

>
```

Figure B.24   The R console

The first thing you need to do is install the `reshape2` package. You do this by typing `install.packages("reshape2")`, then select the CRAN mirror (see Figure B.25) closest to you (CRAN mirrors are the servers where the R source files and packages are hosted).

The `reshape2` package will be installed on your computer. Then to load the library type `library(reshape2)`, as shown in Figure B.26.

Now, you need to pull **rawData.csv** into R so you can manipulate the data. But first you have to tell R where it can find that file. You have to set the working directory to the directory where **rawData.csv** is. I've put **rawData. csv** on my desktop, and I can set the working directory to my desktop by typing `setwd("/Users/ritchieking/Desktop")`.

To load **rawData.csv**, you can use a function called `read.csv()`. That will pull the data in. But to be able to manipulate it (specifically to melt it), you'll need to assign that data to a variable. Try typing this: `data <- read.csv("rawData.csv")`. (In R, `"<-"` is the preferred assignment operator and not `"="`). If you type `data` into the console, you can see what it looks like. Figure B.27 shows a snippet of it.

The variable `data` is what is a called a data frame in R. You can think of it as a table. There are columns and rows, and the columns have names (the rows can have

Figure B.25 Choose a mirror

```
> library(reshape2)
```

Figure B.26 Load the library

names, too, but if they aren't named in the CSV you import, then they will just be numbered). You can see that the names of our columns look a little funny. R doesn't allow column names to start with a number, and when you read in a CSV file where your column names do start with a number, it prepends an "X" to all of those names. It also doesn't like dashes, or hyphens, in column names, because they are reserved for subtraction. So it replaces them with periods. We'll change those values back later, but first, let's do some melting!

Type this into the console: `dataMelt <- melt(data, id="year")`. Then type `dataMelt` to inspect what just happened (shown in Figure B.28).

Amazing, no? Now there is only one data point per row, and each row includes the associated year and age group. You might be wondering what the deal is with the argument `id="year"`. In our original data frame, called `data`, the year already existed

```
> data
   year        X0.4        X5.9       X10.14
1  1950 0.13352371 0.10678043 0.10321438
2  1955 0.14691858 0.11375309 0.09541410
3  1960 0.14316933 0.12606114 0.10179973
4  1965 0.14408711 0.12326364 0.11217040
5  1970 0.14109073 0.12490806 0.10978458
6  1975 0.13295512 0.12332472 0.11182188
7  1980 0.12269527 0.11793309 0.11171039
8  1985 0.12181888 0.10918930 0.10694561
9  1990 0.12116478 0.10872220 0.09913164
10 1995 0.10881275 0.11003914 0.10022900
11 2000 0.09864323 0.10015019 0.10259082
12 2005 0.09433904 0.09145407 0.09387387
```

Figure B.27 A look at data

```
> dataMelt
   year variable      value
1  1950     X0.4 0.133523712
2  1955     X0.4 0.146918580
3  1960     X0.4 0.143169329
4  1965     X0.4 0.144087109
5  1970     X0.4 0.141090731
6  1975     X0.4 0.132955119
7  1980     X0.4 0.122695274
8  1985     X0.4 0.121818875
9  1990     X0.4 0.121164776
10 1995     X0.4 0.108812750
```

Figure B.28 A delicious `dataMelt`

as a piece of descriptive information. In other words, every row had a value for year. We want that to still be the case after melting the data frame.

Pieces of descriptive information are called ID variables in the parlance of the reshape2 package. By telling the melt function to set id = "year" you are preserving year as an ID variable, and keeping the year on every row. This is a good thing.

Now, we can simply export our dataMelt (yum) to a new CSV and then open it up with Open Office and get rid of the Xs and periods. (It's also, of course, possible to do that in R, but R is not quite as intuitive.) Here is the code you need to create a new CSV file: write.csv(dataMelt, "allData.csv", row.names=FALSE). The first argument—dataMelt—is the data frame you want to export, and the second argument— "allData.csv"—is what you want to name that exported file. By default, R will create a column with the row numbers (or, more broadly, row names), but that information isn't useful to us, so we can set row.names=FALSE to tell R not to include the row names.

After you've done this, the CSV file will automatically appear in your working directory, whatever you've set that to be. Go ahead and open it up in Open Office. On the Text Import pop-up (shown in Figure B.29), you'll want to check "Commas" so that Open Office knows your data is delimited by commas.

Check out your data (Figure B.30).

Looking good. We just need to do four more simple things. We are going to change the column header "variable" to something more descriptive—let's call it "age," as in Figure B.31.

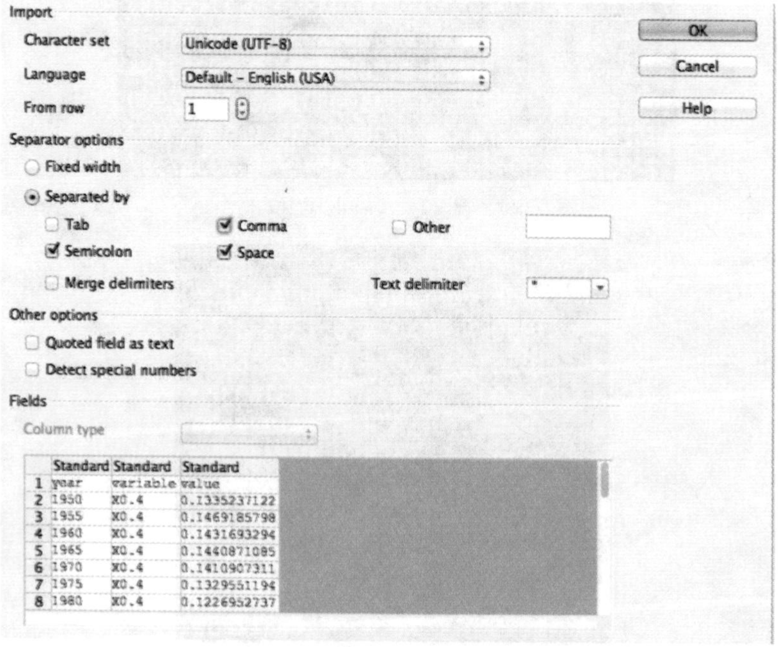

Figure B.29   Pick the delimiter

Then we have to replace those Xs with nothing. We don't want them there at all. Go to Edit > Find & Replace... and then type "X" in the "Search for" bar and nothing in the "Replace with" bar and hit "Replace All" (see Figure B.32).

Goodbye Xs! Now, we have to replace those periods with hyphens. You can use the same find and replace trick, but you have to be careful. For two reasons, actually. The first is that once you replace the periods with hyphens, some of the values will start to look like dates. "5-9" for instance, looks like May 9. Open Office thinks so, too, and

	A	B	C
1	year	variable	value
2	1950	X0.4	0.1335237122
3	1955	X0.4	0.1469185798
4	1960	X0.4	0.1431693294
5	1965	X0.4	0.1440871085
6	1970	X0.4	0.1410907311
7	1975	X0.4	0.1329551194
8	1980	X0.4	0.1226952737
9	1985	X0.4	0.1218188752
10	1990	X0.4	0.1211647761
11	1995	X0.4	0.1088127501
12	2000	X0.4	0.0986432279
13	2005	X0.4	0.0943390378
14	2010	X0.4	0.0928490519
15	2015	X0.4	0.0909373934
16	2020	X0.4	0.0865951491

Figure B.30 Checking out the data

	A	B	C
1	year	age	value
2	1950	X0.4	0.1335237122
3	1955	X0.4	0.1469185798
4	1960	X0.4	0.1431693294

Figure B.31 Picking better column names

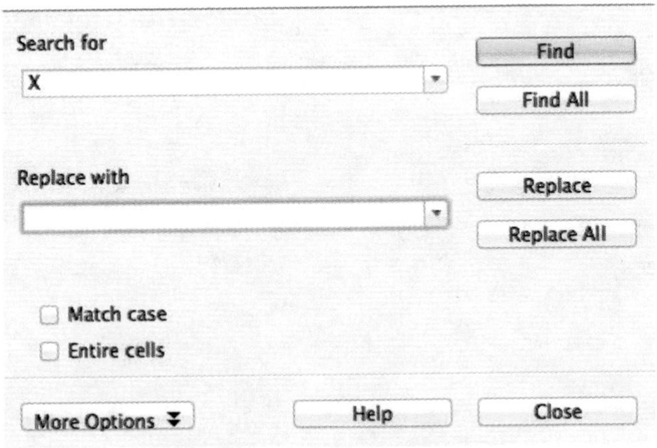

Search for

X ▾   Find

Find All

Replace with

▾   Replace

Replace All

☐ Match case

☐ Entire cells

More Options ⯆   Help   Close

Figure B.32 Get rid of those Xs

anticipating what you want, automatically converts it into a date. But that's not what we want. So, you have to select all of column B (which you can do by clicking on the column letter) and then go to Format > Cells... and select "Text" under "Category" (see Figure B.33). This tells Open Office you want these cells to remain as text and not get automatically converted to dates.

The other issue is that there are also periods in the "value" column, because all of the numbers are decimals. If you replace those periods with hyphens, then well, things will get a little weird. No worries. It's actually possible to limit the "Replace all" that you do to a group of selected cells, instead of truly replacing characters in all of the cells.

So select all of the cells in column B (you can do that by simply clicking on the column letter). Then go back to Edit > Find & Replace... To limit any replacement to the selected cells, you have to click "More Options" in the box that pops up and then check the box next to "Current selection only." Boom.

One more "Find and Replace" left. We want to change all of the 80+ values (which now actually read "80-") to "80 and up." Easy. You know how to do that.

Okay, there's actually once last thing. You can't just save the file, because for some reason, Open Office has a tendency to insert semicolons in CSV files where the commas should be. So you have to go to File > Save As... and when the dialog box pops up, you have to check "Edit filter settings".

Then when the next dialog box pops up, you have to make sure that the "Field delimiter" is set to "," (see Figure B.34). Then you should be all set! Your file—**allData.csv**—is basically good to go for making the bar charts in this book.

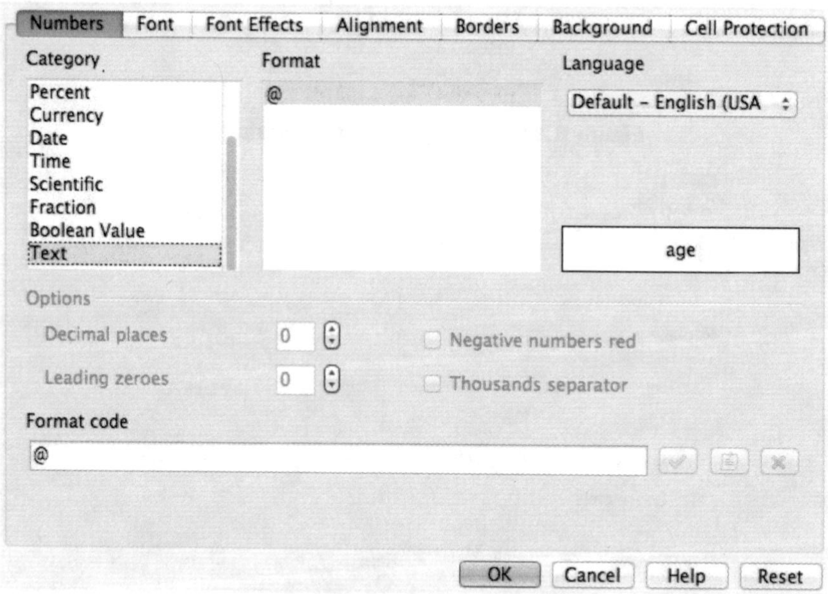

Figure B.33   Keep the dates away

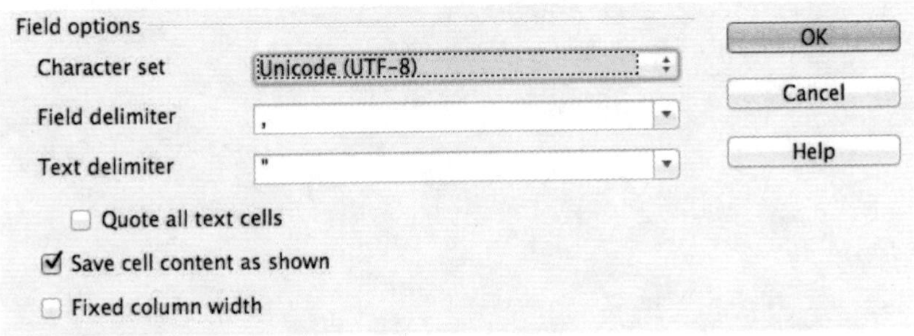

Field options			
Character set	Unicode (UTF-8) .... ⟳		OK
Field delimiter	, ▾		Cancel
Text delimiter	" ▾		Help

☐ Quote all text cells
☑ Save cell content as shown
☐ Fixed column width

Figure B.34   Making sure the values are actually comma-separated

There is one task left. Right now the data is ordered from "0–4" to "80 and up," while the bars in our bar chart are in the opposite order. If you want the bars to be ordered from "80 and up" to "0–4" then you have to sort the data. But I'll leave that exercise to you.

Index

FREE
Online Edition

Your purchase of *Visual Storytelling with D3* includes access to a free online edition for 45 days through the **Safari Books Online** subscription service. Nearly every Addison-Wesley Professional book is available online through **Safari Books Online**, along with thousands of books and videos from publishers such as Cisco Press, Exam Cram, IBM Press, O'Reilly Media, Prentice Hall, Que, Sams, and VMware Press.

Safari Books Online is a digital library providing searchable, on-demand access to thousands of technology, digital media, and professional development books and videos from leading publishers. With one monthly or yearly subscription price, you get unlimited access to learning tools and information on topics including mobile app and software development, tips and tricks on using your favorite gadgets, networking, project management, graphic design, and much more.